THIS WAY TO THE REVOLUTION
A Memoir

By the same author

Non-fiction
Erin Pizzey Collects
Infernal Child
Prone to Violence
Scream Quietly or the Neighbours Will Hear
The Slut's Cook Book

Fiction
The Consul General's Daughter
First Lady
For the Love of a Stranger
In the Shadow of the Castle
Kisses
Morningstar
Other Lovers
The Snow Leopard of Shanghai
Swimming with Dolphins
The Watershed
The Wicked World of Women

THIS WAY TO THE REVOLUTION
A Memoir

ERIN PIZZEY

PETER OWEN
LONDON AND CHICAGO

PETER OWEN PUBLISHERS
20 Holland Park Avenue, London W11 3QU

Peter Owen books are distributed in the USA and Canada by
Independent Publishers Group/Trafalgar Square
814 North Franklin Street, Chicago, IL 60610, USA

First published in Great Britain 2011 by
Peter Owen Publishers

ISBN 978-0-7206-1360-5

A catalogue record for this book is available from
the British Library

Printed and bound in the UK by CPI Antony Rowe

Typeset by Octavo-Smith Ltd in Constantia 10/13
www.octavosmith.com

To all the mothers, children, men and women
who passed through our refuge

NOTE ON THE TEXT AND ACKNOWLEDGEMENTS

Almost all the names of people living in the refuge have been changed to protect their identities. In some cases the identities of Chiswick staff and volunteers as well as victims of violence outside the refuge have been disguised as well. I am inestimably grateful to all those who helped out in the refuge houses over the years, even if they are not explicitly mentioned in this account.

The book was started and finished in a barn in Wales belonging to my friends Karen and Dean James, and I cannot thank them enough for their hospitality. My thanks go, too, to the award-winning photographer Christine Voge for allowing me to reproduce a selection of her evocative pictures of the refuge, soon to appear in a book, *Suffer Little Children*, as well as Wally Fawkes, also known as Trog, for the use of his 1981 *Observer* cartoon. I also want to express my gratitude to my extended family Cleo, Amos, Amber, Mikey Craig, Trevor Shillingford, Richard Lewis (known as Cass), Francis Charles (known as Russ), Darren Vaz, as well as Annie Ruddock and Caron Ramsingh, who all grew up in my home in Goldhawk Road. I am also indebted to my beloved twin sister Kate (née Rosaleen) Gustaven. I also want to thank Wendy Couling, who takes such good care of me, Rosemary Smith, my wonderful neighbour, Jo Pentony, the father of our house, and Dace Brennan, who taught me all I know about making mosaics, for their friendship and support over the years. My gratitude goes, too, to Jeremy Preston, East Sheen Library's manager, for introducing me to Sandra Hempel who suggested Peter Owen as my publishers. I would have struggled to complete the book without the help of the wonderful staff at A to Z Computers near my home in Twickenham. Finally, I want to thank my editor Antonia Owen and her team at Peter Owen for making the publication of this book such a happy occasion.

CONTENTS

ILLUSTRATIONS

between pages 160 and 161

11

Mothers and children in the overcrowded house

Erin meeting the Queen in London, *c.* 1972

Erin at work in her 'cubby-hole' at the refuge

Erin and child, 1978

Erin with members of the refuge community in the garden in Chiswick

Singer Roger Daltry and drummer Kenny Jones of The Who with Erin and children during a visit to the refuge, *c.* 1977

Erin sharing a secret with Phyllis, one of the housemothers

Dormitory with bunks and a mother with her children

Conditions in a refuge dormitory

Children watching fireworks

Fighting closure by Hounslow Council

The original boys' accommodation in a shed at the back of the house

A selection of Christine Voge's 1978 images of the refuge

Erin camping in France while on the run from the law during Glenda's court case to retain custody of her children

Lord Goodman in the 1970s

Trog in an *Observer* cartoon marks the Greater London Council's generous offer to the refuge, 1981, enabling its doors to stay open *(image courtesy of Wally Fawkes)*

Erin's extended family: Cleo's boyfriend Mikey Craig, her daughter Cleo, Annie Ruddock, another family friend, Erin's grandson Keita and her son Amos modelling Boy George's fashions, 1980

Front cover of *The Slut's Cook Book* by Erin, published in 1981

On 19 February 2009 I celebrated my seventieth birthday sitting in my flat contemplating another battle in the courts, this time against the British journalist and writer Andrew Marr and his publishers Pan Macmillan.

Andrew Marr – for reasons I will never understand – referred to me in his book *A History of Modern Britain* as a former member of a terrorist group that bombed targets around London in the 1970s. I was enormously hurt that after thirty-eight years of devoting my life to rescuing people from violence I should be thought of as one who would have associated with terrorists. I was also very anxious that I could find myself banned from entering the United States where I have family.

Andrew's accusation tore the scabs off some very painful experiences many years ago. The tears I cried on my birthday were tears of frustration. The battle that has gone on for the past forty years stems from the time in Britain when I believed the country I loved and supported had gone mad – seemingly overnight.

I think that when I reached seventy I finally accepted that I was officially elderly. Unlike many of my friends, I have never had any problem with growing old. I do mind the aches and the fact that I have had to have a knee joint replaced, but on the whole I find I can bear life's difficulties with a greater sense of equanimity. I no longer declare Third World War on my critics and opponents, and in the case of Andrew Marr's libel I simply picked up the telephone and spoke to Edward Yell of the Carter-Ruck firm of lawyers and left it all in his capable hands.

1

IN THE BEGINNING

It may have been Timothy Leary, the American professor responsible for the destruction of millions of brain cells through his endorsement of LSD, who coined the phrase, 'If you can remember the sixties you probably weren't there.' I remember the 1970s all too clearly but sometimes wish I could forget that whole period.

By the end of the 1960s my husband Jack Pizzey was working for the BBC. As a radio reporter he was sent to cover the rapidly emerging underground groups of young people who seemed determined to destroy the fabric of Western society. Part of me was highly inquisitive about what was going on, and the other part of the convent-educated woman in her late twenties was disgusted.

Jack helped to arrange a television programme that involved flying in leading members of revolutionary groups from across the world. I knew most of these people by name from their inflammatory statements in the British newspapers, and I was curious to meet them face to face. We were asked to collect an American revolutionary from Berkeley University, California, from Heathrow in our dilapidated green van. Most of the others were picked up in Porsches and Mercedes, and our revolutionary went into a sulk when he spied his transport.

The get-together was to take place in a cavernous room in BBC Television Centre in west London. There we were met by more tantrums; one of the revolutionaries from France, Danny Cohn-Bendit (better known in the press as Danny the Red), was screaming at the programme's producer because he didn't like his hotel room and said his expense account was 'merde'.

I couldn't think of anything appropriate to wear for such an occasion, so I took down a red felt curtain in our house in Coulter Road in Hammersmith and fashioned it into a maxi-dress. All around me at Television Centre arguments were breaking out. It seemed as if there was little solidarity among the revolutionaries, and in the middle of the confusion a man approached me waving his arms declaring, 'We must take over the BBC and make our internationally revolutionary demands known to the world!' I recognized him as Ken Tynan, the brilliant British theatre critic who had become notorious for being the first person to say 'fuck' on television. I had been sitting behind him that historic day. I remember he was wearing bright-red socks. He had a stutter, and it took ages for him to say the word; immediately the whole of Britain reverberated with shock. The BBC made a fulsome apology, the House of Commons issued four censuring motions signed by 133 MPs, and Ken Tynan ruined his chances of a future in television.

My next moment in revolutionary history came soon after when a large contingent from the BBC attended a meeting of the Black Panthers in central London. Bernadette Devlin, the political activist and soon-to-be Member of Parliament, introduced the brothers (no sisters), and I watched as one after another dressed in black and wearing black berets assured us 'whities' that we were all going to die in horrible circumstances. I looked down the line of all-white male BBC personnel and was depressed to see them waving their pink fists in the air shouting 'Right on!' The world seemed to have gone mad.

Another close encounter with the so-called revolution took place in a dank basement where Jack was sent to interview Richard Neville, an Australian who was the well-known editor of an 'alternative' magazine called *Oz*. This was one of many 'underground' magazines that had sprung up during the late 1960s. In one edition of the magazine, the 'Schoolkids' Issue', Rupert Bear, a cartoon character loved by many children including my own, was redrawn with an enormous erection. I failed to find the image amusing. I didn't get a chance to talk to Neville that day, as I was left in his slogan-festooned sitting-room while Jack conducted the interview in an inner sanctum.

I did, however, get to meet Caroline Coon during another of the many occasions I trailed round after Jack and his tape-recorder. She ran an organization called Release where young people could get help with their drug problems. During the 1950s, when I first came to live in London, drugs had been almost unheard of, but now, some fifteen years later, they were everywhere. Young and vulnerable young people benefited from Caroline's sympathetic ear and her practical efforts to assist them. Hers was the first project I encountered that actually seemed to be doing some practical good.

It was around then that a Dutch magazine carried a photograph of Germaine Greer with her bare bottom in the air affording the reader an eye-watering image of her anus and vagina. Her narcissistic posturing aside, she was influential in forcing me to think about my role as a wife and a mother of two children after I read her 1970 book *The Female Eunuch* from cover to cover. I also read Betty Friedan's work *The Feminine Mystique* and was comforted to find that the angry, isolated housewife rampaging in my head was not alone. Out there in the universe were millions of women who felt as I did.

I must have been very difficult to live with during my revolutionary birth pangs. Jack and I were regularly invited to dinner parties where most of the women worked for the BBC. I was an embarrassed outsider observing these wonderwomen spouting feminist jargon. Their husbands generally disappeared into the kitchen to attend to the food and keep the wine flowing, while the women held forth at the table. I felt I had nothing to contribute to the debates and often went home in tears of frustration. My problem seemed to be that there was a massive revolution taking place and I was confused because most of it seemed irrelevant to my life and did nothing to address my feelings of isolation.

Jill Tweedie was writing stirring articles in the *Guardian* newspaper during my period of political awakening, and I sat up in bed in the early hours of the morning voraciously devouring her words. Jill and I were to become unlikely friends many years later; even then I could detect a subversive sense of humour in her writing. Much of the other prose I was reading at the time felt like wading through thick black treacle. I would read the articles and books with a dictionary on my lap. Most of the women authors seemed to use jargon that fenced off those less well educated from the important points they were making. I had achieved four O-levels at school; those and a secretarial shorthand and typing course were the sum total of my education. I struggled on, however, and what I lacked in knowledge I made up in revolutionary fervour.

As soon as I finished reading the *Guardian*'s Women's Page it was time to get our two children out of bed and off to school. Jack had his own routine and was out of the front door and off to his office early every morning to pay the mortgage and bills. My contribution was to take care of everything else. There was a problem with this – I hated housework. I was sure that one day I would be found dead on the dirty kitchen floor having suffered an overdose of Nescafé. In my fantasy next to my rigid body was a bucket full of nappies and in the sink a pile of filthy plates. But however much I hated housework I had the bitter taste of office life in my mouth. I had qualified as a secretary in 1956 when I was seventeen, shared a flat in London with other girls my age, and I had worked in several offices. Even more than housework I loathed the daily grind of working all day long at someone else's beck and call. On balance I preferred to stay at home. Besides, a retail revolution was taking place in the high streets, and a shiny new shop opened called Habitat. For a few pleasurable months I threw myself into ripping up all the old carpets in the house and laying down deep-purple cord carpet and hanging washable wallpaper with bright orange and yellow flowers.

For years the drab grey streets and the beige walls of British houses had depressed me, but now the revolution that erupted on the streets flowed into the worlds of fashion, furniture and lifestyle. My kitchen bulged with terracotta cooking pots, and my wardrobe was full of long multicoloured peasant dresses, while our children were allowed to choose their own flamboyant clothes – much to my mother-in-law's disgust. Although I enjoyed the fashions, the profusion of psychedelic patterns and colours and the frenetic atmosphere of upheaval and change unsettled me more than ever.

Jack was lucky to have a job he loved. I was well aware, however, that this was unusual. Some of the typing pools I had encountered had been veritable snakepits. The women in charge pitted one employee against another and forced us to become like rivals in a paternalistic quasi-family. Now that I had given up secretarial life I felt that relatively well-off women like me were lucky in that we had a choice, but I was aware that millions of women across the world were less fortunate: they went out to work and had to come home and work again.

I enjoyed the freedom to cook nice meals and to play with my children. I spent happy hours dissecting fish in order to show Amos, my son, the gills and the liver. I watched children's television with him and his elder sister Cleo, but the dispiriting routine of vacuuming and scrubbing floors sent me into spirals of despair. It never crossed my mind that Jack should help out in the house. After all, he did the washing-up every night, and that was all I expected from him. I saw my role as a housewife to run the house, take care of the children and create a safe haven for our family. I didn't feel resentful about this, because I knew Jack put in long hours and worked hard. I was happy to create three-course meals for dinner and for the two of us to sit down together to discuss his day. We discussed his day rather than mine because I felt I had nothing much to report. Apart from shopping and housework my life was circumscribed by the One o'Clock Club in nearby Ravenscourt Park and, later, the school run. Some days the best I could offer was some scintillating conversational exchange with one or other of our children.

My father Cyril Carney had worked for the Foreign Office, and when we were not living at Her Majesty's pleasure in handsome large houses in hot distant countries my twin sister Rosaleen and I had been incarcerated in a convent in the Dorset countryside where I escaped my beautiful but violent and emotionally cold mother, Pat, who hated me. I was subject to the whims of a malevolent senior nun who made my life miserable – but at least she couldn't beat me. At the convent all the work was done by the most astonishingly gentle, smiling sisters. As shining examples of the joys of leading a religious life those women were inspirational. I think it was their serenity and contentment in their selfless work on behalf of the children at the school that made me realize that caring for others could be fulfilling in itself. I genuinely believed that selflessly caring for my husband and children would lead to its own reward when our offspring were grown up and I had time to myself.

For several years as a child my sister and I had been left stranded in England. My father had been posted to Tientsin in China in 1949. My brother Danny was too young to be left in a preparatory school, so he had accompanied them. Within a few months they were captured by the Communists and held under house arrest for three years. For a long time we didn't know if they were alive or dead, then letters started to arrive, albeit heavily censored. During this period – indeed for six years or so – Rosaleen and I would spend our school holidays at St Mary's, a holiday home run by a huge kindly woman called Miss Williams that took in around forty boys and girls.

I had been born in China in Tsingtao on 19 February 1939. Two years later my father was posted to Shanghai. Mao was already on his long march from the north of China. My parents were friends of Chiang Kai-shek, the Chairman of the Nationalist Party, who was fighting against the Chinese Communists. All of my father's life was devoted to fighting Communism. After his years under house arrest he became even more rabidly right-wing in his politics. He once threw a glass of wine in my face at a dinner party because I said I liked Paul Robeson's singing voice. 'The man's a red!' he shouted at me.

An incident that still haunts me was when a woman and her two small children came to stay with us in Devon while my father was still in China. My mother told me that the eldest child, who was about seven years old, had been encouraged to inform on her father who had been a senior official at the Hong Kong and Shanghai Bank. He was taken away and tortured, and he did not emerge from Communist China until many years after my parents and brother had been released.

My own political awareness was undoubtedly informed by my parents' arrest and incarceration. My father recounted to us the atrocities taking place in China. He talked about the starvation of millions of Chinese peasants and the fact that the benefits of the agrarian revolution had failed to materialize. He told us that women in China were encouraged to have abortions to restrict family size and described, too, the horrors of Stalin's Soviet economic experiment that caused millions to face starvation. He also knew about the gulags that imprisoned and tortured anyone who disagreed with the Communist regime and the 20 million people who had died or were killed.

What confused me in the late 1960s and early 1970s as I read my revolutionary writings was that most of the authors seemed to believe that the brightest future for the West lay in the Soviet and Chinese revolutionary experiments. The intellectuals who came to dinner at our house spoke with revolutionary fervour about what needed to change in society. Their Marxist views left me bewildered. How could people with university degrees advocate Communism of one sort or another as the only way forward?

When I tried to talk about the 20 million murdered by Stalin I was airily told that their deaths had been necessary for the revolution to succeed. I learned to keep quiet, pass the food and wine and to keep my opinions to myself. I soon came to realize that it was all a fashionable game. At the end of a night of furious arguing, smoking, drinking and flirting the dinner guests would return to their comfortable houses to sleep under their Habitat blankets and sheets.

2

THIS WAY TO THE REVOLUTION

I left Jack to babysit our two children while I went off to attend my first Women's Liberation meeting in Chiswick. It was 1969. As I climbed into the car I realized that I was very nervous. This was the first time I had left Jack to mind the children – and it was the first time I had been out at night without my husband since we had wed almost ten years before.

I came from a generation of women that was brought up to believe that marriage was the ultimate goal. Taking care of my husband and my children was my destiny. Some women of my age had gone to university, but at that time most women expected to get married and give up careers to bring up their children. I was quite happy with my choice. I had never wanted a career. I wanted to create a warm, loving home – the home I never had in my childhood. My rather brittle and cold mother had refused to do housework, so when we were abroad we had servants and she would spend her time playing bridge, organizing parties, shopping – she spent money like water – and complaining about my father. When we were in England on leave my sister and I acted as her servants. Our house was a cold mausoleum to a dead marriage and a woman who was unable to mother.

My first liberation meeting was in a tall house in one of the more affluent tree-lined roads in Chiswick, and as my hostess opened the door I felt ridiculously overdressed. In order to calm my nerves I had slapped on more makeup than usual, and I was wearing my only decent dress – the one garment that wasn't stained from interactions with children and pets. 'Artemis,' she said, extending a cold nail-bitten hand. Her eyes raked my face, and I knew she didn't like what she saw. It was too late to wipe off the makeup, and I realized I should have worn trousers. All the photographs in the newspapers showed feminist women wearing dungarees or boiler suits with flat heavy boots.

I followed Artemis's rigid back through the gloomy hall to the kitchen and reflected that unlike the Artemis of the Greek stories I had read as a child she was plainly no virgin – children's toys were piled everywhere and she was plainly a stranger to housework. Torn pages out of magazines were roughly tacked up around the kitchen walls. I saw pictures of women waving their fists, Asian women shouldering huge rifles, and in the middle was was a photo of pudgy-faced Chairman Mao.

There were six of us present, and only one woman looked as out of place as I felt. Artemis introduced us and said we needed to form a local group, call each other 'comrades' and pay her three pounds ten shillings – £3.50 – to join the movement. 'I came here to join a women's movement,' I objected. 'I don't want to join the Communist Party.'

'You're not joining the Communist Party. You're joining a women's movement. If we don't create a movement of our own we will continue to be oppressed by men.' The other four said nothing. 'Anyway,' Artemis continued, 'why are you here?' Her question was hostile. She obviously didn't expect any of us to argue with her.

'I'm here', I said, desperate to convince her of my passionate interest in her new movement, 'because I am so lonely and isolated alone with my children that I want to find a movement where women can meet one another and work together.'

'You're here, even if you don't know it,' she responded coldly, 'because your husband oppresses you.'

'Jack doesn't oppress me. He's at home babysitting. He pays the mortgage so I can stay at home. How can you say he oppresses me?'

The slim, dark woman in the corner was nodding in agreement, and I smiled at her. I felt hugely relieved that she supported me.

'You're brainwashed,' Artemis snapped back. 'That's why you're here. Listen. One of you should hold a consciousness-raising group at home, and I'll come along and help you set up the first meeting.'

I decided that I would offer my home in Goldhawk Road for the meeting, because I doubted if Jack would be able to babysit on a regular basis, and to my relief the others agreed that this sounded a good idea.

'It's terribly lonely,' Jack said when I got home that evening.

'Well, think how I feel!' I responded. 'Night after night I sit here on my own.' For a moment I felt a glow of satisfaction. I never discussed my isolation with Jack; nor did he ever consider it. I took it for granted that he had to work late and that I should be the one to stay home. Maybe I *was* oppressed – but by whom? Perhaps I should blame the BBC because they made him work so late. Artemis said I was oppressed by Jack, but he, like so many other men down our road, could be seen each morning racing out of the front door to catch the Underground train at Turnham Green Station to take him to his workplace. I had held down office jobs in the past – and I could never envy anyone working in one full time. At least I had the freedom to arrange my day as I saw fit. They had no choice. Still, no doubt Artemis would tell us all in good time whom we could blame.

The first official meeting of the Goldhawk Road Group took place in our house. I was very nervous. I had a phone call from the Women's Liberation Workshop head office in Little Newport Street to say that I could expect six women to attend plus Artemis. I was also informed that she would be bringing another 'sister' along. I stocked up on gin, wine, olives and crisps. I decided to wear jeans and a voluminous shirt. I experimented with the clean, scrubbed look, but I couldn't bear the way my face looked without facepaint. I definitely needed help and hoped that some of the others would be wearing makeup. I realized that I was frightened of Artemis.

Everyone arrived together, and I was glad to see my new friend Alison – the group member who had smiled at me – among the women who swarmed through the front door. Artemis told us to sit in a semicircle in the sitting-room. The woman with her from HQ had very long blonde hair, round National Health Service spectacles and a rabbity nose that twitched with disapproval. I got the impression that everything connected with the room, the house and my lifestyle made her cross. In order to break the ice I provided everyone with large drinking glasses and placed several bottles of wine on the coffee table. I had already poured myself a gin and tonic and put out bowls of olives and crisps. I thought the room looked quite convivial apart from the disapproving faces of the already liberated sisters.

The woman from Little Newport Street was called Gladiator, she informed us crisply. There was a general gasp of surprise. 'Did your mother really name you Gladiator?' I felt I had to ask. She said she had been given a very bourgeois name when she was born and she had felt compelled later to rename herself in her own right. We then got a lecture on how we were not to use the patronymics of our oppressors – our husband's names. I tried to say that I liked Jack's surname and that I liked being married. That did not go down well with the sisters. They began a harangue that I was to hear on many occasions. The family, they declared, was an unsafe place for women and children. In the new order to come, when women had defeated the patriarchy, men would no longer rule the world and the family would consist of women and children – men would have become expendable. An appalled silence descended on our little group.

Two of the women got to their feet and bolted muttering about babysitters. I went into the kitchen and poured myself another stiff gin and tonic. I returned and filled the remaining glasses with wine (the sisters declined to drink) and said that I disagreed with their analysis. Most women wanted to be married, I maintained. Yes, some women wanted a choice to go out to work; in fact, most women – unless they were married to wealthy men – undertook some sort of paid work anyway. As for the demand for 24-hour nurseries, I didn't believe that any woman would want to dump her children for long days or nights in such places.

I agreed that abortions should be made legal. I knew a girl who had died following a back-street abortion. She had been given a short metal tube to push up into her cervix and, apart from being in excruciating pain, she almost immediately developed an infection – and I remember how frightened we were of taking her to the hospital because she had committed a criminal offence.

Before I married Jack I had to bring proof that we were going to be wed to my family doctor so that she could provide me with contraception. Everyone at the meeting agreed that contraception should be made available to all and that teenagers should be made aware of contraception. Artemis began a discussion about women's rights to explore their own sexuality.

I saw Alison's eyes widen as Gladiator joined in to explain that truly liberated women should not have sexual relationships with men at all. 'Why would you want to sleep with the enemy?' she asked.

'My husband is not my enemy,' replied Alison.

'Besides, some of us like sex with men,' I put in.

'Have you ever had sex with another woman, Erin?' Gladiator's eyebrows were raised archly.

'It's on my to-do list,' I joked.

It soon became obvious that we were not easily going to be brainwashed at the consciousness-raising session, and the sisters proposed to take their leave of us.

'You live in a cage,' Gladiator hissed as she swept out of the front door.

'I do indeed. A mink-lined cage,' I assured her as she stomped down the front stairs. I watched them ride down the road on their bicycles. 'At least they're not on broomsticks,' I muttered to the others who stood beside me gazing out of the large front windows at their receding figures.

3
SISTERHOOD IS POWERFUL

Alison phoned me the next day. She, like me, had decided we were not going to have our movement destroyed by Artemis and Gladiator. We had both been to boarding-school, and we knew all about bullies. She promised to ring up the five other women and organize another meeting at my house without 'Glad' as we decided to call her – it made her less scary. Artemis was also banned.

Seven of us met a week later, and everyone brought a bottle. Fortunately we all enjoyed a drink. I cooked my foolproof chicken dish based on a recipe by Alice B. Toklas. Actually, I used to prepare most casseroles in much the same way. First I would cut up half a stick of butter, then chop lots of garlic, onions and carrots into an earthenware dish and let the lot cook for a while over a flame before adding the meat. I used to buy a large chicken from the butcher down the road and would ask him to cut it up for me. He was from Sligo. My father's family, the Carneys, came from County Mayo, and I think when the potato famine caused my ancestors to emigrate Ireland deported its most dysfunctional tribe ever. My butcher and I had an erotic relationship satisfied by winks and innuendo – I was certainly satisfied with the extra cuts of delicious meat and huge marrow bones he provided.

I poured a bottle of my best red wine over the vegetables and chicken and left the dish to bubble for an hour or so. The smell was always exotic. I thought we needed a good hearty meal to celebrate the first meeting of our group under its new name the Goldhawk Road Group. In my hand I had the latest copy of the Women's Liberation magazine *Shrew*. On the back it listed all the groups in London, and our group was among them. On the front of the magazine was a cartoon of a woman struggling with an enormous pile of ironing with two small children pulling at her legs. Her husband was standing in the doorway saying, 'What's for supper?' None of us could see the point of the image. Our husbands worked all day, and we cooked supper. That seemed to us a fair division of labour. Jack did the washing-up, and I would far rather cook than clean up.

We were supposed to talk about our lives as wives and mothers. Deidre, who had been a model before she had twins, suggested we called it a bitch session. This sounded much more relaxed than 'consciousness-raising', which is what we were supposed to be doing. We loaded up our glasses with alcohol, filled our plates with the drunken chicken and settled down to a good long moan.

After comparing a long list of our husband's failures, we decided that Alison and I should go along to the Women's Liberation offices in central London to register our demands. We duly wrote a list. Our first demand was that the women's movement should create an atmosphere in which women ceased to compete with each other and learned to cooperate. We all approved of the slogan 'Sisterhood Is Powerful', and I particularly liked the idea that I might engage with other women on an equal footing and not have to listen ruefully to their reports of how brilliant they were at running their houses, how wonderfully behaved their children were and how easy it was to juggle domesticity with work.

I had read an *Observer* newspaper feature discussing domestic short cuts written by the journalist Katharine Whitehorn, who had admitted how if her knickers were dirty and she couldn't find any clean ones she would retrieve the dirty ones from her laundry basket or consider heading out commando-style. 'I'd go out with dirty knickers,' I confessed. 'Reverend Mother, who lives permanently on my left shoulder, would strike me dead if I went out knickerless!'

Everyone was sympathetic except for Soraya from Iran who sat there looking shocked. 'In my country we don't do that sort of thing,' she said crossing her beautifully shod feet at the ankles.

'I'm afraid some of us do in our country,' I said. 'Actually I think I'm a bit of a slut.'

We then embarked on a discussion on the difference between a slag and a slut, and Deidre told us about a friend of hers who was terribly promiscuous and who had the habit of stubbing out her cigarettes in her jars of cold cream. Slags, we decided, were promiscuous and sluts were faithful in relationships but would probably stub out their fags in inappropriate places.

Gillian lived across the road from me, and her husband also worked for the BBC. He presented programmes, so he was at home more than Jack, but she felt as I did about the competitive women she used to meet through her husband's work. Bernice, who was tiny, pretty and French, spoke for us all when she said we should make it clear that we loved our husbands and were happy to be married and to bring our children up at home. That left Sonia who so far hadn't said very much, but now she agreed that we should make our statement but emphasize that we wanted women to have a choice as to whether they went out to work or not. We all agreed to this, and I typed up the list of our demands. One of the big mistakes a woman can make is to admit she can type and do shorthand. By default I became the Goldhawk Road Group secretary, and that was the main reason I accompanied Alison to head office.

We really should have left the whole thing at that, but after several bottles of wine we decided that we needed to devise our own poster and take it along to the office. At that time it seemed that all radical groups had posters or banners, and I remembered Richard Neville's basement festooned with posters and slogans – much like the walls of Artemis's kitchen. I offered to consult Jack who was good at art, and the design of the poster was left in my hands.

I asked Jack to draw an outline of two naked revolutionary women cradling guns and leaning against a sign. It pointed two ways. The one to the right said 'This way to the revolution' and the other facing the left said 'This way to destruction'. Our revolution was all about women joining together to change society in cooperation with men, and the left path was all about hatred and the destruction of men and families. I decided to give the woman underarm and pubic hair made out of patches of black Velcro. After Alison and I finished painting the poster we agreed it was a far better effort than the ones we had seen on Artemis's wall. We labelled it the work of the Goldhawk Road Group.

4

TAKING ON THE SISTERHOOD

I was going to drive our white Ford van up to central London. I disliked using the Underground, and after a discussion with Alison I realized that neither of us was used to going into town anyway. As young mothers we tended to stay pretty close to home, with our lives devoted to bringing up our children. I often felt as though I had lost contact with life outside the confines of my house on Goldhawk Road, the One o'Clock Club in Ravenscourt Park, our children's school and my husband's social sphere of orbit.

I think part of the huge attraction I had for the newly emerging movement was that it offered isolated women like me a chance to rewrite the rules. Why, I used to rage at my kitchen cupboards, was I relegated and made to feel anonymous? I had always struggled with these rebellious feelings. I tried joining a writing group where we created a monthly journal. The idea was that you filled in an account of your life and then mailed the journal on to the next woman on the list. I was embarrassed to find that I wrote long rants, and my pages were covered with red wine and cigarette ash. I gave the group up when I realized that the other women were not happy with my explosions of rage and frustration. 'Erin needs to sort out her priorities' was the phrase that came up more and more frequently.

It wasn't that I resented my children or my husband. What I most missed after a childhood spent in the Far East and Middle East were the teeming, swarming families that lived cheek by jowl. Even if my parents chose to live in huge isolated houses their three children spent most of their time in the servants' quarters. Here we were incorporated into these families' lives and went shopping in the local bazaars with our minders. Now my life was slipping away with no one to talk to for hours on end. My only adult company before Jack returned home was after school when, now and then, mothers took turns to sit in one another's kitchens watching our children play.

Since my daughter Cleo had been born my brain had turned to mush. To find the time to struggle through dense books meant that I had to crawl out of bed in the early hours of the morning before the children awoke and I had to start the daily ritual of cooking breakfast and taking them to school.

Like many husbands, Jack found it difficult to understand how I could complain about having time to myself. He assumed I had all the time in the world during the day to entertain myself. I often stood in front of him red faced and angry. I was quite happy to do the bulk of the housework and ensure he had a decent meal waiting for him when he came home. After all, he worked hard and he put in long hours to make it possible for us to have our comfortable lifestyle. However, he had no idea how tedious it was keeping a three-storey house clean and a kitchen well stocked with food. The house was a joy, the garden was beautiful, I loved my husband and my children – so why was I so desperate for more?

I really believed that the women's movement could provide an answer. I think that is why I decided to fight so hard to make it what I wanted it to be. I had a vision that there could be within every community a place where we could come together and be usefully occupied; a place in which women who were stratified by the jobs their husbands did could meet women from different backgrounds instead of being segregated by the rigid British class system. In my imagination a communal meeting place would offer a key to any woman who wished to work there. We would make space for a playgroup so our children would be welcome, and together we would work for our community. In those days there were few opportunities for mothers who remained at home with children to get together. The only places were the One o'Clock Clubs. There we would sit and watch our children play. I ached to be useful, to feel at the end of the day that I had achieved something worth while. I know I was supposed to feel fulfilled because I was sublimating myself into the lives of my family, but I wanted more. What was wrong with me? Maybe nothing, I began to feel. Maybe there were millions of others out there who felt the same, and I need no longer feel such a freak.

Such thoughts kept me awake the night before our visit to the

Women's Liberation office. Alison chose to wear her smartest and most severe business suit that, after childbirth, pinched somewhat around the waist, while I decided to hide my rolls of fat beneath a long black PVC maxi-coat. The weather was grey and chilly, and the late-autumn wind whistled through the trees outside my house. I wore an ancient fox-fur hat, and a long-dead fox hung from my neck, its lethal white teeth clamped to its tail. I felt defiant and confident. Just to make sure, I wore long black boots. 'You look like something out of *Star Trek*,' joked Alison.

'And you look as if you are about to give someone a good thrashing,' I countered.

The thought of delivering the poster with the two naked ladies and their Velcro pubic hair was beginning to alarm me. I gave Alison several sideways glances while I was driving into town, but she wore a look of such cheerful resolution that I decided to rearrange the butterflies in my stomach so that they all flew in the same direction.

Little Newport Street in Soho was unsalubrious and grimy. The houses were narrow and with steep staircases. We pushed open the front door to the office and climbed upstairs. We could hear women's voices and eventually came to a door that was ajar. Alison pushed it open, and I followed her into a small room. I saw posters much like those on Artemis's walls with vengeful women waving guns. Sitting on the floor were a puddle of young women. Ensconced on the only chair was Glad. She didn't look pleased to see us.

'Hello,' I said wondering if there were secret revolutionary greetings we knew nothing about.

'Welcome, sisters,' Glad replied without much enthusiasm. She motioned towards the women sitting on the floor. 'We're having a planning meeting about the first Women's Liberation march.'

Four faces looked up at us blankly. We introduced ourselves, and the four gave us their names in a perfunctory manner and went back to talking among themselves.

I took a deep breath and asked about the policy for putting up posters in the office.

'If your group's voted to put up a poster and there's room on the wall, you're welcome to put up anything you like. If anyone finds it offensive we'll have to contact all the groups for a decision to take it down. So far nobody's put up anything offensive, so I don't think you'll have any problems if you have something for the wall. There are no hierarchies in our movement, and all decisions are taken communally.'

I fished out the poster from its cardboard roll. Alison found a free space on the wall, and I produced a roll of tape. After we had finished putting it up we stepped back to survey our artwork. There was a sharp intake of breath and a gratifyingly stunned silence.

Alison handed several copies of our demands to Glad, who for once had nothing to say. 'Our group wants you to circulate our demands to the other groups,' she said decisively. 'The two of us will come and help out in the office three mornings a week. This way we can keep our group in touch with everything that's going on.'

'Thanks,' said one of the women. 'We could really do with some extra help. There's so much to do.' I liked the look of her. She had very curly black hair and deep-blue eyes. She looked as if she was enjoying the shock momentarily experienced by the others. 'It takes all sorts of women to make our movement,' she continued. 'I'm glad to meet you as representatives of the Goldhawk Road Group. We need everyone to assist with the march. The next big Women's Liberation meeting will take place in a few months' time, and you can help us organize it.'

With her on our side Alison and I escaped downstairs and fell into the nearest pub.

'Did you see their faces,' I crowed.

'I did,' Alison said, 'and I expect there'll be trouble!'

'Ah,' I said, 'there are no hierarchies, and no one is in charge, so we can do what we like.' Those words spoken in 1969 would later come back to haunt me.

5

THE SISTERHOOD FIGHTS BACK

We gleefully reported back to our group at the next meeting. Artemis telephoned me a few days after our jaunt to head office and was furious. 'You made a fool of me,' she snarled.

'I don't see how.'

'I introduced you to Gladiator, and she believed me when I told her you wanted to find out more about our movement. And all you've done is take the piss.'

'I'm sorry you feel that way' – and indeed I was genuinely sorry. I could tell Artemis was mortified. 'You shouldn't think that I'm not interested in the women's movement. In fact, I'm passionate about it. It's just that you don't leave any room for women like me and the rest of our group to feel that we belong. We were just trying to get your attention.'

'You have our undivided attention from now on, Erin,' she said, her voice dripping with menace and sarcasm. 'We'll be watching your every move. We are circulating all other groups for a vote on whether we can take your poster down or not. Your new issue of *Shrew* is in the post.' With that she banged down the phone, and I went off to pour myself another glass of wine. Why was the women's movement so difficult to join? What had happened to having a good time and women laughing together? So far most of the ones I'd met through Women's Liberation seemed to have a serious humour deficit.

At our next bitch session Alison gave a vivid description of the Little Newport Street office and told everyone that our poster was now tacked up on its wall. *Shrew* magazine, put out by each collective in turn, lived up to its name. That month's writers lived in Islington, which had a number of large communal squats. We passed the copies round, and we agreed that we resented being preached at and that its far-left stance and the political jargon just gave us a headache.

We did spend some time discussing an article called 'Kinder, Küche, Kirche'. Sonia understood German and translated it as 'Children, Kitchen and Church', which, according to *Shrew* magazine and the Nazis, represented women's position in society. 'We don't need Germans to tell us that,' Deidre snorted. 'My husband says my place is barefoot, pregnant and in the kitchen.' We howled with laughter.

'Yes, and Jack's position in society is suited and booted and chained to a desk.'

That set off another bitch session, and we decided that as a group we owed it to the sisterhood to attend a big women's conference scheduled to take place in two weeks' time in Central Hall, Westminster. Here we would get a chance to meet others; perhaps some of them would prove to be kindred spirits, and we could link up to form an alternative women's movement that didn't hate men or want to destroy family life.

Two weeks later we packed into my van and set off. We had made a collective decision at the end of the previous meeting to dress in what we hoped was a liberated style, and to this end I bought jeans and a big hippy shirt in Shepherd's Bush Market and completed my ensemble with a pair of workmen's boots. Everyone else wore suitably feminist attire, and most of us did without makeup except for Bernice who said she couldn't possibly be seen outside her home without eyeshadow, mascara and lipstick. She vowed that if ever there was a fire in her house she would leave the children and grab her makeup. We believed her.

The conference proved a miserable experience. We passed through the front hall that had a group of rather weedy-looking men trying to corral wailing children into a corner, and we followed a huge crowd of women into the main hall. The first speaker stood up and began an impassioned speech on the position of women in society, and someone at the back started waving her arms and yelling that the speaker on the platform didn't represent the views of the majority of the women – and then the general yelling began.

The day dragged on until we took a break for the first workshop. We split up, and Alison and I decided to go to the 'Family' session. We felt we might have something to contribute. As it turned out we didn't. A dictatorial woman from the Maoist group from Hemel

35

Hempstead read an enormously long and tedious paper on the collec-
tivization of people living in China. When I told the workshop that
my parents had been captured by the Communists for no good reason
and held under house arrest and that thousands – if not millions – of
others had been tortured or oppressed by the Chinese state and that
Chairman Mao had a lot to answer for, she got very cross and said my
parents were enemies of the revolution and deserved everything they
got. She then asked me to leave, declaring me a CIA agent.

Alison and I mooched off to the dining area where we gloomily
contemplated plates of vegetarian pasta and rice. Eventually the
other members of our group found us, and we shared a table and
decided to make a stand at the final plenary session. I spotted Glad
who was rushing around clasping a clipboard to her flat bosom
and barking orders. 'So,' she said eyeing me with distain, 'you
want to read a statement from the Goldhawk Road Group from the
platform?'

'Yes,' I said, 'the whole group is here, and we want to make our
position clear.'

I didn't like the smile that crept over her face. 'I'll see what I can
arrange,' she said. 'Be at the platform at 4.30 sharp.'

I was shaking with nerves, but I promised the others that we
would make our views known, and I was comforted by the fact that
they looked just as scared as me. How could a movement that pur-
ported to unite women create such fear? We were soon to discover.

I found myself on the platform with the others ranged behind me.
They had decided I should speak on their behalf. I guessed we looked
like total misfits compared with the massed feminists gathered
before us. There was an icy silence, and I started to speak. At first
my voice wobbled, but as I went on some of the passion I felt for my
vision for society came through. 'We love our husbands,' I said
firmly. A wave of jeering and whistling spread around the room. 'I
don't care what you do or what you say. Our group represents far
more women in this country than any of yours.' By now the noise in
the hall was drowning out my voice, and looking behind I shrugged
and said to the others, 'We might as well go home.'

'I'm not giving up,' I told them on the way back. 'I'm not letting
those bitches take over our movement.'

There was silence in the van.

'I'd like to carry on meeting at your house,' said Bernice eventually. 'I think we can go on being part of the movement, but I don't want to get involved in any more fighting.' There was a murmur of assent.

'I'm still going into the office,' I said. 'I feel I must give it one more try.' I couldn't bear the idea that we should abandon our vision for women to come together to offer one another support. Bolstered by kindred spirits and new ideas I whipped through the housework. I was patient with the children, and for once I had something to say about my day. I was not going to give up that easily.

6
MARCHES AND BOMBS

I knew my days in the office were numbered, because by now word was round the collectives that the Goldhawk Road Group was trouble. It reminded me of when I had joined the Brownies. I signed up because I thought they would have penknives, make camps and teach us how to light fires with magnifying glasses. I soon discovered that none of that applied to girls – only to the Cubs and Boy Scouts. We were expected to get our badges by learning to knit and sew, dance round toadstools and to do household chores. To add insult to injury I had been made to wear a badge with a blue tit on it, and all the little boys sniggered when I wore my uniform. The others quickly realized I was a rebel, and before long I was drummed out of the group. I left, but I learned a very valuable lesson about girls. Girls hunt in packs, and they hunt those who dare challenge them. They grow into women and behave in much the same way.

This pack mentality is what underpins the profitable financial markets that prey on the majority of women's desire to conform. If the leader of the pack says 'Jump', women ask 'How high?' If fashion dictates that they have to wear five-inch heels, they wear five-inch heels.

I honestly believed in the assurance of the early women's movement that women would no longer have to follow the herd. We could become individuals and do our own thing. We would no longer be defined by our relationships with men, and through cooperating with one another we could overcome the isolation of our lives as mothers who were stuck at home on our own with young children.

I could see that the women's movement meant that we were going to swap one set of rules for another. We had already been told that we shouldn't wear makeup and not use deodorant. I noticed that many of the women in the office no longer wore bras and smelled of sweat. Liberation meant rejecting our feminine natures and reaching for male power.

The new movement saw women as victims of men, but I saw women's role in the family and in society as equally important but different. I was concerned that if women demanded that they be more like men we would end up throwing out the nurturing, altruistic side of women with the bathwater. For millions of years women had created the hearth and home of family life. In creating this we had offered domestic comforts, meals and the unselfish provision of our time to our men and our children. Our partners played their part in working elsewhere to provide for our material needs and give support to their families. In the new world vision of the feminists I saw danger in a future where women would compete aggressively in every sphere of life and men would retaliate by withdrawing their goodwill and support. With the accessibility of the contraceptive pill, feminists trumpeted that sex was as much a liberating and pleasurable casual recreational activity for them as it was for men, and men gleefully agreed. But I could foresee a world where men and women could become rivals and love and cooperation between the sexes would become a thing of the past.

Many of the women working in the office lived in the large politicized communes of north London, and an air of acute paranoia was beginning to develop. They complained that their phones were being tapped and accused one another of being members of MI5 or police informers. There was a daily ebb and flow of women through the office, as plans were afoot to organize the first Women's Liberation march. I sat in the background typing letters to desperate women from across the country who sent in their £3 10s. to join the movement. Most of the correspondence was torn open by the sisters who pocketed the banknotes, scooped the letters together with many of the cheques into carrier bags and threw them into a filing cabinet.

I was appalled at this misuse of cash, and I resented the cavalier attitude the sisters had to the sad, lonely women who poured out their hearts in their letters. I spent all my time answering them – often with tears in my eyes because I wanted a movement that would genuinely reach out to them and offer them help. Most of the letters told of the isolation of women trapped in their homes, often in miserable relationships. All I wanted of the movement was a vision of how to form communities where women could get together to offer friendship, understanding and mutual cooperation. My view was that the solution was not to destroy the family but to reinforce it by offering support. Reading the hundreds of letters that arrived weekly committed me to continue at the office for as long as possible – even if my presence was not welcome.

The Goldhawk Road Group decided to go *en masse* to the first women's march since the days of the Suffragettes to be held on 6 March 1971. I read in the books now pouring off the printing presses that the Suffragette movement had also been riven with splits and political disagreements. Christabel Pankhurst was far more radical than her mother Emmeline. However, the Suffragettes had never been anti-family like the Women's Liberation supporters. Marriage was at that time regarded as the best way to protect women and children from the evils of society.

Before the march theatre groups drew up ambitious plans for floats and costumes that would raise the consciousness of the crowds expected to line the streets and the millions of people watching on television. I observed as women in Little Newport Street jostled to pick up the telephone in case someone from the despised media might ring. Some of the office workers were ransackers of the money that came through the post. The point of the movement was that women learned to offer mutual support, and here was an example of them cheating each other in the basest way.

One of the ways that the workers at headquarters retained dominance within the avowedly non-hierarchical movement was to make sure that whatever they learned from telephone calls they kept to themselves and their particular cabal. Thus the more aggressive groups such as the Maoists dominated the office at this time and would privately make appointments for journalists to interview them away from the building. This divisiveness made for a tetchy and sour atmosphere, no different to that which I had experienced as a typing-pool secretary. As far as I could see, women, even if they preached liberation, behaved no differently from before, except that now they could blame their ills on men.

The left-wing in-fighting between the Maoist, Trotkyist and Stalinist factions was all too apparent in Little Newport Street and elsewhere. Even within the Trotskyist camp could be found dozens of rival groups such as the International Marxist Group, the International Socialists, the Workers' Revolutionary Party and myriad offshoot sects all jostling for dominance. Their members expended extraordinary amounts of energy trying to gain control of educational establishments, local councils, unions and workplaces to further the revolutionary aims of their particular group. What became known as 'deep entrism' into the Labour Party and other institutions became commonplace as revolutionaries tried to conceal their far-left allegiances and try to change the labour movement from within.

I gloomily reported back to the Goldhawk Road Group that the word in the office was that the march could become violent. The Trotskyites were at war with the Leninists. The Maoists hated everyone, and some of the theatre groups were accusing others of 'capitalist revisionist' performances.

We agreed that I would drive the van and that Deidre – who wore the highest of heels so could not reasonably be expected to take her place on foot among the crowds of liberated women – and Alison would take sandwiches and flasks of hot chocolate to distribute to the children who accompanied the demonstrators. The other members of our group would participate in the march itself. None of us had ever taken part in a demonstration in our life, and I was glad to be safe in my van.

The day arrived clear and very cold. I decided to wear my ancient fur hat and stole. I knew it would annoy the anti-fur brigade, but the foxes had died long ago. Anyway it was too chilly to worry about that. Alison and Deidre arrived, and we piled sandwiches and flasks into the van and set off. There were endless lines of policemen along the route. We arrived a little early before the main phalanx of the march and joined the other groups streaming across London.

Very soon the van was surrounded by women adorned in all sorts of bizarre outfits and carrying banners. Even though it was bitterly cold, many of the children were underdressed and wailing. Before long we started handing out the hot chocolate and sandwiches to as many as we could. We got a shock when suddenly a policeman crashed his truncheon down on the roof of the van. I stopped the engine and got out. I was wearing high wedge heels, and as I drew myself up, towering over him, I noticed that, unusually, he was not visibly displaying his badge. I guessed that this was intended to make him less accountable for his actions. I glared at him, and he backed off. Fortunately the other police we encountered on the march seemed to take the day's events in good humour.

One of the floats displayed a giant birdcage with a scantily dressed woman cavorting inside. This was meant to illustrate the gilded cages in which we middle-class sisters allowed ourselves to be confined. At that moment I would have given anything to get back to mine in Goldhawk Road. I longed to be ensconced in my centrally heated house with a stiff gin and tonic. The march seemed to go on for ever. There were dozens of banners extolling Maoism, Lenin's foxy face appeared on many placards, and the Trotkyists, too, were out in force. Considering that it was the first women's march in England for decades, I felt there was rather a lot of sloga-neering on behalf of male Communist leaders. Still, there were no actual fisticuffs, and we returned home frozen stiff but feeling we had been part of history. I watched the march on the BBC news that night. Inevitably the cameras and the journalists captured the more outlandish exhibitionists, and I feared that to the average women in the country the march looked like a freak show.

The end of my time in the women's movement was not long in coming. I had become increasingly aware of a small group of much younger women who stood in the corners of the office whispering among themselves. Mostly I ignored them and got on with answer-ing letters, but at times I could hear them talking in hushed voices about the Angry Brigade. This was a small group of anarchists I had read about who were planting bombs mostly around London. The bombing of the BBC van outside the 1970 Miss World Contest had been attributed to them, and the police were frantic to track them down. The whispered discussions that really worried me were ones mentioning the clothes store Biba. This was a large shop in Kens-ington owned by the fashion designer Barbara Hulanicki. I loved it and often went there with my children and other friends. I thought of it as a glamorous and liberating place. One lunchtime the young women were sitting in a circle on the floor of the office sharing packed lunches. I heard one of them describe Biba as 'capitalist deco decadence'.

'I love it,' I contributed.

There was a frosty silence.

'I've heard talk of planting a bomb there,' I said, stung by the contempt in their faces. 'If anyone seriously means to bomb Biba I'll go straight to the police. Thousands of women and children shop there, and I can't believe anyone would be so irresponsible!'

The women got to their feet and walked out.

I couldn't sleep that night. The women weren't even willing to engage with me, and I felt that if I didn't try to do something to prevent even the remotest possibility of a bombing attack I would carry the guilt for the rest of my life. The next morning I telephoned Hammersmith Police Station. Within a few hours there was a knock on my door, and a policewoman asked me if she could come in. I explained that I was worried about rumours I had heard but emphasized that they were only rumours. I added that it was my impression that some members of the Women's Liberation organization were soliciting contributions to the cause under false pretences. I voiced the opinion that, as far as I was concerned, the movement was less to do with liberating women than a front for activists to line their own pockets and recruit support for their own far left political groups.

The policewoman heard me out. I knew I probably sounded hysterical and overwrought, but I had been awake all night with anxiety and felt exhausted. I hated the idea that I was sneaking on women in the movement, but I felt that if there was a plot to attack Biba or other similar targets tragedy could ensue. The policewoman pulled out a sheaf of photographs and placed them on the table. They were images of the Little Newport Street office, but the women in the pictures were unknown to me. They looked as though they were pasting up a journal or newspaper. I shook my head. The policewoman left, and I sat and gazed out of the window. I had one thing left to do – and I wasn't looking forward to it.

Alison had considerably more political experience than I. She was married to Patrick, and they had grown up in Ireland. I remembered with huge embarrassment that my father liked to sing 'The Wearing of the Green' and 'Oh Danny Boy' with tears pouring down his face. His Republican sympathies enraged my mother who pointed out that he had never even visited Ireland. Anyway she felt it wasn't seemly for a diplomat to support the Republican cause. I, however, thought it was all rather romantic.

My only first-hand experience of any sort of IRA-style activity had been in the late 1960s when our Irish chemist was arrested on suspicion of terrorism and taken into custody. At the time Jack was away on business, and I was telephoned by the chemist's wife. She explained that the police had raided their house and dug up their garden, and she asked if we could stand bail for her husband. Of course we would, I said. I very much liked her husband, as did all our neighbours. He had been a great help, especially when my children had minor ailments. I was also very fond of his wife Maria and their bright, friendly children.

When I went round there she explained that her husband had been trying to get some guns to his father and the family they had left behind in Ireland who lived in an overwhelmingly Protestant area and who had no means of defending themselves. Now she wanted to get him bailed from prison.

I had no idea what setting bail involved, and Maria explained that she needed to raise a sum of money to offer the court as a surety pledge so that her husband would not be remanded in custody. She said the money would not need to be paid unless her husband absconded. I immediately offered to post bail with £5,000 I didn't have. She told me that when she had told the Reverend Mother at her children's school of her husband's arrest the nun had put her hand comfortingly on Maria's knee and said, 'Ah, but, to be sure, everyone in Ireland had a gun stashed somewhere. Ours was under the baby's bassinet!'

When Jack came home I told him what had happened. Jack looked extremely dubious about my offer to help, and, of course, he was right. He was working for a television news programme, and to have one of its reporters standing bail for a man accused of being a Republican terrorist was not a good idea.

In the event, Maria's husband wasn't permitted bail anyway, and he was sentenced to gaol. I was devastated for his wife and family. I was told that the police had been watching their house for months and they had received a tip-off that arms were buried in the garden. Jack went to visit him and came back saying that half of Hammersmith Grove seemed to be banged up in gaol with him. I had visits from men with caps pulled down over their foreheads for months afterwards asking for donations for the cause. Given Jack's position, I felt I had to refuse.

That was my only encounter with radical politics apart from Women's Liberation. Alison was a great support to me when I found myself bewildered by the seismic changes taking place in our lives. The new movement that seemed to promise so much had gone sour. All around me I saw women pitted against one another. The women's movement seemed riven with bitter rivalry, when what I was seeking was cooperation and harmony.

'I should go to the office and tell them I've spoken to the police,' I told her.

'They'll eat you alive,' she warned.

'I don't care. I just want to warn those young idiots they are being watched. If they don't want to listen, it's up to them. I just don't want them getting involved in violence. They might think bringing about the revolution is exciting, but I reckon they're being used. If they get involved in bomb attacks it won't be the organizers who go to gaol – it'll be them!'

I duly went into the office on a day I knew the conspirators would be present. I finished typing a letter and swung round on my chair to tell them that I had been concerned about what I had heard them discussing. I said their preoccupations seemed to have little to do with normal women, the sort who wrote telling us about their lives, expressing support or asking for advice. 'You don't ever bother answering their letters. You just pocket the cash and dump their letters in a drawer. I think that's stealing.' I told them about my meeting with the policewoman and concern about possible terrorist activity – and I knew at that moment that my days in the Women's Liberation Movement were over.

7

GOODBYE TO THE SISTERHOOD

The Goldhawk Road Group collectively agreed that we were no longer interested in belonging to the national Women's Liberation organization. The women's movement seemed an excuse to break away from the traditional political left and to create a new power structure. To this end the feminists recruited relatively apolitical women in their campaign against lovers and husbands. The idea seemed to move the goalposts so that women were no longer pre-occupied with fighting just the old enemies of capitalism and class but were being co-opted into fighting 'patriarchy' as well.

One wine-sodden evening we decided to ignore a summons for someone other than me to attend a grilling at head office and that we would now get on with the matters that really affected our daily lives. One of our concerns was the weekly shopping hell. On a Saturday morning I usually went to our local Sainsbury's in Chiswick High Road. Jack would give me a list because he said I was an irresponsible shopper – and he was right. I regarded shopping as drudgery. I almost never checked prices, and I would throw whatever caught my eye into the trolley with abandon. I was, however, aware of impecunious and elderly people who crept around the shops assiduously seeking out bargains, and I suggested that we start a price war.

My idea was that we should stand with a blackboard outside the parade of shops in the high street. On it we would write a list of the main shops and the prices of staple foodstuffs. We decided to concentrate on eggs, bread, milk, bacon, butter and packets of cereal. The poor and the elderly, who trudged up and down the road trying to save pennies, would be saved time and energy. Everybody agreed that this was a good plan.

Deidre suggested that, in addition, we should consider holding a meeting in the town hall demanding legal abortions for all. The law then required two doctors – usually men – to determine whether a

46

woman should be allowed to have an abortion. We wanted the decision to terminate a pregnancy to be placed into the hands of the woman concerned. This, too, was passed by vote as a worthwhile project for our group.

The evening ended with all of us feeling a lot more positive about where we were going, but I still felt betrayed by the movement that I had joined with so much enthusiasm and hope.

I was not surprised when a letter arrived from Little Newport Street office telling me that forthwith I was to be banned from the women's collectives. I knew that most of the groups were paranoid about security, and the idea that someone would talk to the police branded that person as an informer. The gulf between my reality and theirs was too wide for me to be able to explain that being party to a bombing incident was abhorrent to the majority of people. To the feminists it was just part of the process that would sweep away the old class system and liberate the toiling masses so they could take their place in the glorious world revolution led by Maoists, Stalinists or Trotskyists.

I found rejection hard to bear. Alison knew how I felt, but she pointed out that we were now free to create our own movement without worrying about head office approval. We could approach Hounslow Council to request the use of a vacant house in our neighbourhood for a community project in return for a peppercorn rent. Now that I was no longer engaged in activities at the Soho headquarters I threw myself into developing this scheme.

We felt instinctively that the Women's Liberation analysis of what was amiss with society was wrong. On one occasion I had been taken to task by a woman who demanded to know how I felt about staying at home while my husband was on the nightly BBC television current-affairs programme *Nationwide*. 'There you are, the little woman, propping him up while he's covered in glory!'

Her attack took me by surprise. 'My children and I are proud of him actually . . .' Her look of disgust on her face shut me up. In fact, I didn't envy Jack. I was grateful because he gave us a secure family life. What I prized was that I had the freedom to do what I wanted for a greater part of the day. Most working men had very little free time to themselves back then.

What was, however, becoming increasingly clear to me was that by choosing to bring up young children by myself I had opted for a lifestyle that doomed me to a largely solitary existence. I had given birth to my daughter Cleo in Singapore in 1961 after my marriage to Jack in the UK earlier that year. There I lived in the heart of the city, and when we moved to a large flat at the top of an old colonial house I found two young Malayan girls with their own children to work for me. Very soon I not only had companions of my own age and a gang of small children but was part of their family life.

Back in England with a husband and small child I discovered the extended family did not exist. And at this time, in the West, women were valued only if they worked outside the home. What we needed, I thought, was some way in which we could extend our lives into our local communities – whether we went out to work or not – without jeopardizing the welfare of our children.

One evening I was with Jack at a dinner party in a film director's house feeling frumpy and child-soiled among the sophisticated fellow guests. The hostess described how her au pair had let her three-year-old son fall through a missing banister at the top of the stairs. He had broken his jaw. 'If you hadn't left your child with a seventeen-year-old girl it wouldn't have happened,' I heard myself say. I could feel myself blushing, and I knew that my dig was made out of spite. The rest of the meal was subdued, and I realized that I had upset our hostess, but I didn't feel able to apologize.

I remembered early days in London when Jack had just joined the BBC as a trainee and money was so tight I had to go out to work. I would race out of the flat each morning to get Cleo to the childminder on time and then head off to the office. I would go shopping in the lunch-hour. I rushed back after work to collect her, then hurried home to get her ready for bed. Often I fell asleep while reading her a story. Then it was time to get supper – and I often had to bring work home from the office to get through the workload. Weekends were a nightmare of running round taking my daughter to the park while juggling washing and cleaning. One weekend I heard her repeating the jingles from the advertising commercials she had heard that day. I knew that she must have been sitting in front of the television for far too long. My exhausted, guilty days as a working mother were over, and I quit work to do what I knew was far more valuable in the long run. I chose to have a child – and she had to be my first priority.

8
MAKING A DREAM COME TRUE

I was thirty-two in 1971 when we began our revolution in the leafy streets of Chiswick. I was meeting women from all walks of life. One who joined our group from the abortion campaign launched at the town hall was a qualified plumber. There were teachers, secretaries and people who worked in schools as dinner ladies as well as several who considered themselves middle class. It didn't matter what background they came from; what mattered was what they could offer. My own upbringing was middle class, but in my heart I always felt an alien.

My mother used to tell how when she first met my father she worked in Peking as a senior nurse. She and her best friend Barbara had left Canada to find eligible husbands. They dated two young men working in the Foreign Office Chancery. My father Cyril dated Pat, and Barbara dated Allen Vetch. Barbara and Allen became our god-parents – and Barbara got the better deal. Still, neither of my parents had been entirely frank with each other about their backgrounds. My mother said her mother had died in childbirth, which was true, and that she had been brought up in a huge town house on 343 Sherborne Street in Toronto by elderly wealthy relatives, which was false.

My father had a litany of horror stories about his own childhood that dripped into our lives like vials of poison. Every Christmas Eve he made it a point to tell us about his terrible childhood. He was the seventeenth child of a huge Irish Catholic family. He said he had hated his mother but admired his father, who seemed to spend most of his time drunk and fighting. Apparently my powerful grandfather could pin five men against a wall at once and drink a quart of whiskey a day. He ran several pubs around Hounslow in his time and used to race horses. His jockey was his eldest son Jack, and if he won all was well, but when he lost the horses would have to pull coal around the neighbourhood. I have a photograph of my grandfather in a porkpie hat looking huge and menacin g. My mother told me that my paternal grandmother had been a prostitute and that she had died in an insane asylum weighing seventeen stone. According to my mother I resembled my grandmother, and I was destined to follow in her footsteps. Actually I was entranced by the stories of my grandparents and would have loved to have met them.

Birthdays also set my father off. He was jealous of the few presents my mother bothered to get together for us children. He had never received any gifts. All his clothes were threadbare, and he walked to school with holes in his shoes. He was always hungry, and he did his homework by the light of a candle. I was an avid reader of Charles Dickens, and I understood that my father had really suffered from poverty, but his self-pity and incessant moaning meant that his three children found his wallowing in the past distasteful. As far as we were concerned he had escaped his background; he now lived in large houses with servants and plenty of money, so why did he need to drag his resentment about his background into the present?

My mother never really recovered from the fact that when she married my father in a double ceremony with Barbara and Allen she had mistakenly believed that she was marrying into the upper classes. She presented her husband with two first-class tickets to sail around the world, and she packed forty trunks of matching luggage and set off with him on their honeymoon and to visit her in-laws in England.

She soon found her airs and graces were cancelled out by my father's 'in the gutter' behaviour. He dominated conversation, and if people interrupted him or, worse, tried to argue with him he declared war on them. She had to admit that he had a brilliant mind, and undoubtedly his bosses in the Foreign Office recognized his phenomenal grasp of international politics, but, as far as enhancing her reputation as a society hostess was concerned, most of the people they met socially tried to avoid his company altogether.

When they reached Canada my mother made sure that her friends and relatives met their train at the stations, and a brief conversation would ensue while they handed over their wedding presents. My father never got the chance to meet any of her family or friends there properly. When it was his turn to introduce my mother to his own family he took her to visit Auntie Nita who was married to Uncle Will in Devon. Will came from an aristocratic family, so my father hoped to impress my mother. Unfortunately Nita forgot to mention that Will had lost all his money on the stock exchange and they now lived in a hovel of a cottage. Will spent his days smoking and reading *The Times*, while Nita administered to his every need. Nita, like my father, had a broad Hounslow accent, dropped her h's and cocked her little finger when she held a cup of tea. My mother felt that she had been wed under false pretences, and her grievances about her marriage marred her life.

Their relationship became even frostier when my mother discovered there was no manor house attached to the Carney name and that Auntie Mary lived in Manor Road in Ealing in a small back-to-back with an outside lavatory. Years later my mother left me with Mary in her tiny home. My mother could barely bring herself to drink a cup of tea before she fled – as though Mary's 'commonness' might somehow be catching. However, it was Auntie Mary's lack of pretensions, her warmth and openness, that endeared her to me – as well as her big soft double bed with its shiny purple satin eiderdown. There was where I felt I belonged – with Auntie Mary with a cigarette dripping ash between her stained yellow fingers and her cough resounding off the blackened wall behind the cooker. For once I didn't feel out of place. Mary was unselfconscious about who she was, and I was more than happy to stay with her for as long as possible.

Looking back, I realize that my mother and father had no proper parenting. When my mother had her three children she was unprepared. After her own mother had died in childbirth my grandfather had married a woman who hated his three children and who was violent and cruel towards them. My father was also devoid of parental love and affection. His father either ignored him or beat him. All he knew was the rule of the boot and the fist, so it was no wonder that we suffered the same lack of parental care. The result was we three children felt like outsiders. We broke the rules and were deemed 'difficult' and 'obstructive', but in truth we didn't understand the rules in the first place. All three of us were disastrous at school. My brother Danny had a reputation for knocking people out if crossed. He had to live with the fact that his father was indifferent to him and his mother dumped him in a preparatory school when he was seven and thereafter never paid him any attention. Eventually he was to follow his own star in Africa and would write the novel *The Wild Geese* that was made into a major film.

My own life was to change course in November 1966 when I saw a moving BBC television drama called *Cathy Come Home*, written by Jeremy Sandford, in which a homeless couple are torn apart and the mother has her children dragged out of her arms by social workers. After the programme ended I wept. I made a vow that I would try to make a difference. But how? In 1971 I hoped this question might be answered by opening a small community centre where we could improve our own lives and those of other women.

9

MARGARET THATCHER, MILK SNATCHER

My idea of the shopping price war was to make the local super-markets compete against our blackboard on the high street instead of persisting with surreptitious price-fixing. Our efforts to aid local shoppers were so successful that I received a menacing phone call from someone called Jack Cohen.

'I own the Tesco you're picketing,' he said. 'Stop now, or I'll sue.'

'So sue me,' I answered – not at all sure what I was saying. My bluff worked, and I learned that meeting a bully head on is often the best way to proceed.

Another supermarket manager wrote a letter to the *Richmond and Twickenham Times* saying that we were ' an irresponsible body of women trying by sheer sensationalism to get publicity'. When that didn't stop us picketing his supermarket he organized a meeting. We sat around his highly polished table and tried to talk to him about the realities of everyday shopping. He wouldn't listen to what we had to say, and as we left he stood up and patted me on the head. 'Don't worry your pretty little head about such things,' he said, and his condescension convinced me that we had a long road to travel to get ourselves heard.

An even more controversial event was our first mass meeting on abortion held in Chiswick Town Hall. We were aware of the antagonism we were likely to face, because in 1971 abortion and contraception were taboo subjects. I knew of two women who had attempted to undergo illegal abortions; both ended up with infections, and one had died. None of us in the group had personal experience of abortion, but all of us felt that it should be a woman's right to chose. I knew I would never have have one on religious grounds, but I also knew that I should not impose my beliefs on anyone else.

We were surprised when about fifty people came to hear us speak. We were nervous, but the crowd were genuinely interested, and a two-way dialogue ensued that greatly increased everyone's knowledge of the subject and related issues. I came away feeling that the work we were doing was definitely benefiting the community. In addition, I was meeting people I would never normally encounter. We still needed a community centre, so we continued to badger Hounslow Council for premises we could call our own.

In the meantime Margaret Thatcher, as Education Secretary under the Conservative Prime Minister Edward Heath, decided to end universal free school milk in primary schools in 1971. All children used to receive a third of a pint of milk mid-morning, regardless of family income. I was outraged because I was aware that in our neighbourhood and elsewhere in the country this milk was the main source of nutrition for pupils until their school dinner, and I couldn't believe that a woman could be so ignorant as to how impoverished families lived. In those days if a child was entitled to free school dinners it meant that they had to stand in a different queue from the paying students, and it was obvious to everyone that they were poor. I recalled all too clearly how my mother couldn't be bothered to provide 'mufti' for my sister or me at boarding-school. We were allowed to wear our own clothes on Thursdays after classes finished, and my mother asked the nuns at the convent to buy second-hand clothes for us. Thus we we stood out as different, so my rage against Thatcher was personal as well as political.

I decided to write to the Conservative Party to request a picture of Thatcher. By return post a glossy mugshot arrived showing her sporting a string of pearls. I took it to our local newsagent's shop, and they helped me to design a poster. Underneath large black letters proclaiming 'WANTED' we placed the photograph; at the bottom, in the same type, were the words 'MARGARET THATCHER MILK SNATCHER'. I was thrilled with the result and had the poster photocopied. I stuck two copies on the doors of my car and drove off to collect the children from school. On the way I was gratified at how many drivers hooted and waved. At a red light a man leaned over and yelled, 'Where I can get a copy of your poster?' I peeled one off my door and passed it over. For the next few days I handed posters out of my car window at red lights all over west London.

At one of our meetings I suggested we should organize a milk march. I telephoned the Milk Marketing Board and asked them to assist. To our surprise, they offered to loan us a milk float full of cartons of milk – as well as a beautiful Jersey cow. We set a date, notified the press and invited as many local councillors as we could. We knew many of them personally because we had been trying for months to get a community house donated by Hounslow Council. Many were sympathetic to our request, and many felt as we did about the withdrawal of free school milk.

The day of the march was a beautiful if windy one. Many more people turned out than we expected, and as I walked alongside the cow displaying our poster I looked back to see a gratifyingly long line of families marching behind us. Mothers, fathers, children and anyone else who supported our campaign were welcome. There was no aggression, there were no divisive political slogans and no raised voices. We laughed and strolled along the streets until we reached Chiswick Green.

As we marched on to the green some councillors came over to meet us. I was standing by the Jersey cow and her handler. An unsmiling man introduced himself as Alderman King and put out his hand. I shook it but was immediately puzzled. From his expression I realized that this was not what he expected. 'Where's your petition?' he demanded.

'I didn't think we needed one. We have all these people here to meet you all. Isn't that enough?' Actually I had no idea what a petition was.

'You have to have a signed petition,' he told me. Just then the cow lifted her tail and dumped several steaming cowpats right next to his brightly shining shoes. Most of the marchers managed to keep straight faces, but as the smell wafted forth guffaws could be heard rippling across the green. The cow batted her eyelashes, and after a few embarrassed minutes of attempting to discuss the issue of school milk the councillors headed off and we were left to disperse and make our way home.

Britain's schoolkids never did get their daily free milk back – even though I was told years later that the Education Secretary had been upset when she heard she was being taunted with the jibe 'Margaret Thatcher, Milk Snatcher'. Remarkably, to this day our campaign is recalled by those with long memories, and our slogan has passed into political history.

10
CHISWICK WOMEN'S AID
OPENS ITS DOORS

Mary Smith was a local Chiswick councillor and an ardent champion of our efforts to get a centre to engage in community enterprises. She was a large, ebullient woman who helped drive our project through the labyrinths of bureaucracy that swamped Hounslow Council. Finally, towards the end of the summer of 1971, we were offered a house. We arranged to meet at 2 Belmont Terrace in Chiswick. When I saw the derelict semi-detached I burst into tears. At first I thought it was a joke. Perhaps we had got the wrong address. No, it was the house designated for us. Of course, had we been less naïve we would have realized that we were not meant to have decent premises. Alderman King was going to see to that.

We stood inside the tiny house in silence. 'Well,' said Alison, always the optimist, 'we can do this place up in no time.'

I was not so sure. The walls were filthy and in need of repair. There was nothing on the floors. There were four little rooms, a galley kitchen and a small outside courtyard with a lavatory at the end. Then I remembered Harry Ferrer. 'I'll ask Harry if he'll help us.' I was sure that Harry, a big soft-hearted man who had helped me do up our home in Goldhawk Road, would advise and support us. Harry became our saviour. 'Don't do the work for us,' I told him with remarkable prescience. 'Some of us might find ourselves on our own without a man, and if we can learn how to fix things it might come in useful!'

Under Harry's tutelage we covered the floors with hardboard sheets, then we painted the boards with coats of varnish. We painted the walls bright orange and bought yards of light-brown hessian to make curtains. Meanwhile the house was painted inside and out. Finally, on the night before our opening, we put an office desk with a typewriter in the little room on the top floor. We had a telephone, a working kitchen and a playroom. Outside the little toilet was now immaculate and the tiny courtyard swept. We went to bed elated.

The next morning I went straight to our little community centre in Belmont Terrace after dropping the children off at Unicorn, their new school.

Education was a major worry when the children were young. When we moved to our first home in Coulter Road I sent Cleo to the local primary school in Hammersmith. It wasn't the school I would have chosen for her, but by then the professional middle classes in England were beginning to feel the pinch. Most couldn't afford to pay for private education. This meant that they descended on local state schools and elbowed their way into the ones with the best reputations.

The ferocity of the mothers was awesome. Very soon the schools of choice in our area became like bear-pits, with mothers taking control of the Parent–Teacher Associations. The headmistress of our children's school was delighted that she now had a posse of women who would help run the place and organize fund-raising. Who could blame her? She wanted the best for her pupils, but to me she was betraying the less-well-off families who had lived near by for years by favouring the affluent newcomers buying up local houses in order to obtain the best free schooling for their offspring. Soon there were the 'good schools', which by now had a majority of middle-class children, and the worst or 'sink' schools, where the poor and 'problem' families were forced to send their children.

Much the same thing happened with the doctors' surgeries. It didn't take the pushy new residents long to work out which were the best general practitioners so that long-established locals started to be turned away. The GPs were pleased to have nice middle-class families in their surgeries. It made a change from the nits and the scabies.

In 1971 I heard of an adventure in education that was taking place in a church hall in Kew. Two women who had worked as teachers in the state system had a vision that they could create a new education system that would include children from the age of three and allow each child to learn at his or her own pace. We met up with several other parents, and the Unicorn School seemed to develop organically. The two teachers were appointed, and their youth and enthusiasm energized the whole project. I was delighted. Amos, aged four, had been unhappy in his playgroups . Now I had found a scruffy group in a church hall run by an eccentric woman who was amazingly good with children. She removed Amos from my arms, packed him into a sling on her back and fed him biscuits over her shoulder. I was able to go off for a few precious hours. He was almost old enough to graduate from playgroup to school, so Unicorn seemed like a miracle of good timing.

Cleo, aged nine, hadn't been happy at her primary school. She was a sociable child, but the strict discipline made it hard for her to fit in. I was a fairly bohemian mother. Our presence at the school gates with Amos in his pushchair, two Staffordshire bull terriers and my eccentric dress sense probably made her an outcast. In those days the John Betts School was run by disciplinarians, and the students were expected to conform to myriad rules unknown in our house. So in her case, too, Unicorn could not have come at a better time.

Once the children were ensconced at the new school we were invited to other parents' houses. At John Betts all the mothers used to stand outside on the pavement. Our only involvement with the school was to chaperone our offspring there and back, apart from a few times a year where we sat on tiny chairs and were frowned at by largely indifferent teachers. In those days the school was not one particularly favoured by the middle-class incomers, and many of the mothers were shabbily dressed. I knew life was a struggle for them.

Our home in Goldhawk Road became a magnet for local children who came to know it as the 'White House'. It was a Georgian dower house built when Ravenscourt Manor was still standing. Our front door was usually ajar, and not long after we moved from Coulter Road in 1970 friends of our children would drop by and were always made welcome. For me it was a life-changing experience. I grew very fond of them and soon made friends with their mothers in the streets around us. Some of the families lived on welfare benefits in chilly homes where the furniture was worn and battered. We lived in a largely poor area with a multi-ethnic community. The realities of these families' everyday lives contrasted sharply with our own relative affluence. Fighting to get single-parent mothers grants from the local welfare department was a first step that readied me for epic battles with bureaucracy in years to come.

I liked living in a racially mixed community because before coming to London when Jack was in the Navy I had lived in a Cornish village where I had been cut dead by most of the locals as an outsider and dismissed as an oddball by the officers' wives. I had been very lonely. In Hammersmith I loved the smell of exotic foods being cooked in nearby houses, and I enjoyed watching the brightly dressed African women sailing like galleons up and down Shepherd's Bush Market. Soon after I arrived in the area I did some childminding to make a bit of money, and two of the children were mixed race. Our trips to the market were frequently spoiled by people making racist remarks. On several occasions I even got spat at by passers-by.

Now that Jack was earning more money I longed for the sun. As much as I loved England I missed the blue skies and hot weather of the Middle East and the tropics. When Amos was born he contracted a virus. Each day I dreaded going into his bedroom and finding his eyelids stuck tightly together. His nose ran continually, and he needed course after course of penicillin for ear infections. One morning in 1971 I picked him up, and I saw that his mouth was full of candida from all the antibiotics. I telephoned Jack at work and said we had to get Amos to the sun straight away.

It was April in Majorca. As soon as we unpacked, we took Amos down to the little beach in Puerto Pollensa and splashed him with sea water. There were no other tourists because it was out of season, and the tiny villa was barely furnished. I had brought Alice B. Toklas's cookbook along with us on holiday and spent the two weeks cooking as many of her recipes as I could cram down my family's willing gullets.

Within a few days Amos was on the mend. The sea dried out his sinuses, and the sun and fresh air put colour into his cheeks. The tiny beach fringed with pine trees was tranquil. I loved walking along the busy evening streets of Pollensa with Jack and the children. Laughing women, accompanied by their families, tugged at my tie-dye skirts and exclaimed with wonder at their bright colours. Swinging London hadn't yet reached Spain.

I was happy to be in a place where family ties were so evidently strong. In the restaurants grandmothers, mothers, fathers, brothers, sisters, aunts, uncles and children sat together at big tables stuffing their faces with oily, garlicky food redolent with spices. The thought of going back to chilly, grey London made me despondent. I hadn't realized how much I missed living in hot countries, but for the moment there was little alternative. Jack was climbing up the BBC career ladder. For now my life was set on its course, and with a heavy heart I packed our bags to return home.

Part of my malaise was the dearth of family to call my own apart from my twin sister who lived near by and who was a beloved aunt to my children. Jack had a huge family with lots of relatives, but I did not fit in.

I had started off on the wrong foot. I had met Jack in Hong Kong in 1959. My father was Consul in the Portuguese colony of Macau, a ferry ride from Hong Kong. I first spotted Jack on a beach. I heard a voice inside me say, 'That's the man you are going to marry.' Before long I found myself drawn to him. He was so different from the chinless public schoolboys who were officers in the services or who worked for the Hong Kong and Shanghai Bank. In those days Jack played in a jazz band and painted. He told me that his mother wanted him to be an admiral, and so he had left grammar school and gone to the Britannia Royal Naval College in Dartmouth, but now that he was a sub-lieutenant he didn't want to pursue a career in the Navy; he inclined to one in music or the arts.

My parents were posted to Macau on the Chinese mainland, and I was working in Hong Kong as a secretary. My mother thought she had developed a slipped disc, but the specialists told her she had terminal cancer. She duly flew home to England. I felt I should join her to offer moral and physical support. My sister was already studying occupational therapy in Exeter, and my brother Danny was at a public school in Devon. I couldn't leave my mother to my father's bullying, so I travelled on one of the Elder Dempster ships sailing to Southampton with our furniture and belongings, while my father flew back separately.

In 1961, at the age of twenty-two, I married Jack in Kensington Register Office with my best friend Sonia Sword and her friend Mary as witnesses. Jack had promised his mother that we would attend a family get-together afterwards. I had assumed that I had managed to escape the Pizzey tribe that day because, much as much as I loved 'Pop', Jack's kind and gentle father, I regarded

Jack's mother Gwen with great wariness, and as there was no way she was going to welcome me into the family war was mutually declared. Jack dragged me off to the Rubens Hotel somewhere near Victoria after the ceremony, and we walked into a plush red-carpeted restaurant where the clan was assembled, sitting in a sepulchral silence around an enormous dining-table. Their stony faces revealed their disapproval – and I inherited the mother-in-law from hell.

11
DREAMS BECOME NIGHTMARES

As soon as the little semi-detached in Belmont Terrace was ready women started streaming through the door to ask for our help and advice. I was energized, and I began to accompany women who needed to collect money from the local Department of Health and Social Security. I quickly realized why they were soliciting our help. Acton Social Security Office was a forbidding concrete pile, and when I paid my first visit there with a young woman called Brenda who lived in terrible conditions I was dismayed at the treatment she received.

We entered the dingy portals and took our place on shabby chairs lined up in rows. In front of us were men and women stationed behind glass. One by one people shuffled up to the desks, and everyone else waited as long as it took to collect their money or try to argue their case when the accounting was wrong. I went up with Brenda to help her sort out the mistakes that had been made with regard to her benefit payment. The woman behind the glass shield informed me that she was prepared only to deal with Brenda. She was told to go away and to write in if she had any complaints. On our way back to the centre in Belmont Terrace Brenda told me she couldn't read or write. I asked if she had been sent a list of grants or Social Security entitlements, and she said she had received nothing in the post apart from the meagre payments the DHSS had determined she was due.

Now that I frequently escorted women to the DHSS offices I discovered that the people behind the desks treated the vulnerable and often brutalized mothers as if they were criminals. There was a sneering condescension in the attitudes of those dispensing payment and advice to them that seemed to be a hangover from Victorian times. It was as though the staff blamed anyone who had the misfortune to end up in need.

At this point I came across a fiery anarchist called Nicholas Albery. He had created, with a bunch of fellow anarchists that included Nicholas Saunders who wrote *Alternative London*, a community with an alternative lifestyle and had opened an information agency known as BIT. He had been passed a document called the 'A list' and had illegally made copies. This was a secret document that must have been leaked by someone working for the DHSS. It listed all the grants and rights of people who were receiving Social Security benefits. Nicholas also ran a pirate radio station which gave the addresses of local housing that could be squatted all over England. All this was to prove invaluable to me and others involved in the Belmont Terrace project.

Brenda was a classic example of how the system failed the people it was designed to protect. Her husband was in gaol on the Isle of Wight. She had lost her home while he was inside because she failed to make regular rent payments. She was now rehoused in a derelict house behind our community centre. When she came to us she was looking for clothes for her two small children. I went back with her to her house to see what else she needed. I had witnessed poverty in the streets of Hammersmith when I lived in Coulter Road, but I had never seen conditions as appalling as hers outside the Far East. Families, mostly young women and children, had been dumped into these back streets and largely left to their own devices. Brenda's tiny terraced house had a leaking roof and mould growing down most of the interior walls. She had tried to get social services to do something about her accommodation, but her efforts were largely ignored. These terraces had originally been occupied by generations of Hounslow families that had been forcibly moved into newly built high-rise flats in Brentford because the council declared that the houses were about to be demolished. This was untrue. Hounslow Council had realized that Chiswick was going to become an affluent part of their borough, and the housing department wanted to renovate the houses to sell off to young upwardly mobile professionals. Before this happened the council dumped people on their housing lists into the rapidly decaying or derelict former homes in these streets.

Brenda was allowed a visitor's voucher to travel with her children to the Isle of Wight to visit her husband. However, the logistics of such a trip, involving a ferry across to the island, were bewildering to someone illiterate and so unworldly. By the time she arrived visiting hours would be over, and there was no question of an overnight stay. We therefore organized volunteer drivers to take her and the children to the island and bring her back. I offered to do the first trip. Her husband was doing time for robbery, but they were a close family, and she and her children missed him enormously.

This was the first time I had visited anyone in prison. I didn't go into the visitors' room but remained outside. Even there conditions were awful. All around me were crying children and harassed women, some with relatives, nearly all exhausted after long journeys and with just an hour to spend with their partners. I thought Brenda's husband had the better deal. He was at least warm, fed, with people around him. She had nothing but a daily soul-destroying struggle to take care of herself and her children on a pittance.

Once we had a copy of the 'A list' in our hands I decided to go to Acton Social Security and kick up a fuss. The mothers and the volunteers who made frequent trips to the offices invariably returned furious about the despicable treatment they received. We made copies of all the grants available to those on benefits and took the list down to the Social Security office and stood outside the front door handing them out to those entering the building. I then went into the offices with a few other volunteers, and we leafleted the men and women waiting patiently to be interviewed.

We stood at the back of the room after we finished handing out our literature, and, like the Red Sea rising, a wall of people rose to their feet and rushed to the booths. I could see the look of panic on the faces of the staff. People were banging on the counters and waving the leaflets. Very soon a small man erupted from a back office. He was spluttering with indignation. We stood our ground, and I waved at him in a friendly way. He ran across the room towards me demanding, 'Where did you get this information?'

'Can't tell you. It's secret.'

'Get out! Get out!' he yelled.

'You'll have to carry me out,' I retorted. I had an adrenaline rush. Over the past few months I had become used to being pushed around while trying to get fair treatment and justice for the women who had sought our help. This was a moment to savour. For a split second before he called the police we had won. The claimants in the building had ammunition. Shortly afterwards we were escorted out by a benign policeman, and for the next few weeks we made it our business to stand outside the Acton Social Security offices and hand out information to passers-by and those entering the building.

As a result of our activities we made contact with the Claimants' Union. This was a group of people who came together to oppose mistreatment by Social Security offices around Britain. We found we had common ground with this organization and could offer mutual support.

My approach from the start was that I didn't care about people's backgrounds or their political views unless they were blatantly racist; all I was adamant about was that no one had the right to bully anyone else into accepting particular political or religious views. Left, right, pink, blue or in the middle – if they wanted to help that was fine by me.

My beliefs were simple. I felt myself to be a lover of God in all his aspects. I loved him with all my heart and tried to the best of my ability to love my neighbour as myself. This attitude, I knew, was regarded as old-fashioned if not actually insane.

I was convinced that no one should go through the bullying I had experienced at the hands of the radical feminists. We were a motley crew of men and women who genuinely liked working together. Our group included a woman I had met in Ravenscourt Park at the One o'Clock Club. She was sitting in the corner of the hut watching her two young children play. She was older than the other mothers around her, and she looked rather lonely. I sat next to her, and we got talking. She told me she was a nurse and lived near me. I told her about the little house in Belmont Road, and she promised to come down and visit us. Her name was Ann Ashby. She was to become my right-hand assistant, and when I eventually left England she took over the running of the refuge.

Our links with organizations such as the squatting movement grew, and I went home at night full of indignation at the injustices that existed in one of the wealthiest countries in the world. Gradually I became aware of tension at home. Jack was still working as a reporter on *Nationwide,* a BBC evening television programme that frequently covered social issues. When he came home at night he plainly did not want to be regaled with a litany of my activities. I agreed that I would leave my day-to-day experiences outside the house.

I collected the children from school and prepared supper for them. After they had done their homework and got ready for bed I would prepare a meal for Jack and myself. He never came home before eight, so we would sit down to eat on our own, but I found conversation becoming increasingly stilted. We had little to say to one another, especially since I couldn't discuss my community work. Very soon we resembled the couples I used to watch in restaurants when we were first married. 'We'll never sit in silence like that!' I had said – but I was wrong.

Another problem was his formidable mother, Gwen, who would visit us in Hammersmith to see her son and grandchild. Her husband Pop was embarrassed because of her open hostility towards me. He loved food and was more than happy to eat one of my big meals, but Gwen always flourished her digestive pills after dinner and made pointed remarks about rich food and other digs about my lifestyle. I finally got up the courage to tell her that I wasn't happy to spend weekends in Eastbourne in their immaculate home.

In retaliation she pursuaded Jack that Cleo, then aged three, was better off spending most of her holidays and half-terms with her grandparents. I was devastated. Cleo loved staying there, and undoubtedly Pop was a loving grandfather, but I was concerned about Gwen who, I knew, had a tendency to bully. When Cleo returned during term time she was understandably resentful at giving up her spoilt, affluent lifestyle in Sussex. It was several years before she grew out of wanting to live with them. By then she would have been six.

My sister often came round to spend time with us in the early years of my marriage, and when she was there I felt less alone. When Cleo was a few years old I tried to see my father Cyril and his new wife Marjorie. He had remarried six months after my mother died. I felt that Cleo had a right to know her grandfather, so Jack and I drove to Purley where he had bought a property. By then he had sold our old home, Hunthay House, near Axminster. The visit was a disaster. Within a few minutes he started to rant about my ungrateful behaviour, and I saw a look of fear in my daughter's eyes and decided that there was no point in trying to re-establish any sort of relationship with him. My daughter was not going to be brought up in fear as I had been. We left, and I didn't see him again until the day in 1982 I carried his ashes to my mother's grave. The wind blew the piles of ash high up over the peaceful Devon grave-yard, and I stood there thinking that the grey cloud floating around my head was the man who had terrorized me for so much of my life. A sense of peace descended over the church, and my sister and I headed off to the local pub to celebrate.

Through much of our married life Jack was away a great deal, and I found myself living like a single mother. It was a bitter pill to find that the women who were happy to entertain us as a couple were unwilling to receive me in their houses on my own, especially at weekends when their husbands were present. My world was made up of couples. Uncoupled, I was ignored. The little house in Belmont Terrace became as much of a refuge for me as it was for those who came for our advice and help.

Jack had friends who lived in a lovely house in a place called Boulter's Island in Maidenhead. The house was an old shooting lodge which had been previously been owned by the television broadcaster Richard Dimbleby. Before long the couple had embarked on divorce, and the wife, Georgia, asked me to take care of the house while she went home to the United States.

The lodge became a valued retreat for me and the children. It was perched over a weir that thundered outside the front door. The swimming-pool, filled with water from the Thames, was a delight in summer, and I would make the family large meals in the lovely kitchen. The bedrooms had french windows leading out on to the lawns. In order to get to the house it was necessary to row across the river. There were two boats; one was a flat-bottomed dory with a powerful engine that enabled us to roar up and down the river, while the other was a sedate rowing-boat.

Having access to the house made a big difference to my life. After a week of struggling with other people's problems I could sit on a chair in the garden on the tip of the island and watch the spray through the sunlight refracting the colours of the rainbow. All I could hear was the bickering of ducks; occasionally swans passed by looking disdainful but giving sidelong glances to see if we were going to reward them with scraps from our table.

Back in west London the little house was now full of activity, and then one day a woman walked into the little office on the first floor and changed my life for ever.

12

SOMEWHERE TO GO

I can clearly recall Kathy's arrival. I was sitting behind the small desk in the office at the back of the house in Belmont Terrace. She had dyed black hair, a thin lined face and intense brown eyes. She told me that she had been beaten regularly by her husband. She took off her jumper, and I could see livid purple bruises from her neck to her waist. 'No one will help me,' she said, and I felt such a jolt of rage that it was as though I had been electrocuted.

She plainly couldn't go back to him, so I had no option but to take her home with me that night. Her children were old enough to take care of one another, she assured me, so we collected my children from school and returned to my house.

After giving Kathy something to eat I put her to bed. She was tired and, as far as I knew, fell asleep immediately. Later on Jack came home and asked if anything had happened that day. 'Nothing much,' I said sticking to the pact we had made not to go into details about my activities. He was standing on the stairs on his way up to change for the evening when there was a loud banging on the front door.

'Oh,' I added casually, 'there's a woman asleep in Amos's room. She's been badly battered by her husband.'

The hammering continued, and I opened it to find Kathy's husband standing on the doorstep. I stood there looking at him and realized I was not afraid. That was the moment I discovered that I was afraid of no male apart from my father – whom I hadn't seen in years. I could face this man quite calmly.

'How did you know she was here?' I asked.

'She rang me.'

'Well, you're not coming in. You beat her very badly – I've seen the bruises! Go home, and I'll talk to you tomorrow.'

He was crying and shaking. 'I can't be without my Kathy,' he sobbed.

I felt the rage rising in my chest. 'You'll have to manage,' I said curtly and shut the door in his face. Watching his behaviour reminded me of the times as a child I had seen my father crying and unsteady after a particularly ugly session of bullying and screaming at my mother. It roused feelings of disgust rather than sympathy in me. As I walked back into the sitting-room I mused over the fact that Kathy indeed must have phoned the man she claimed had beaten her so badly that she was afraid for her life.

As a child I had been incredulous that my mother never made any serious attempt to leave my father. Often, during the seventeen years of our lives with her before she died, she had taken breaks from him of several months while we were at boarding-school in England. I hoped that these would become permanent, but soon she would pack her bags and be on her way back to him. I was too frightened of her to ask her why she didn't leave him for good when most of her conversation about him consisted of a litany of his wrongdoings. Moreover, she swore she hated him.

Now here was Kathy summoning her husband when for once she was safe and he had no way of knowing her whereabouts. I was confused, but I grasped that she, like my mother, was not simply a victim fleeing her husband's violence; somehow she was complicit in the relationship and unwilling to extricate herself from a dangerous situation.

Unravelling the mysteries of Kathy's emotional life proved complex. I found myself making appointments with her doctor, her psychiatrist, her housing officer and other agents in an attempt to try to comprehend the couple's situation. I met a wall of hostility. As far as I could understand, she had been offered solutions by everyone involved in her case but had always chosen to return to her husband.

The psychiatrist told me that she 'provoked' violence in her husband. I knew my mother had provoked my father to insane outbursts of rage. But even if Kathy were somehow complicit in the pain and violence done to her, surely the psychiatrist should want to understand why the couple behaved as they did and make them aware of the damage they were inflicting on their children. He was adamant that such 'dustbin' families could express their feelings for each other only through violence. I restrained an urge to smack his face and told him through gritted teeth that my parents had been well educated but still destroyed one another through violence. My argument fell on deaf ears.

If Kathy had parents who had validated her with their love, maybe she would not have made a relationship with an extremely abusive man. I knew that my own childhood had not allowed me to experience a warm loving relationship with my parents. What I learned from them was to do battle every time I was crossed. It was Miss Williams, who ran the holiday home, and a few other warm, caring adults who had taught me how to love. Maybe it was possible to create a sanctuary in which women like Kathy could learn better ways to relate to other adults. I didn't have much time to ponder. Within a few days Kathy had returned to her husband, and other women came to the door with their children asking for help.

What was obvious from the the day we opened our advice centre was that while there were a great many genuinely caring people working in the statutory agencies their job was made impossible by red tape. This meant they had to treat their clients according to a set of rules laid out in manuals by civil servants and academics who had never actually dirtied their hands with life's problems.

In the early days of most of these agencies staff were drawn largely from the educated middle classes. Their attitude towards clients tended to be patronizing and based on their own values. Their powers were so absolute as to make those who needed help reluctant to consult them, which is why we quickly attracted many women who came direct to us because they felt they would be less likely to be judged for their lifestyles.

Ros made her way to us claiming to be the victim of violence. She was closely followed by her bewildered husband. He swore – and I believed him – that he had never lifted a finger to her. He was disabled and on benefits, and I could tell from the way he behaved that he was not a violent man. I suggested that she stay with us in the house, and we would ask him to come over so that they could discuss what was bothering her and see if she really wanted to leave him.

She was frightened of everything. She was a worn, hunched, dried-out stick of a woman. Her lank fair hair lay limply around her face, and her big bony hands were constantly fidgeting with something in nervous anticipation of disaster. After a while she told us that she had been left on the doorstep of a mental hospital shortly after she was born. She had grown up in the hospital. She said that that during her years there she had been raped by inmates and had given birth almost every year since puberty to so many babies she had lost count. One by one the newborn infants had been taken away from her.

Gradually she relaxed at the centre until one day I arrived at the house and she told me there had been a telephone call from a social worker who was looking for her. 'He says he has one of my sons in his office, and he wants to come and see me.'

'Maybe we should think about seeing the social worker on his own, and then we can discuss the best way for you to meet your child.'

'I told him to come tomorrow morning,' she said, beaming.

I was dreading the meeting. I knew the boy had probably fantasized about meeting his mother for a long time, and he was going to be faced with a woman who looked like a wraith from a rubbish heap. We spent the afternoon sifting through piles of clothes for something nice for her to wear, and someone promised to do her hair first thing in the morning.

The social worker entered our office with a tall, good-looking young man. Ros and her son scrutinized each other, and the atmosphere grew tense as the boy could not hide his disappointment as he gazed at his mother. She stood helplessly twisting her hands, and before long he stumbled out of the room. We heard him pounding down the stairs and out of the front door.

'Couldn't you have arranged to meet Ros first before bringing him here?' I asked the social worker.

He shrugged and turned on his heels. His job was done. He didn't care about the outcome. The box on the form was ticked, and he could return to his office. The feckless mother and her illegitimate son; a botched reunion. Who cared?

Ros did. She was devastated. Gradually she began to recognize that her long-suffering husband really did love her. With our support she returned to him, and they visited us when they felt the need to talk about their relationship. I was glad she was not alone.

Matilda was a much older woman. She arrived at our door lugging an enormous battered suitcase. She had a thick Irish accent and no teeth. She sat down in the office and asked to stay the night since she was homeless. None of us had the heart to turn her away. Ros was then still living in the house and said she would be glad of the company.

In time Matilda took over the running of the community centre. She scrubbed and cleaned and before long became a tyrant. No one was allowed to walk on her newly washed floors or stub out a cigarette without immediately washing the ashtray. If she was crossed she cursed like a navvy. 'All I want', she said when I arrived at the office, 'is a room of me own.'

I decided to help. I spent hours searching the advertisements at the back of newspapers for a room and eventually found something that sounded suitable. The day arrived, and I took her to her new accommodation. I left her sitting on a single bed in a freshly painted bedsit. She had her suitcase at her feet, and she was hugging the radiator. 'T'anks,' she said, giving me a gummy smile. I went home feeling virtuous. I had made an old lady happy. I paid her first month's rent out of my own pocket and arranged for an agency that took care of the homeless to take on her case.

About three weeks later I got a call from Matilda's landlady. She was concerned, she said, because Matilda was never there. There was just the suitcase sitting unpacked in the middle of the room. I contacted the agency who tracked her down to Charing Cross Station where she had been spotted begging. Matilda sent me a message to say she was fine. The room was somewhere to keep her possessions safe. I realized I had a lot to learn.

Very quickly, as word got round that there was a place that would take in women and children, the little house started to fill up. One of the first to arrive was Becky, pregnant and with a small child. When she turned up she was calm and composed, unlike many of the women who came for our help who seemed bewildered and unable to cope with the hand they had been dealt. She told us that her partner was a drunken brute and she no longer wanted to live with him. He had beaten her so badly that he had detached a retina and left her partially blind.

Becky was to stay for a long time and become a big part of my life. By the end of the morning she had organized herself with a bed in the small office and a crib for her two-year-old daughter. I left the house that night feeling relieved. At last I had someone who could stay in the house at night and take responsibility for the running of the project.

Another very young woman arrived with a small baby. Elsie told me that she had rebelled against her loving family and had run away with a man who turned out to be violent. They were living on a caravan site in an adjacent borough, and she had seen an article about us in the paper and decided to escape. She told her partner that she had a doctor's appointment – and for once he let her go off alone. She was absolutely terrified of him. He was enormous and known to the police for his violent attacks. He had bitten off a man's nose in a fight. I was not in a hurry to meet him and hoped she could remain undetected.

Ann Ashby used to push her two small children from her home near me down Chiswick High Road to help out at least twice a week. Another helper was a young and beautiful blonde called Sonia. She arrived with two daughters and a book of self-published poetry. There was a luminous quality about her, and she was one of the most loving, gentle women to come to Chiswick Women's Aid. I was in awe of her resilience and good nature.

We discovered that she had been savagely battered by her mother as a child. She believed that her mother hated her because she was adored by her father. The mother had also been violent to Sonia's father and had run the home along military lines. To others she seemed a prim and proper working-class woman. The front step was always polished and the windows gleamed. As soon as Sonia was old enough to clean the house she was bullied by her mother into endless housework to maintain the pristine cleanliness and tidiness. Eventually Sonia's father decided to leave. The daughter remembered her father coming downstairs with a suitcase in his hand. He sat down and apologized to her. He told her he had to leave and he hoped that once he'd gone her mother would be kinder to her. Sonia watched him walk out of the house and never saw or heard from him again.

She married the first man who came into her life when she was sixteen to escape her mother; also because he was much older and reminded her of her father. José was a self-employed builder. She soon discovered that he was as physically abusive as the mother she had left behind. Very soon she was pregnant with her first daughter – and then she was trapped. José was morbidly jealous of her. If they were out he accused her of flirting with men who worked in shops or who passed her in the street. He would work himself up into huge rages and attack her. On one occasion he broke her nose, and before it was healed she was back in hospital after he broke it again. In those days no one asked any questions.

She had tried to get away from him, but her social worker's sole suggestion was to take a room in a local homeless-family block of flats. Her husband soon found out where she was. He broke into her room in the middle of the night and dragged her out. This time he beat the eldest child as well, and Sonia was convinced that she had to get away or he might kill them both. Her social worker told her about our project, and Sonia duly made her way to Chiswick with the girls.

Becky, Elsie and Sonia made a great team as full-time residents in the little house. By now several national newspapers had picked up the story of our women's project, and the press started referring to the occupants of Belmont Terrace as 'battered women'. Indeed all the women who had recently been through the door had been physically beaten, but some of them – and that included Becky – were perfectly capable of being violent themselves. Becky, I discovered, was a wonderful person except when she had a few drinks. Then she became a monster. It was as though a very powerful rage lay dormant until alcohol let it loose.

Everyone loved her, and the mothers and children were grateful because she was a brilliant administrator. If there was ever a problem with Social Security she could sort it out. We discussed her violent tendencies with her, and she promised to try to stay off the drink. One day she told me that she had given away seven other children. At first I thought she was joking – but she assured me she wasn't. It seemed that Becky was only happy when she was pregnant; once the babies were born she dumped them. She literarily gave them away to anyone who wanted a child, and in one case, she told me, she left a toddler in a shop. She also told me that one of her children had died when very young – a cot death, she said.

There was a cold aspect to her. Even while she discussed the death of her child her face remained impassive. She did have an irrepressible sense of humour, and she was always ready for a party, but

I was aware that something had happened to her that cut her off from normal emotions. I knew I had to wait until she was ready to tell me more about her life. I learned not to push women into telling me about themselves until they were ready. Some wanted to open up almost immediately after they arrived, but for others it could take months or even years before I could fit the missing pieces of the jigsaw.

One of the most important lessons of those early days was learning how to listen – not just to what a woman was saying but also what she omitted. Sometimes it was not the words but the silence between them that was significant. They were telling me things they felt unable to tell anyone else. They spoke about deep, dark secrets of terrible sexual abuse – and sometimes confessions of their own deviant behaviour at times of their lives during which they had felt trapped and confused. These could include acts of sexual perversion, masochism, incest and bestiality. I learned not to react. Sometimes it was hard to prevent tears welling up, but it was the person pouring out her secrets who really needed to cry. Occasionally I would feel nauseated by the stories I heard, but a woman might be confiding in me because it had dawned on her just how appalling her life had been. I would get home, run a very hot bath and scrub myself clean.

I learned to ask a woman who was ready to talk to tell me her first memory. From there we began a journey together. I would take her hand, and we would go back to when she could first remember pain and suffering. We would stop whenever she wanted. Slowly each day we would take up the story once more. It was hard work, and I recognized how brave those women were who were prepared to make that journey of exploration into their pasts.

I came to believe that the seeds of destruction are sown in early childhood – possibly in the womb. We know that every cigarette a woman smokes when she is pregnant is shared by the baby. Every drink also crosses the placenta. It may be that emotions of fear and rage also damage a developing foetus. When pregnant women came into the house worried that their babies seemed not to be moving I would generally reassure them. Your baby is frozen with fear, I would explain, and if you wait a day or two until you've calmed down you will almost certainly feel the infant move again.

13

THE CYCLE OF VIOLENCE

The overcrowding in the refuge was becoming a major problem, and the hostility towards our our little house presented practical problems. Hounslow Council decided to charge us rates, and with our virtually non-existent budget there was no way we could pay this. Even though money was coming in from the public, there were many mouths to feed and clothe, so we had very little cash left to spend on anything. Our major financial worry was that the Department of Health and Social Security insisted that most of the women coming to us had homes and men in their lives who wanted them back and who could provide for them. Even if a man was violent he could demand that his wife and children return because he was offering them accommodation and financial support.

In order to get welfare benefit a woman had to embark on divorce proceedings. This took for ever, because without money she had to apply for free legal aid. While that was coming through I had to find the money to take care of her and her children mostly out of my own pocket. The only assistance offered to a desperate woman trying to flee from a partner was for social services to take her children into care, leaving the mother to find accommodation for herself. With no access to money this meant that women were either forced to return to their violent partner or lose their children into care.

Fortunately I had the assistance of a helpful accountant, Allen Cohen. He was our family accountant, and David Morris was our solicitor. The two of them advised me to set the project up as a charity so that people who wished to send us donations could obtain tax relief, which would benefit all concerned. Thus Chiswick Women's Aid came into being.

Every morning the post was opened in the tiny back office, and we would sit around reading out the letters that accompanied them and working out how much we had in the kitty to keep the house going. At first, because I believed that the money coming in belonged to the mothers I would leave money in the cash-box with a stash of IOU cards in a pile near by. The problem was that, although the money visibly dwindled, no one ever bothered to fill in an IOU. Becky laughed at my naïvety, and of course she was right. She took command of the cash – and I grew up fast.

I wrote to Sir Keith Joseph who was the Conservative Secretary of State for Social Services and told him about the plight of victims of domestic violence. I explained that we were living in a small house and that the overcrowding was giving rise to major complaints from the neighbourhood but that there was nowhere else to go. I got a letter back from one of his staff to say that it was the press attention causing the overcrowding and that I was trying to make myself a media cult figure. I was upset, because not long before in 1972 Joseph had given a speech in which he talked about the cycle of deprivation; as a result he was vilified by the far left, and he had only just managed to hold on to his job.

I, too, was thinking about cycles of deprivation but seeking to develop the notion in order to explain how in a violent and dysfunctional family patterns of behaviour learned in early childhood could damage and destroy the next generation. The problem was that in the early 1970s the radical-left intelligentsia placed the blame for society's ills squarely on the class system and the policies of the ruling Conservative Party, then led by Prime Minister Edward Heath. This gave birth to the idea of a 'victim mentality'. I was informed by the feminist social workers who came to the house that their clients were 'victims' who required their solidarity – because 'all women were innocent victims of their partners' violence'.

On one occasion a male social worker was in our office talking to his client. I heard her screaming and shouting, so I went to see what was going on. The social worker was backed up against a wall. He had his hands stretched out ineffectually in an attempt to stop her hitting him. 'I understand your hostility,' he was gibbering.

I grabbed her by the collar and dragged her off him. 'Give over, you silly bitch,' I said. 'You promised you'd give up fighting!'

It grieved me to hear social workers and others parroting the belief that in a violent family only the male children would grow up to become aggressive adults. Already I had evidence that all off-spring were affected by violence in their homes, not just the boys. I knew that my own family could trace at least three generations of violent parenting on both sides of our family tree, and I could detect the same violence in many of the mothers entering our refuge.

A few weeks later I was summoned to attend a meeting in south London's Elephant and Castle where the headquarters of the Department of Health and Social Security was based. I took Ann and Becky along. We entered the grey concrete gulag and were ushered into a room with a long oval polished table. We were met by scowling civil servants, and after initial introductions I was asked by a granite-faced woman how I thought I was going to run my project. 'I will pray,' I said – because that is what I did in an almost continuous stream of pleas to God every day. There was a moment of unbearable silence. I realized that no one wanted to say anything facetious because it might sound blasphemous, but clearly few present believed in a god or in the efficacy of prayer.

The meeting really never got off the ground. Becky explained her position within the project and her own personal circumstances, but no one was listening, as they wanted to force us to close our door for good on grounds of overcrowding. From the beginning the three of us were adamant that there was no way we were going to comply. We got up and walked out. Behind us we left a very hostile bunch of civil servants. I was to discover later that I had made a long-term enemy of the stony-faced woman.

The following year, 1973, proved a momentous one. We had a telephone call from a man called Neville Vincent who said he owned a construction firm and would like to help us. He came down to the house in Belmont Terrace, sat on a mattress and asked what we needed. We explained our pressing space problem and the threat that I would be taken to Acton Magistrates' Court on a charge of overcrowding.

He told us to find a suitable house and said that he would buy it for us. We were jubilant, and once the older children were in school we went down to Chiswick High Road to an estate agent and found a property that would become known as the Big House. It was a huge derelict building, but Neville promised to do it up, and before long we were able to move in.

The general belief was that it was only the 'lower classes' that beat their wives. A judge was heard to remark in the case of a middle-class man who was found guilty of beating his wife, 'If he had been a miner in South Wales I might have overlooked it. There are some sections of the community where beating one's wife is not the same as others.'

One middle-class wife I met gave us her account of her life at home. 'I can't turn up looking as if I've boxed several rounds with Cassius Clay, can I? Imagine my friend's reaction if I said, "Sorry to look like this, but John thumped me last night." They wouldn't believe me – or they would think he'd caught me with another man and had been full of so-called righteous indignation. Why should they take my word for what happened at home? They see him as the genial teacher on speech days or at the golf club – or when he's cleaning his car on Sundays and greeting neighbours. What can I do? I'm dependent on him for every coin that comes into the house. And I don't hate him. This is an awful thing to say, but I've fallen into a pattern. It's like an equation. John upset equals I get thumped. It's pathetic, isn't it? I love him, though – and he never lets the children see.'

June, a waitress with no children, gave me this explanation before she returned to her violent partner. 'If you love a bloke, a thumping every week or so can't stop you loving him, can it? I got mad with him because he went to the pub with his mates, and I played him up when he came home. So he slugged me. He's good to me, mind you. I never go short if I want a bit extra for the house-keeping, so I shouldn't grumble. As I say, if you love someone a thumping every so often can't stop you loving him, can it?'

Every time I heard a woman use the expression 'I love him' after describing terrible bouts of violence I would remember my mother's unwillingness to leave my father. He didn't batter her physically, but he rampaged and abused her verbally. Her hysterical tears blighted my childhood, and here I was faced with the fact that some women given the option to leave brutal partners refused to do so. This is what agency workers were mainly complaining about: many really tried to assist the women who sought their help. They did their utmost to get woman and children away from violent and brutalizing domestic situations, but after all their efforts, when they thought they had settled the families elsewhere, the mother would choose to go home. I understood their frustration. Now I felt I needed to understand why some women seemed to become dependent on violence. From everything I had seen I developed an idea that the answer lay in their early childhood.

One day a tiny woman, Lucy, burst into the refuge with a beautiful little girl. I was struck by the mother's aggressive demeanour. She loudly denounced her husband Ron who she claimed had attacked her. She said she and her daughter had been brought to us by the police who believed the two of them were in danger.

She had met Ron at a bowling club. He had seemed a quiet and steady man who owned his own flat. He had fallen in love with her. She had never really loved him, she maintained, but realized that she needed security and wanted a child. She claimed that he had regularly beaten her and that she lived in fear of her life.

Lucy proved a very difficult woman to have in the community. During the morning meetings there were complaints about her rudeness and outbursts of temper. She was irritable with her daughter, and one of the mothers expressed anxiety that if Lucy were alone with the child she might beat her up.

I got a phone call from her husband Ron. He had heard of the refuge through the media publicity and contacted me to see if his wife and child were at the house. When he arrived – a tiny man almost as small as his wife – his version of the story was very different from hers. He said she had moved in with him shortly after they met and soon after told him she was pregnant. He very much wanted the child, but even in those early days of the relationship he recognized that she was quick to lose her temper and scream at him. Once the baby was born she started lashing out physically.

He worked as a caretaker for the block of flats in which they lived, so he was at home for much of the time, and it was he who mainly cared for the little girl. Soon after she was born she exhibited a number of worrying symptoms and was treated at a children's hospital. The child had a 'nervous' stomach and was not putting on weight. At the time none of the health professionals suspected that Lucy was violent and the baby was exhibiting emotional stress.

Ron begged to see his daughter, and the mother reluctantly agreed, so I said I would supervise the visit.

He was in tears as he reached out to cuddle his daughter. The little girl clung to her father, and I could see that she had a far stronger emotional bond with him than with Lucy. Later he told me that his wife was going to get a solicitor to start divorce proceedings and didn't want him to have access to the child. I sent him home saying I would see if I could make her see reason. He was willing to agree to a divorce and to pay whatever she wanted in maintenance as long as he could see his daughter on a regular basis.

I was not surprised when Lucy refused to comply. I said we could not support her claim to be a victim of Ron's violence. From watching her behaviour and seeing her relationship with her child there was no doubt in my mind that the little girl would be better off with her father.

Not long after this Lucy gathered up her daughter and their possessions and left us for a newly established refuge in Acton. As soon as I knew she was there I telephoned them and asked to see someone to discuss the case. There was no case to discuss, I was told in icy tones. This woman was a victim of her husband's violence – and that was that.

Any refuge was better than none, but it concerned me that people working at such places should spout the notion that all women were innocent victims of men's violence. Of the first hundred women who came through our doors sixty-two were as violent as the men they had left behind. I had to face the fact that the males were always going to be blamed for violence within a family and that, like poor Ron, false claims would be made against them and that the women would always be believed.

In most cases the violence was both physical and mental, but sometimes there were no blows – just cruel and damaging words. I always used to say that bruises can fade and bones can be mended but words can destroy the soul. Even the most balanced of women needed time to recover from the emotional damage that had been meted out to them by callous and vicious partners. It could take time for a woman to recover her sense of self and rebuild her confidence.

I think that deliberately to take away a person's sense of self-worth is a form of soul murder, and I am extremely glad that these days courts take emotional violence into account. Before the advent of 'no fault' divorces a woman had to produce signed and witnessed photographs of her bruises and other injuries as well as a report signed by a qualified medical doctor before she could claim divorce on grounds of cruelty. There was no possibility then for divorce on the grounds of emotional violence and abuse.

Where women were violence-prone themselves because they had experienced violence and often sexual abuse as children, they needed long-term therapeutic care. All children were affected. It was ludicrous to assume that little boys didn't suffer from such experiences and that only little girls were victims. It was naïve to think that children were unaffected by the screaming and crying and the thumping that went on when a couple were fighting.

Normal women who get into violent relationships unwittingly tend to get out as soon as they can; they take more care when forming future sexual relationships. Violence-prone women usually return home many times and often use a refuge as a revolving door in their continued battle against their partners. If they do leave, the chances are they will very quickly find themselves in another violent relationship. These were the women who most needed our help, and I decided that however much I might be reviled for telling this unwelcome truth I would make clear the differences between the two types of women who asked for our help.

Predictably, this theory turned me into a figure of hate, and female journalists who came to interview me generally refused to publish what I had to say on the subject of women with violent tendencies. Most of the interviewers were feminists, and I got the impression back then that our findings from our work – controversial as these were at the time – were never going to be allowed to emerge into the light of day.

14

LOVE – OR ADDICTION?

Jack Ashley, the Labour Member of Parliament, used to visit us regularly and undertook considerable research into domestic violence in his constituency with the aid of his wife. In July 1973 he rose to his feet in the House of Commons to talk about the subject. This was only the second occasion the matter had ever been raised in Parliament. The first time was back in 1878 after Frances Power Cobbe had written a paper on 'Wife Torture in England'. She had addressed her appeal to the Prime Minister Benjamin Disraeli. He wept tears on hearing her evidence and promised that something would be done. He set up a Select Committee to examine the problem, but eventually the issue faded into oblivion.

I was in the Visitors' Gallery in the House of Commons with other women from the refuge when Jack got up to speak. We looked down on an empty chamber. He made the point that had the House been discussing cruelty to dogs the place would have been packed. I was cynical by this time, and, sure enough, the outcome of Jack's impassioned plea was that a Select Committee was formed to gather evidence and report on its findings. We were the first women to give evidence to the new committee, but I felt that, like the one a hundred years earlier, this would make endless recommendations with no powers to follow them through and that the issue of domestic violence would be swept under the carpet once more.

When we returned to the refuge after giving evidence we decided that this time we would not allow ourselves to be lulled into a false sense of security that things would change. We needed to take action ourselves as well as keep the subject in the public's eye. Even if Hounslow Council was trying to close us down I knew that what mattered was the strength of public opinion. Moreover, it was press attention that would keep the door of the refuge open and sufficient funds coming in to pay the bills.

I was struck by how many of the social services and agency workers involved with families at the refuge saw themselves as harbingers of revolution. Under Edward Health the country experienced the three-day week during which electricity was limited to certain hours in the day and uncollected rubbish piled up in the streets. It felt as though Britain was on the brink of anarchy. However, while London and larger cities such as Manchester and Liverpool were reverberating with calls for a communist or socialist revolution I knew that the vast majority of the public wanted no such thing.

The trouble with much of the brainwashing that went on in the name of sociology courses in universities was that all those in need of state support had to be convinced that they were 'victims'. No one was responsible for anything. If you were poor it was because you were oppressed by capitalism – even if you refused to work under any circumstances. If you were a criminal it was because you were oppressed, so, if money was taken away from the undeserving rich and given to you, suddenly you would mend your ways and become a model citizen. If you were a woman and obviously violent you could excuse your violence on the grounds of self-defence. This was the new religion, and there was no point in arguing with left-wing fanatics.

I scoured public libraries seeking information on domestic violence. There was nothing to be found. I was starting to think I should commit some of my own ideas to print, but meanwhile we had to keep the refuge door open. Many weekends when Jack was away I would load the van with my children and with as many mothers and their offspring as we could cram in. Sometimes it would take several trips down to Maidenhead, but once on Boulter's Island we could relax, and the children loved roaring up and down the Thames in the motorboat. We would put the babies in bathtubs as makeshift cots, and everyone else bunked up in the luxurious bedrooms. It gave us time to talk and to think. I cooked big meals, and we sat down to eat in splendour at the large antique dining-table. When my friend Georgia eventually sold the house she donated most of the furniture to the refuge in Chiswick, so, for a while, until the hordes of children managed to destroy it with their boisterous antics the Big House looked remarkably grand.

The mothers who accompanied us to Boulter's Island were by

now close friends. Becky, Elsie, Sonia and I were a very tight team. I felt particularly close to Sonia, perhaps partly because we both had had cold and violent mothers. I remember one evening when she was sitting with me on the tip of the island and we were watching the sunset and listening to the roar of the weir I felt an instant of great happiness. Such moments tended to be few and far between. Ahead of us was a long, pleasurable night of feasting and drinking wine. I will always remember that idyllic evening – thanks to the kindness of our host Georgia in letting us take over her home.

During that visit Sonia told me about her childhood with her father, but what I most remembered was her describing the effect her husband's voice had on her. She explained that if she heard it she knew she would go back to him. 'There's no need to worry,' I said, 'because he has no idea where you are. We'll give your address in confidence to the divorce court judge, but it won't be on his solic-itor's papers – so you are perfectly safe.' I was about to go on holiday with Jack and the children, and I wanted her to feel secure because her divorce case was due to come up while I was away.

I was in Spain when I got a phone call from Ann. She said that a mistake had been made and that the refuge's address had been included in the divorce papers. Sonia's husband had tracked her down, and at night, when was all the occupants of the house were asleep, he had phoned her and begged her to return. One morning Becky discovered that Sonia and her two children had gone. She had left a letter for me, but shortly after she returned home she had a car accident. Apparently while driving up a steep hill her vehicle smashed head-on into a tree at the side of the road, killing her outright. What occurred the day of her death I will never know; something had caused her to lose control of the car.

The news was devastating, and for days I walked around bereft. I felt we needed to find Sonia's children and comfort them, but Ann said they had been taken off by the local social services, and they refused to tell me where they were.

As soon as I returned to England I tried to track the girls down because I wanted to offer them a permanent home. I was met with a wall of silence. All I was told was their father didn't want them and they were in care. I reread the letter Sonia had left behind. One sentence especially disturbed me. 'I need to be loved by him for some unknown reason – by him alone.' Here was a highly intelligent woman who was gentle and caring yet seemed unable to leave a man who had nearly killed her on several occasions. Not only had she risked her life living with him but she had allowed her children to be brutally abused and battered. She told me how the children had witnessed her being tied up and beaten. And her local hospital was used to her being admitted with broken bones.

The only thing that seemed to make sense to me was that, for some people, violence was in some way addictive – they became dependent on it in their relationships. I would say to a woman, 'Think of him as your pusher. The only way you are going to get over him is to go cold turkey – like a drug addict.' I recalled Sonia describing her husband's voice and saying that she would feel compelled to follow him if he summoned her. That was when I first started thinking about addictive relationships. 'Co-dependency' wasn't a term in use back then, but from my discussions with women emerging from violent relationships I came to realize that not all of them were unreservedly relieved to walk out on their abusive partner and that, for them, splitting up could be a complex and confusing matter.

I often used to joke that the first day a woman came into the refuge she was on a high because she was safe and so were her children. The second day she was busy getting their lives organized, but by the third day I would notice that the high had dissipated. That was the day she was most likely to think about going back to her partner.

I wished I had listened more attentively to Sonia's descriptions of being abandoned by her father. The day he walked out of the house, she told me, she made a vow that she would never ever leave the man that she had married. Certainly she adored her father; her bond was with him and not her violent mother. Was there some memory of this bond in her relationship with her violent and much older husband?

Sonia wasn't the only woman at the refuge to die. I had begged Jenny not to go home to her husband. She was a big, laughing Afro-Caribbean woman with six children who joined us because, although a judge had given her the right to the family house when they separated, she couldn't remain at home because her husband continued to harass her. We took the matter back to court, and the judge warned the husband that he would go to gaol if he disobeyed the injunction to leave her alone. I wasn't happy about her returning home. I knew that most injunctions were not worth the paper they were written on if a man was truly violent.

Jenny's husband exhibited all the signs of being compulsively violent. He told her constantly that he would kill her. He was morbidly jealous and followed her everywhere. I regarded it as dangerous for her to leave the refuge for this reason. Jenny argued with me about this, rationalizing that, although they jointly owned the house, she paid the mortgage and all the running costs because her husband didn't work. Most of the time he took drugs, and the only money he earned was from some drug dealing. She had come to Britain from the Caribbean with her family years before, and her house represented the fulfilment of a struggle to get an education and a successful working career. She was particularly proud of her hard-earned furniture, and the idea of losing her material goods together with her home devastated her.

Before long her husband's solicitors went up in front of the judge and told him she had not returned to the property. He ordered that she either returned there or the house would be put up for sale. She duly went home with her offspring. Within a matter of days her husband had got into the house and stabbed her to death. She lost her life – and six children were left without a mother. Their father went to prison, and the children went in care. After her death I put Jenny's picture up in the little cubby-hole next to that of Sonia and wondered how many more faces of women I had loved would come to line those walls.

Some days I found myself in despair, because the threats of prosecution for overcrowding at the Big House were getting more and more difficult to fend off. Legally we were meant to have no more than thirty-six people living there, but we never turned any family in crisis away.

Now and again when women and staff received bad news about a court case during which a judge had made a poor decision we would dress up in our oldest clothes and take ourselves down to the local green to cheer ourselves up by playing football. Ann and I, being the biggest of the women, would play in goal, and the mothers would play against the male staff – we always included men among the twenty or more staff and volunteers; indeed the men would often work and play with the children.

The football match usually restored our spirits. Sometimes if it was raining staff would play guitar for the mothers, some of whom recalled the old East End songs. I had never realized that 'My Old Man Said Follow the Band' was a song about bailiffs arriving at a poor family's door. Apparently tenants would lean out of the slum tenements, see bailiffs heading up the road and loudly sing the song so that their neighbours would hear and not 'dilly-dally on the way' while escaping surreptitiously out of the building to give the bailiffs the run-around.

We had parties, lots of parties, at the church hall. We always celebrated birthdays. We needed to laugh and play. Many of the mothers and children had lost their ability to relax and have fun, and some had never known what it was like to get together with others without drunken fights breaking out and a beating once the family returned home.

Since cooking was close to my heart I was always happy if any of the women enjoyed making meals and were willing to teach the rest of us their recipes. In the early days in Belmont Terrace there were cookers in most of the dormitories. Rota systems took care of the cleaning and the washing-up, but it was left to individual women to decide how they wished to sort out mealtimes. I was adamant that we were not going to become an institution and that the mothers should have control over their domestic lives. As they made new friends little groups would form to prepare meals for one another, and I often would watch as mothers showed us recipes for exotically spiced curries, West Indian chicken, rice and peas or a delicious new variation on toad in the hole. For many of the women previously isolated by violent partners or perhaps their own antisocial behaviour, to find themselves among a group of well-wishers and non-judgemental mothers was a new experience. It was gratifying to see them befriending one another and cooperating with domestic arrangements and childminding.

After we moved into the Big House in Chiswick we retained the system of allowing women to sort out their own shopping and cooking arrangements, although in due course the kitchen facilities improved considerably.

As a community we were always busy. Visitors from all over the world would throng through the front door. It became the duty of the mothers to show them around and answer questions. Photographers would also turn up now and then. The community agreed that it was fine for them to take pictures but that if anyone did not wish her photograph to be taken she should stay out of the way.

As representatives of the world's first refuge I encouraged the women to go out together and speak on our behalf about our community. Some of them became excellent public speakers – as did many of the volunteers. Sometimes we would get together to create banners and placards and take to the streets to publicize the refuge and campaign against violence in the home.

Visitors were often amazed at the positive and happy atmosphere within the community. Women who moved on into their own accommodation were always welcome back, and the Big House was always there if they needed company, solace or support.

The vexed issue of alcohol was a perennial problem. I have always enjoyed a drink, and all my life I have drunk more than I should. I don't defend this except to say that it has never affected my ability to work or care for people, but it has certainly been the cause of some of my most outrageous behaviour. So when arguments broke out about drinking alcohol I simply said that it was up to the residents to make their own rules. The only rule I insisted on was that there was to be no physical violence in the refuge.

Some of the women who turned up were brought there by disapproving social workers who termed them 'alcoholics'. It was often assumed that they had contributed to their abuse by their drunken behaviour. Usually I would hug the miscreant and suggest we go inside and discuss our addiction to alcohol over a cup of tea or coffee and a cigarette. Those who wanted to give up boozing were encouraged to attend Alcoholics Anonymous, and women who wished to carry on drinking had to abide by the rules of the house.

This system usually worked well when the majority of the women in the house did not have a drink problem, but if a large number of heavy drinkers banded together they could sway the house vote. My first memory of a disastrous night in the refuge came when Becky – who generally drank very little but who got completely out of control when she did – banded with others and insisted that, since it was Guy Fawkes Night, after the children had let off fireworks outside the mothers should be allowed to throw a party in the house. Staff were not invited.

I voiced my concerns about this, but the house had voted, so the staff and volunteers stayed until after the children went to bed and then left the building to the mothers. The next morning I returned to a very subdued house. The sitting-room was packed with women, and after the playstaff took off the juveniles not attending school I sat down to listen to the accusations and tales of woe. One mother, Gillian, was missing from the meeting because a fight had broken out between her and Becky. Usually these two were best friends; indeed, Gillian acted as a second mother to Becky's little girl. The catalyst for the row seemed to be that some of the mothers had decided to invite boyfriends to the party. Meanwhile Becky had knocked back more than a few drinks and took exception to something Gillian had said or did.

The next morning Gillian stayed upstairs in bed. After a few suppressed giggles I was asked if I would go up to see her. I climbed to the top of the house to find her sitting up and looking glum. She had a saucer on her bedside table full of hair and sported a pink strip of bare scalp on her head. Gillian was hoping to be backed up by the other women as she vehemently declared her innocence in starting the fight. I went back down. The house deliberated for a considerable time, and eventually it was decided that the two women had behaved equally badly.

At least the less dominant members of the community had learned to find a voice and speak up for themselves. One aspect of living in a shabby, packed hostel was learning to take responsibility for one's own behaviour. I had known that there were bullies in the house, and the decision to allow alcohol on to the premises was by no means a popular one, but, by refusing to speak up for their rights, the less vocal section of the community had failed themselves and their children. This was redressed at this morning meeting, which resulted in a total ban on alcohol in the house and very clear expressions of disapproval of Gillian's and Becky's behaviour. The two women were a huge asset within the community, and no one wanted to see them evicted, but they were given notice that there was to be no second chance.

Gillian was furious to hear that she had been included in the general motion of censure and sent a message to the meeting that she intended to stick her head in an oven. The house had recently been converted to natural gas, so, after putting her head in an upstairs oven with the gas taps on, nothing happened. By the time I went to check on her she had got bored and given up her attempt to gas herself. This was just as well, since even natural gas is toxic – as well as highly inflammable. As it was, she eventually joined the meeting to general hilarity and was made to shake hands with Becky, which she did, albeit grudgingly.

Jack Ashley went to work for Barbara Castle who was appointed Secretary of State for Health in 1974. He kindly offered to make an appointment for a few of us to see her to seek her help in our fight to stay open until there were sufficient refuges across the country to offer shelters for women to escape their violent partners. I was particularly keen to meet her because I knew she was already fighting hard to ensure that victims of domestic violence could receive financial redress by the Criminal Injuries Compensation Scheme. Up till then such women had been excluded, since members of a family couldn't claim against one another.

Jack took us to her office in Whitehall, and we filed in and sat down to discuss the issue. We had high hopes for this meeting after being brushed off by the civil servants at the Department of Health and Social Security. I knew that for all of us, however nervous we might feel, there was a sense of achievement in getting this far and a sense of reassurance that our voices would be heard.

The Minister bustled into the room and briskly shook us all by the hand. She took her place at the head of the table and pointed to one of the mothers and said, 'You begin.' She sounded rather irritable and impatient, and I immediately wondered whether she felt coerced into meeting us. One of the mothers was explaining how she had been taken to hospital on a stretcher several times after attacks by her violent husband when the MP stood up, smoothed her skirt and said, 'That's enough. I've got to go and talk to my nurses.' With that she swept out of the room.

The mothers were bewildered, and I was furious. Then it dawned on me. The Minister would have already been briefed by civil servants, including the granite-faced women I had encountered at

DHSS headquarters in south London who refused to acknowledge that we were doing an important job. The growing militancy within the feminist movement meant that many professional women held views similar to hers. Because I had said that women could be as violent as men and that we were prepared to help men in trouble as well as women, we would inevitably experience hostility from people like her and Barbara Castle. Moreover, my posh accent made it more likely that I would be written off as a middle-class do-gooder undeserving of support, and our refusal to accept all aspects of the dominant feminist ideology meant all those involved in running the Chiswick refuge were regarded with suspicion.

The next morning the mothers voted that we should hold a conference in our church hall, inviting groups across the country to share their views with us. It was hoped that we might form some sort of loose federation through which autonomous regional groups could support each other and share information. There were groups we were aware of, in particular Dublin Women's Aid, who shared our aims and who would send us mothers and children, because in Dublin a determined man could trace his wife quite easily. Church groups were also trying to set up shelters, and one was in the process of being set up in Liverpool. We hoped for a meeting of minds so the mothers could share their experiences and those running refuges could seek advice on the issue of overcrowding.

In the event the conference was an unmitigated disaster. None of us had any idea that the Women's Liberation Movement, aware of our plans to create a federation of refuges, was seeking to get us ousted and to present itself to the Civil Service as the national charity representing British women and children fleeing domestic violence.

On the day of the conference I walked into the church hall to find the Dublin group already there, and I was pleased to see they had a few men with them. Most of the mothers in our refuge were still busy with domestic affairs, as it was a Saturday and their children were at home. Chiswick Women's Aid was thus represented by a small group that included Ann, Becky and Elsie. Before long the spacious room was crowded with women, some of them dressed in men's suits and ties whom I recognized from the London Women's Liberation conference. My heart sank, and Elsie left after whispering that she was going back to the house to get reinforcements.

I kicked myself for being so naïve, but it was too late, and within minutes one of the representatives from Women's Liberation established herself as the conference leader, found a microphone and began to rant. Most of us sat on the floor because there were not enough chairs, and the conference raged around us. Proposals were made and votes taken.

More and more mothers from the Big House joined us. The room was electric with tension, but I just felt depressed. I had failed to take into account the emerging national domestic-violence movement because I had chosen to concentrate on meeting the immediate needs of the women and children we were encountering in Chiswick. By failing to acknowledge the national movement's rapid growth and attempting to get involved at its inception we had left a power vacuum – and the women at our little conference were intent on filling it.

After a particularly aggressive tirade from a huge radical lesbian who demanded that men be banned from the refuges altogether and that boys should be excluded after reaching puberty one of our mothers could bear it no more. 'Go 'ome and get your dildos!' she bellowed. There was a moment's stunned silence, and then a woman from Acton Women's Aid took the floor to argue on behalf of 'working-class women'.

'The only working-class woman you know', interjected one of the mothers from Chiswick, 'is the one who cleans your floors!'

At this point Ann and I decided we might as well leave the feminists to it. Our group got up *en masse* and returned to the refuge. Over tea and cigarettes we agreed that we would work as we always had done and if there were groups that we could work with so much the better. We realized that we needed to team up with refuges elsewhere offering accommodation for women who just needed a leg-up to become independent of their partners. We would then be able to concentrate on aiding women who were violent or who needed long-term therapy and support after really traumatic domestic experiences.

Years later I found a mention of our little conference and myself in a book written in 1982 by Beatrix Campbell and Anna Coote called *Sweet Freedom*. In it the authors said of me that my views diverged sharply from those of other groups involved in the refuge movement. They said that I saw wife-battering as a psychological problem and maintained that certain kinds of women were violence-prone and invited physical domestic abuse. They carried on to say that this was regarded as 'dangerous nonsense' to feminists who regarded domestic violence as an expression of the power wielded by men over women in a society in which female dependence on men was evident in every aspect of daily life. The authors concluded that from feminists' 'extensive experience' of working in refuges at that time they had concluded that wife-battering was not merely the practice of a few deviant males but behaviour that could emerge within normal marital and heterosexual relationships.

I was, however, to stand by my analysis.

15

SCREAM QUIETLY OR THE NEIGHBOURS WILL HEAR

My book *Scream Quietly or the Neighbours Will Hear* was due to be published in 1974. This proved a depressing experience during which I ended up arguing with my editor and refusing to allow her to put a heavy political spin on the text. The problem was that it was coming out as a Penguin Special. For a long time anything to do with human behaviour had been hijacked by left-wing academics who insisted that all society's ills were caused by Western capitalism. My premise that violent and abusive behaviour within the family occurred because the children of violent families learned inappropriate behaviour from their parents was in direct contradiction to the prevailing left-wing ethos, and I was too naïve to realize I was stepping into a minefield.

I was asked to dinner to meet the managing director of the Penguin Special imprint. It was not an enjoyable meal for either of us. I had been warned that he had far-left political leanings, which didn't mean much to me except that his views were likely to be diametrically opposed to mine on a number of issues, but in the late 1960s and early 1970s I didn't find this particularly unusual. I believed the family was essential to society and should be protected; I also believed in couples being faithful within marriage, and I passionately believed in my unorthodox God. By this time I was beginning to realize that my views seemed out of step with the times and anachronistic.

Whatever the outcome, I was pleased that my book was going to be published, and I hoped that once it came out it would encourage serious discussion and analysis of the issues surrounding domestic violence in place of the sensationalist horror stories that appeared daily in the tabloid newspapers. I was concerned that readers would become indifferent to the issue and fail to support our call for major changes in policing, legislation and the social services with regard to domestic disputes.

While I was writing the book a young film-maker just out of film school knocked on our door and sat down with the mothers to discuss the idea of producing a film about the refuge. We had been inundated with communications by television companies who wanted to make a film, but we had resisted their approaches because we knew that we would have no control over the final result. But Michael Whyte was different. He promised that he would collaborate with the mothers in the making of his documentary and allow them to help shape the resulting film.

Just after my book came out the film was made, also called *Scream Quietly or the Neighbours Will Hear*. Everyone who participated was happy to be involved. Many of the women felt a sense of pride in giving testimony, in that they felt they might help other women find sanctuary as a result of the resulting publicity. Michael Whyte decided to allow the women to tell their stories in their own words, and he accompanied their testaments with moving and beautifully composed shots of daily life within the refuge. I was interviewed, too, but the main emphasis was on the women and children themselves. There was no commentary, and the result was immensely powerful, giving the viewer an accurate impression of the realities of communal life and its attendant hardships and rewards.

Once we saw the preview we believed our troubles were over. The scene that most moved me was the shot of the mothers and the children sleeping on the floor of the sitting-room of the Big House in tightly packed rows – much as they had formerly done in the little semi in Belmont Terrace. Nearly five years had gone by, and nothing had improved in terms of the residents' material conditions. The government resolutely turned a blind eye, ignoring the hardship and discomfort of the women and children. It merely colluded with Hounslow Council in its attempts to gaol me for running an overcrowded house in the hope that the problem would go away.

One of the ways we registered a protest at the government's indifference was to keep an eye on political engagements in the press, and when we saw that Commonwealth leaders or other international dignitaries were invited to lunch at 10 Downing Street we would pile into our van and drive towards the Prime Minister's residence. At that time there were no gates at the ends of the street preventing us from sending the refuge children with communications to post through the letterbox of Number 10. We became a familiar sight standing in dignified silence with our banners and placards reading 'Battered Women Need a Refuge', and we made friends with the good-natured policemen on regular duty there.

The film was sold to Thames Television, and we waited for it to be shown. In the end the film was scheduled for transmission very late at night at a time in 1974 when the country was plunged into darkness during the many power strikes that bedevilled Britain during Edward Heath's administration. It was the only time the film has ever been broadcast in Britain. Despite this, it made a huge impact when it was shown on national television.

The success of the publication of the book *Scream Quietly* was also in doubt because little advance publicity was planned. Launch-party invitations were sent out without our address on them, so very few journalists found their way to the refuge in Chiswick. It was the *Daily Express* that saved the book from sinking without trace by buying extracts which they published over several days.

Once the film and the book had been released we started to get a great deal of support.

We received a huge number of letters from all over Britain, and people came in to volunteer their help. We had almost no money to pay anyone except for a playleader and a housemother, but the volunteers were given petrol money and their travelling expenses. I claimed petrol and some of my telephone bills. The majority of the men and women offering to help in the refuge signed on and gave their time for free.

The bulk of the work in the refuge was done by the mothers themselves. For some who had grown up in care or spent time in gaol it came as a shock to discover that they were expected to contribute to the everyday running of the house. In institutions people are quickly depersonalized and made to feel that they are objects to be managed. They are used to having staff around who dictate how they behave, what they will eat and administer discipline. The only people who had a say in how people behaved in the refuge were the women living there as residents, and all decisions were left to them.

Women who had been in violent, controlling relationships often found it hard to know what to do with their newfound freedom. For some, even the idea of being able to leave the refuge without asking permission was too much to begin with, an d some took days or even weeks before they felt confident enough to venture out on their own, so used were they to being confined at home by their violent partners.

Even more exciting for many was the fact that, provided they had someone to babysit their children, they were encouraged to go out dancing or to the local pubs or cafés.

For some visitors the chaotic atmosphere at the refuge came as a shock. 'Mrs Pizzey,' one volunteer said on her first day, stunned, 'there are women running up and down the corridors throwing teabags at each other.'

I laughed. 'Isn't that great? So many of the mothers and the children here have never had time to let their hair down and have fun.'

'Mrs Pizzey,' she rejoined over her shoulder on her way out of the front door, 'you are a hippy!' She would have been even more scandalized had she attended any of our parties in the church hall. These nights were passed in riotous drinking and dancing, although it was my job to evict anyone whose behaviour got seriously out of hand. I loved watching the faces of the women who had been abused for so long alight with laughter and happiness.

Of course, the would-be volunteer was right in a way. The refuge would never become a typical institution hidebound by rules during the years I ran the place. I felt that just because a woman had found herself in a violent situation didn't mean she was subsequently incapable of taking responsibility for her own life and making her own decisions. The house was a place of healing, and I know of nothing more healing than good company, laughter and fun.

One day a stunningly beautiful young woman came in with two small girls. The eldest must have been around four years old and the baby a little over a year. The mother, Isuleta, proved an extraordinary character. She had grown up in Barbados and been abandoned by her parents when she was very small. She was passed from relative to relative and didn't seem to have learned any life skills from anyone. She blithely told me she had never been to school and couldn't read or write. There was nothing she was willing to do in the house except fill her baby's bottle with milk and feed the children on chips from the shop across the road. From the first day she arrived she left the children in their bunk bed and went out. The next morning the mothers brought up her desertion of them in the house meeting.

Kathy, who was wonderful with infants, offered to help Isuleta, and she was happy to go along with this. Kathy soon found herself Isuleta's full-time nanny. The mother fascinated us by her behaviour. She could be funny and even witty but behaved as though she were the same age as her eldest child. She was completely irresponsible, and as far as I could make out she had made her way in life by flitting from one man to another. She was on the run from a very violent man who was due to come out of prison after a sentence for bank robbery. Mercy, the youngest girl, was not his child. Isuleta planned to give her to social services, but so far her negotiations had not succeeded in getting the toddler removed into care.

Now she wanted me to speed things up on her behalf, because she wished to to return to her house and the honeymoon she was anticipating with her newly released partner. I was dubious. 'What if your eldest daughter tells him about Mercy?'

'She don't tell,' she blithely assured me. Nothing I could say would move her. Mercy was the most gorgeous little girl. She had a very distinctive little hooked nose and thick straight black hair. She was a happy, sunny child, and whenever she saw me she stretched out her fat little arms. I couldn't bear the idea that she might have to go into care. I knew from so many of the mothers and children how devastating the British care system was for children. One day I asked Isuleta if I could take Mercy home to ask my husband if we could foster her for a while. One reason for my suggestion was to see if she might change her mind about letting her go, but Isuleta was more than happy with this plan.

That evening I took Mercy home with me. She sat on my lap in the sitting-room and gazed at Cleo and Amos. Sam, my Staffordshire bull terrier, licked her feet and Ella, our cat, purred on the arm of the sofa beside us. The children loved the idea of having her in our family, but when Jack came home he was adamant that Mercy must be returned to her mother straight away. I begged him to reconsider, at least to let me keep her while we tried to sort something out with Isuleta. But there was no reasoning with Jack, and I think from that moment the cracks in our relationship widened perceptibly.

We were becoming very different people. He still had his crowd of friends and his glamorous social life with media folk, but now I was creating a world of my own in which I felt comfortable. Of course, I understood that he was well within his rights to refuse to take on someone else's child on what might end up a fairly long-term basis.

'Most people, Erin, would agree with me.'

'I'm not most people.'

The little girl needed me, and I needed her. It was if I'd always known this child, and she had come into my life like a gift. I had to take her back to the refuge that night and hand her over to Kathy. I drove home in tears, and eventually both children went into care.

Isuleta danced out of the refuge on her way to a new man, her bank-robber lover forgotten, and to this day I remember Mercy. I can still see that lovely child sitting in my rocking-chair on a white sheepskin smiling up at me.

By the mid-1970s we seemed to be awash with research workers wanting to interview the mothers about their experiences. None of us had much idea of the use they were making of their findings, but during a house meeting it was decided because I was the biggest woman it would be my job to evict any researchers who harangued the mothers on the joys of Marxism, as well as feminists who told them that all men were potentially dangerous and the Irish priests who ordered their parishioners home on the grounds that they were breaking their marriage vows and would end up in hell. Several researchers ended up at the bottom of our stairs encouraged by a hearty push from me.

A psychiatrist called Dr John Gayford would later remind me that my first words to him were 'Who the fuck are you?' I had not been warned he was coming, and I walked into the sitting-room to find him perched on a sofa. The mothers had voted to allow him to undertake the first in-depth research on the refuge because, they reasoned, since he was a practising Christian he was less likely to distort his findings to suit his own agenda. Gayford did publish his research but failed to honour his promise to tell the whole truth. He omitted to mention that some of the women in his survey were violent and others were prostitutes. Later he tried to put things right, but it was too late by then. His study had been cited extensively by the radical feminists in their literature. He was to admit afterwards that had he tried to examine the notion that domestic violence could be consensual and that in many cases both partners had violent tendencies he would never have been granted his doctorate.

He undertook an enormous amount of work, and all the women in the refuge answered his questions honestly. He and I also spent many hours together discussing the results after everyone had filled in his questionnaires. I, too, filled one in, and like so many of other women I could trace my family's violence back through to my parents and my grandparents. To us the patterns were quite simple to detect, and we would promise each other that we would try to overcome our propensity to violence and make sure that our children were protected from aggression.

On one occasion I discovered that a teacher at Amos's school was making his life miserable, and when he told me about her bullying I flew down to the school and shoved her up against a wall. 'Don't you ever,' I said through clenched teeth, 'ever bully my son again!' I saw the fear in her eyes, and I walked away jubilant. But I needed to recognize that I, too, had violent tendencies, and I had to work hard to overcome that first moment of exhilarating rage.

Once I had calmed down I was ashamed and returned to apologize. I certainly knew by then that rage was not an appropriate response to my dismay that someone should upset my child. I also knew that there were moments when I might genuinely need to summon anger but that these were very rare.

One morning a man was shouting outside the refuge. He was standing at the bottom of the steps, having previously run up and pounded on the door. The mothers and children were terrified. I looked out of the window. He was tall and athletic, so I went to the front door with Mike, one of our volunteers, and asked him what he wanted.

He pushed me back into the hall but had not reckoned on Mike's burly shoulders. Mike rugby-tackled him round his knees, and I crouched down. He began to cry softly, and I put my arm around him. He had recently arrived from Nigeria and had picked up a prostitute. She had become his only friend, and she had visited him regularly. One night she stole his wallet and car keys and slipped out of his room before he awoke. She had told him she lived in a battered wives' refuge in Chiswick, so he was able to track her down. It seemed he was more upset by her treachery than the loss of his money or keys.

I knew whom he was talking about, and when I entered the

sitting-room I could see her sitting in the small alcove grinning at me. She had the keys by her side and held out his empty wallet to me. 'Here. You can give these back to him.'

'No,' I said. 'You go and give him his stuff back – and apologize. That was a shit thing to do.'

'Make me!'

There were several other women crowded into the little side office watching with interest.

'OK,' I said, and with that I pushed my fingers up through her hair on the back of her head, threw my considerable weight against her and propelled her backwards across the room and out on to the front doorstep. 'You sort it out!' I yelled.

Mike and I could see her on the forecourt of the refuge. She was apologizing to the man, and I was glad to see them leave together. Social workers would no doubt have suggested more appropriate methods of resolving such a situation, but I knew that whatever happened in the refuge had to be based on mutual respect. From then on Diana did not challenge me again in this way, although on many occasions I had to challenge her.

I was no stranger to violence, because as a child I was a lethal fighter. Much of my rage was directed at my father. My mother physically beat me badly at times and obviously disliked me, but I always felt a need to protect her from my father's verbal rage. I wasn't frightened by her, but my huge monster of a father terrified us all. His three children lived in a state of suspended terror. When there were outbursts of rage there was actually a sense of relief. It was the suspense that was most agonizing. When one or other erupted we children reacted very differently. I would plough into the battles between them and take on my father. My sister retreated to the furthest corner of the house, and my brother usually stood in a catatonic silence. We knew that once the fighting was over there would be a period of calm.

Sometimes my life took a sinister turn. My father had arrived on leave for several months when we were living in Hunthay, an old house outside Axminster in Devon that my parents had bought in 1952. He was bored and friendless and had no office work to preoccupy him. He spent much of his time haranguing my mother and us, and the sound of my mother's hysterical weeping flooded my heart.

My sister was covered in eczema sores from stress; my brother's face was pinched and white with fear. I lived in a permanent state of rage. After one particularly violent night I decided I would have to kill him, and I told my sister that there would be no peace for any of us while he remained alive. At fourteen I had very little idea of what to do, but I had every intention of killing him. I could no longer bear to lie at night and listen to his powerful voice spewing hatred and jealousy against us all from his bed. And there was no peace even when he was asleep. His snores made sleep impossible.

My mother made it clear that she, too, was at the end of her tether. She implied that she could no longer bear to go on living. There was a tacit acknowledgement in the family that it was my responsibility to save the four of us from this monster. Did I think that his death by my hand would mean that she might love me at last? Possibly.

One night I took the big kitchen carving knife from the drawer and sat on the landing in front of my parents' bedroom door which was ajar. They had separate beds. My father's huge carcass threw a deep shadow on the wall. He leaned across to my mother, and I squatted on the ground outside the door with the knife raised. 'D'you want a cuddle?' he asked her. His false teeth were in a glass on the side table. 'No,' she said and turned her back on him. I rose to my feet to go to her aid if required, but he didn't insist on his marital rights. He subsided back into bed and saved his own life. I didn't kill him that night, but there would be other times ahead when it was a near thing.

To live on a knife edge of wanting to kill is a little like being a piece of elastic stretched so badly over time that it can never return to its original shape. That sense of murderous rage will always remain deep within me. That is why, when faced with violent situations at the refuge, I was safe. Even the most violent of men who came to the house found their threats dying on their lips as they confronted me. And women who had killed their partners or others in a paroxysm of rage recognized that I understood what had happened and why. There is a comfort for all of us in knowing that you are not alone in your violence and anger.

16
CHARITY OR EMPIRE?

In the early days of the refuge I was often incensed by the people who came from the so-called 'helping agencies'. Many of them were highly educated, but most were naïve because they came from normal, loving backgrounds. For many of the women seeking refuge, it was only when death stared them in the face that they decided to leave their abusive partners. Surrounded by violence and brutality, and mostly isolated on the sprawling housing estates that sprung up to replace the slum tenements, the idea of a life filled with joy and harmony was an alien one.

'Peace', I came to understand, was to them a very bizarre and unsettling state of affairs. It was between the bouts of violence that my siblings and I had been at our most anxious. I remembered how I had felt and how the feverish anticipation of the next outburst of rage between our parents had kept me awake for days at a time. Thus I knew the refuge worked best for violence-prone women and their offspring when it was packed with people and full of energy. A crisis refuge, I believed, always needed to be bustling, busy and full of activity until the families were ready to be moved on to a more tranquil way of life.

In the 1970s to say that some women were as responsible for the familial violence as their partners was to invite abuse and derision. Feminists were trying to establish their own refuges – and we were glad whenever anyone did. With the Big House often cramming in over a hundred women and children, extra beds were a blessing. Everyone agreed that any refuge was better than none. However, I was aware that a tide of feminist anger was threatening to engulf me. After the publication of *Scream Quietly or the Neighbours Will Hear*, whenever I was asked to speak publicly I was hounded by pickets with banners proclaiming that I hated women and said they wanted to be battered. Phone-in radio programmes on which

I appeared would soon find their lines jammed with my detractors. Dislike bordered on hysteria, and I learned to approach newspaper features on my work at the refuge with apprehension.

In the very early days we were often contacted by well-meaning families who offered to take a mother and her children into their own homes. This was very kind of them but unworkable because, for a start, the mother would lose her housing rights if she was no longer regarded as homeless. Losing such rights was a serious matter, as it meant one would fall off waiting-lists for council housing and no longer be eligible for housing benefit. Even staying at our refuge could cause problems. Because there was a log-jam of women looking for shelter, the London boroughs argued they had no responsibility if families left their borough boundaries; moreover, many of the councils tried to argue that because the women were in our refuge they were not technically homeless.

The second reason it was a bad idea was that even if a mother could cope with adjusting to living with a normal family she rarely had children who were not violent and disturbed, and their behaviour would threaten the host's family and offspring. The few times we tried to settle mothers and children into private homes proved disastrous.

In 1974 the National Women's Aid Federation went to the Department of Health and Social Security and met our detractors at the Elephant and Castle headquarters. Despite the fact that we had already been registered as the national charity for homeless women our grant was reallocated to the federation. We were too busy to waste much time fighting the decision, but I knew that this meant few would listen to what we had to say from now on. Domestic violence would be regarded as something that men do to women. Money would be diverted from the care of victims of family violence and placed in the coffers of the women's movement. This would fund jobs for women in refuges, in the field of women's studies as well as bankroll conferences barred to men.

For those of us at the Chiswick refuge it seemed alarming that feminists could potentially abuse their role as providers of refuge for vulnerable and damaged people because of an agenda to bolster a movement born out of hatred of half of the human race.

We all had fathers, brothers, uncles, lovers or husbands, and we knew that most of them were protectors, friends or partners who would never raise a hand to anyone weaker than they. Women fleeing violence might end up as the cash-cows that could fill the coffers of a movement with relatively little broad-based support. There was never any mention of male victims, and no one ever asked whether women could be victims of a mother's violence – or whether same-sex violence was even possible.

My main concern was that in the early days when we opened the little community centre in Belmont Terrace and I began to mix with helpful groups such as the Claimants' Union and the squatting movement I became aware that many of the larger national charities I had supported for years had been targeted by political activists. Well-known charitable institutions were moving away from working directly with the people they were meant to help and becoming massive empires with all their energies expended in lobbying Parliament and competing for funding. Time and again I telephoned organizations such as the National Council for Civil Liberties only to be told that they no longer took on individual cases. They were concerned only with national policy.

I tried to address this issue in my book *Scream Quietly*. I quoted a case in which I had struggled to get help for a couple and felt that the charity Shelter had failed them. Shelter decided to sue me. I was dragged into a meeting with the barrister who had read the book on behalf of Penguin before publication and who had declared it free from libel. He now changed his mind, and I was told that Penguin was not going to support me. I told them all to fuck off – in so many words – but Jack, mindful of the imminent arrival of bailiffs at our front door, refused to support me in my stand. The headline in London's *Evening Standard* later duly read 'Erin Pizzey Apologises'.

What I saw happening all too often with most national charities – with the shining exception of Save the Children – was that, once money started flowing in, the charity's founders would deem it necessary to give its workers grand-sounding titles and high salaries, establish prestigious new office premises and massively extend its staffing, especially at the top. This quickly turned a charity into a small business and thereafter a large and top-heavy empire. Thus the selfless impulse that caused its founders to reach out to those who needed help soon became ossified, and a surfeit of committee meetings, conferences and endless political debate meant the original intent was swamped in a sea of bureaucracy and lost to sight.

17
MEN CAN BE VICTIMS, TOO

I was busy struggling with my day-to-day life and, like many working women, wishing I had a wife at home to take care of the children and housework. I vowed that we should try to make the working conditions at the refuge family-friendly, and to this end we decided that none of the staff or volunteers should start work before 10 a.m. so that we had time to take our children to school without getting caught up in the crush of rush-hour. For me it meant I had time to have a proper cooked breakfast with Cleo and Amos. I was also able to collect them from school. I can't pretend that I had as much time as I would have liked with them because the telephone at home rang all the time. The people in the refuge knew not to disturb me unless something was really urgent, because the mothers were capable of running the place by themselves, but there were times when legal decisions had to be made immediately or I needed to be informed about a a situation.

JoJo Polaine, our first housemother, was able to deal with the daily running of the the refuge. She was brilliant at coping with any dramas that might erupt, and she was a warm loving presence in the house. Ann, too, was indispensable to me from the first few days that we moved into the Big House. I knew that I could leave it in good hands and return to my children, but the time was soon approaching when I needed to travel abroad to help others establish shelters.

By 1976 I had succumbed to employing au pairs who could be with Cleo and Amos when I had to stay late at the refuge. The children welcomed them, and we were lucky because all of them proved a great addition to our family. Still, I minded having to spend so much time away from my daughter and son, and I also worried about their welfare.

Meanwhile I had long been preoccupied about the court case due to be heard in Acton Magistrates' Court. The problem had started one afternoon when two men arrived with a summons for me to attend court on grounds of overcrowding at the refuge. I pulled it out of the envelope, read it, tore it to pieces and stuffed the scraps back in the envelope. I asked the two men to hand it to Alderman King whom I knew was behind the summons.

The men were transfixed. Seemingly they had never witnessed anyone tearing up court papers. I told them I planned to ignore similar communications from Hounslow Council. By this time Chiswick Women's Aid had a huge following across Britain. I don't think the council was aware of the support we had amassed since we had opened our doors. Our supporters ranged from members of The Who and, later, Stuart Copeland of The Police in the world of music to little old ladies who wrote enclosing fifty-pence pieces. The comedian Spike Milligan was another great supporter of our cause. He would visit the house and sometimes telephoned me at home when he was in the depths of despair. He would talk to me for hours on end. He admitted his own violence towards women and talked about his hatred and rage towards his controlling mother. All those years later he was still driven by his obsession with her, and he admitted that other women had borne the brunt of his violent rages. He would send envelopes of cash to the refuge which we used to buy treats for the children.

Whether I liked it or not, I was so often featured in the newspapers or viewed arguing with pundits on television that I was becoming notorious. I had a number of implacable opponents working within the Borough of Hounslow, although there were some very caring councillors who supported us – in a few cases possibly at the cost of their careers. Jim Duffy was one of them, and he was to become a personal friend. He was a local health inspector who not only brought me bunches of flowers but tipped me off when any large houses fell empty in the borough that we might be able to squat.

He was not our only secret saviour. Paddy O'Connor, once a homeless dosser on the streets of London, had been elevated to a position of seniority at the Greater London Council. He had a well-stocked drinks cabinet in his palatial office and dispensed booze liberally to those who visited him. We were regular drinking companions. One day he appeared outside the refuge in a long black limousine and drove me to an old shooting lodge surrounded by a high brick wall in Putney.

The plan was that Paddy would come by to show me properties left empty by the GLC. The shooting lodge was one of these. In the dead of night we would enter the houses with mothers and children, and I would pin a notice on the door stating that we were officially squatting the building. Paddy would then join in the general outcry at the GLC at our trespass. When the police arrived they knew that squatting was merely a civil offence, so the borough council was left with the decision to leave us alone inside the property or evict us in the full glare of the press. It would then be responsible for rehoming the families. They left our squats alone.

I loved Paddy. We were both of Irish descent; we both drank far too much and on occasions behaved very badly. I had the appalling habit after imbibing a bottle or two of red wine of saying exactly what I thought, and the results could be disastrous, but Paddy would always forgive me. And, from his own experiences of sleeping rough on the streets, he cared passionately about the plight of all those who found themselves, for whatever reason, without a roof over their heads.

Despite the overcrowding problem, I knew that many of the mothers and children were too emotionally vulnerable to be pushed out of the refuge straight into substandard accommodation to manage on minuscule amounts of money and experience the corruscating loneliness that is the lot of most single parents. I suggested in a house meeting that perhaps some of the women would prefer to share with each other until they could be rehoused on their own with their children. In our early days any family that came into the refuge had no immediate chance of being rehoused, hence squatting became a necessity. It was obvious that we needed to squat in large numbers, so that Hounslow would leave the families alone instead of picking them off one by one. This suited us, because I knew that the two or three years it would take for a mother to be rehoused from one of our 'satellite' or 'second-stage' squatted houses, such as the Putney hunting lodge, meant that she had time to heal and to learn to share her life with her new friends.

Some of the social workers who moved mountains to rehome their clients were furious when the women returned to violent partners. They failed to realize that regarding their clients as a 'housing problem' missed the point. Certainly some more of the stable and resilient families were able to move on and create new lives for themselves, but there were many at our refuge who were so traumatized by their pasts that transferring them into isolated housing often resulted in their heading back to violent partners or falling prey to dangerous and predatory strangers. By sharing a large house women could also split the domestic bills and organize themselves into those who wanted to work and those who would provide child care. Above all, there would not be the long days and night shut alone behind doors with their traumatic memories.

I was particularly touched by the gift of an old vicarage in Bristol which was donated to us by a young millionaire called John Pontin. Sadly the house was vandalized before we were able to move in, and I said a good many prayers because there was no money to spare on repairing and refurbishing it in order to make it once more fit for occupation.

Soon after this I had a telephone call from a woman who said she wanted to talk to me privately, and I agreed to see her at my home. A small quietly spoken blonde, she sat on our sofa and presented me with a neatly folded cheque. 'I've inherited this money. I don't believe in inherited wealth, so I have decided to give it to the refuge.'

I unfolded the cheque and saw it was for £10,000. I was astounded. All I could do was smile at her, take a deep breath and say, 'Thank you, Lord!' When I had collected my thoughts I told her that I would like to use some of the money to open a refuge in Bristol. She looked pleased and left. The next morning I rushed into the Chiswick house to tell the mothers of our incredible luck. 'God does answer prayers,' I said to the raucous laughter of the unbelievers.

The mothers designated to live in the Bristol house moved in even before the renovation work began. I was offered a room at the bottom of the stairs that was used as a guest room and supervised the work by the builders and decorators to restore the lovely old building.

Outside the house was a large walled garden, and one of the first things I did was buy some chickens. We had a pen and a henhouse at the bottom of the garden, and at weekends one or other of the children would take me by the hand to collect the eggs. They were so enthusiastic about the hens that at the slightest indication of a chicken squatting and being about to lay she would be surrounded by a sea of little faces – and the boys and girls would rush triumphantly back the house with every egg produced.

When the Bristol house was finished and the workmen were due to leave we decided to throw a party the following weekend in their honour as they had been so very helpful in making the property habitable once more. I offered to make a chicken curry, but none of us wanted to kill our hens ourselves, so we gave the job to a workman. He promised to do the deed before I returned the following Friday from a week in London. He kept his word, but none of the mothers had any idea how to pluck them. They decided to stick the corpses, giblets and all, into the deep freeze in the larder. After dinner that Friday I raised the subject, and the birds were disinterred from the freezer still fully feathered, frozen solid with their little eyes glaring at me reproachfully through a thick sheet of ice.

I spent most of Saturday laboriously plucking them and wondering how anyone could get all the stubbly tiny feathers off. In the end I decided to resolve the problem my own way. I covered the kitchen table with bottles of wine and beer and placed small candles down its length. I duly cooked a big curry, swamping the jointed chickens in thick sauce and served the dish only after keeping the workmen waiting sufficiently long for everyone there to be sloshed. We ate by candlelight. One of the workmen looked dubiously at a morsel of chicken on his fork and pointed out some stubble. 'Black pepper,' I told him firmly. He duly tucked in. It was then I decided that one day I would write *The Slut's Cook Book*. Not everyone had time to be the perfect cook and housewife. It dawned on me that the slut's best friend was a tin opener and that many women would welcome shortcuts to making good meals with the least expenditure of effort – and without breaking the bank.

Many of the women in the London and Bristol refuges admitted that they were violent and needed help with their relationships with partners. Those men who asked for help were often as vulnerable as the violence-prone women. Where the violence was part of the family culture and children grew up in households where their parents, like mine, used physical and verbal violence as a form of control I knew it was possible to teach other methods of child-rearing. However, where violence was the result of a personality disorder or mental illness the parent's issues could not be addressed without recourse to psychologists or psychiatric social workers.

I asked the Greater London Council, by then a booming business with a number of colourful characters working from the banks of the Thames, to give me a house for men. The idea was to provide shelter for men and teenagers who had been at the receiving end of violence or serious abuse from partners or parents. I was duly offered a huge vacant house in north London, which I was delighted to accept. I rather naïvely assumed that the wealthy men and women who were willing to support refuges for women and children would feel the same way about vulnerable and fragile men.

I very soon discovered that no one was willing to give me a penny for my men's project. We opened the house, and I faced another stark reality. Whereas filling a house with women and children resulted in the women quickly forming a community and taking charge of their own lives, filling a house with men resulted in them disappearing into a room and sitting helplessly on their beds or else sulking because there was no one to run the place and take care of cooking and other practical matters.

In vain we talked to them about the set-up in Chiswick. We talked about self-help. We talked about how we would decorate the satellite houses ourselves as well as do minor repairs. We talked about their responsibility to take care of one another. We met with blank silence. The men were not only unwilling or incapable of caring of each other in the house but we were unable to get any male volunteers to help out. The men's project petered out, and I gave the property back to the GLC.

We went back to the old system of relying on volunteers who were willing to visit the partners of refuge women in their homes or wherever else they were staying. Meanwhile I learned a big lesson. Women are naturally tribal. They will organize and help one another and take care of each other's children. Men are different. Most are solitary and invest their emotions only in their partners and their offspring. The problem with the men's house was that we did not have the resources to send a posse of women to work there to teach the men how to look after themselves. Indeed, the Chiswick refuge had been successful partly because we needed so few paid members of staff. The women ran the house, did the cooking and got on with their daily lives. For the moment I had to put the men's needs to one side.

By the mid-1970s British law had been changed in relation to domestic violence, so now the police had the right to intervene in fights that went on behind closed doors. An Englishman's home was no longer his castle. It seemed to represent a new dawn where the police were able to remove violent offenders. It soon transpired that the police could only remove a man, even if he was not the perpetrator; there was no provision for the removal of women, because the feminists had dinned it into the legislators that female violence was an impossibility.

One morning I arrived to find a tiny little woman in the refuge's sitting-room with her nose squashed across her face. As soon as I sat down she exploded with rage and told me her nose had been broken by a policeman who had come to arrest her husband. She said she wanted to sue the police. I let her rant on and offered her one of my Rothman's. She calmed down somewhat but was adamant that she intended to sue. Before making an appointment with our solicitor I telephoned her local police station to check her story.

'Yes indeed,' the officer on the end of the phone agreed. 'We do have a record of an arrest at that address. The female partner of the man arrested had called to ask for assistance, and because of the man's record for brutal violence a police squad arrived to take him away. The lady in question did suffer a broken nose, but this was the result of an accident when she engaged in battle with her partner against the police officers.'

'Why on earth did you attack the police?' I asked her as soon as I got off the phone.

'Because I changed me fucking mind!' She agreed the account I had received was substantially correct and that she had attacked one of the policemen she had originally asked to protect her from her partner.

'In that case,' I said risking a punch from her balled fist. 'I will go into court and give evidence against you if you try to sue the police. You know you are living with a very dangerous man, yet you keep leaving him and then going back. Each time you decide to leave you call the police – and then there's a massive fight! You risk everyone's lives, and then you go back to him again! If you want to stay here at the refuge and work on why you feel the need to lead such a reckless existence, then you are very welcome.' I knew I was wasting my breath. She wasn't ready to give up her chaotic and violent lifestyle. I watched her walk out of the room and wondered how long it would be before she would end up dead. Sometimes I wondered if what she was doing wasn't just a slow sort of suicide. Eventually her partner might kill her – if only by accident during one of their regular fights. The likelihood was that he would spend years in gaol and come out leaner, fitter but just as angry. His rage against women would remain undimmed.

Through lack of available time I ended up having to leave campaigning for further legal change and in the provision of more accommodation for victims of violence to others. I knew that to effect such changes took years of work and energy, and I didn't have that sort of time to spend on paperwork. My job, as I saw it, was to spend my time mostly working directly with mothers and children. I still felt I needed to understand why people create such disastrous relationships. At an elementary level I comprehended that people with backgrounds similar to mine were likely to fall into the patterns of domestic life they had experienced in infancy and repeat these unless someone came into their lives and showed them a better alternative. At the refuge this was what we were doing. However, sometimes I recognized that the law had to be changed and that I needed to intervene directly.

What I found especially bad was that we had to escort the mothers to the High Court in the Strand or to county courts in order for their divorce and custody cases to take place. I would usually accompany the women with the most violent partners because I discovered that we were expected to stand outside the court next to the men and their cronies. This seemed one way the court system would brutalize those who come through their doors seeking justice. The only security offered to the vulnerable women was from the tipstaff and bailiffs – and they were in short supply.

The most dramatic case we experienced was after a man had stabbed his wife in the neck on leaving London's High Court. She lay on a marble floor in a pool of blood trying to scrawl 'I am a Jehovah's Witness – no blood transfusion' before passing out. She survived the attack but on leaving hospital was not seen again. I was left with her four beautiful children. I knew that they would probably be split up if they were sent to children's homes but that they had caring relatives in the Caribbean where their mother had been born. It was a matter of arranging passports, finding the money for their airfares and dispatching them to their West Indian relations before anyone official got wind of what was going on. Their father was gaoled for a considerable time, and I got a telegram from the Caribbean to say all was well and that the children were safe. The father was not happy and threatened violent retribution. I very much hoped that a long spell in prison might calm him down but never heard from him again.

After establishing the Chiswick refuge I realized I needed to learn a great deal about alternative ways of thinking. The emotionally damaged and vulnerable women who sought my help often had fallen through holes in the state's safety net, and often the solutions I worked out left me sailing perilously close to breaking the law.

One day an American woman came into the refuge with a small baby and toddler. A warrant was out for her arrest, as her violent partner had been given custody of the two girls. This was because he owned the house, and she had no claim to it. As an American she had no right to any financial support or services from the state. The judge concerned decided that although her partner beat her he didn't have a record of attacking the children. The fact that the man's daughters might have been seriously affected by witnessing their mother being physically battered apparently never entered the judge's head.

I knew we would have to move fast. One way of getting a mother out of the country was to send a posse of mothers and children down to the coast to catch a ferry for France, ostensibly for a day out. We could get a group ticket, and usually in the hustle little attention was paid to individual tickets or passports and everyone was waved through. Once in France a mother who needed to disappear could head off to one of the European refuges and eventually make her way back to her own country, but this time there was a problem. I didn't realize that the ports and airports in England had been told to watch out for the American. God was on our side, however, because a sympathetic official turned the woman back but let her go free so that she could return to the refuge in Chiswick. I immediately sent her off to an airport in Scotland, since it took several days for an English court order to be imposed on airports there, so she was able to fly back to the United States with her children and safely rejoin her family.

Many years later her grown-up children returned to England and contacted me. They brought with them their father's ashes. They told me he had mellowed with age, and eventually they felt secure enough to spend some time with him. He had died leaving a will stipulating that his ashes should be scattered in Richmond. I drove the children to Richmond Bridge. As he requested, his ashes were scattered under the bridge in the swiftly flowing dark-brown water of the Thames.

These are the times when daily cares fade away – and I rejoiced in the company of the two poised and well-adjusted girls whom I had not seen since they were vulnerable infants.

18
PARTING OF THE WAYS

It was almost inevitable that my marriage would break down as a result of the changes in my life. I could well imagine how difficult it was for Jack to accept that the woman he had wed had turned into a mountain of frenzied energy and determination to change the world. For most of our married life I had been a housewife, and he was used to the idea that he went out to work and I looked after him and the family. Now the telephone rang incessantly – and the calls were mostly for me. He dealt with much of the change in my lifestyle by being home less than ever. Then, one day in 1976 when we had spent the weekend in the Bristol house, he sat up in bed and confessed that he had been having affairs.

I was shocked when he told me because I never thought that either of us would have extramarital relationships. I had always felt really sorry for friends with partners who cheated on them; to find I was one of those naïve, unsuspecting woman came as a surprise. Oddly enough, I felt almost a sense of relief. I had no good reason to break up my marriage, and, indeed, I took my vows very seriously. I could never have asked for a divorce out of the blue, but now I could see a way in which we could consider a separation.

Over the years we had become estranged. I found it difficult not to be able to discuss my work at the refuge with him, but Jack had declared a moratorium on the subject. I discovered that he was not happy if I was on television or radio, so I would turn the programme off straight away. I also hid any newspapers containing features about me or the refuge. Of course, I could do little about the people who approached us in the street to ask if I was Erin Pizzey. He was on television, but meanwhile I was gaining notoriety and becoming recognized in public as often as he. He was famous, and I was infamous – but we were like strangers to each other.

I knew divorce would be devastating for our children, so we

decided that Cleo, who was living in the basement with the au pair, would move upstairs and take our bedroom, and I would create a partition across the sitting-room for my bedroom, and Jack could live in the basement in a newly created one-bedroom flat until he felt that he was ready to move out and live on his own. This way the children would not be brutally torn apart from their father.

I knew that any divorce, however civilized, is damaging for the children concerned. Jack was very clear after admitting his affairs that the only marriage he could envisage was an 'open' one, but in my book that was no marriage at all. I had seen too many men and women make a mockery of the marriage with their sexual philandering, and I wanted none of it. The vows I had taken in 1961 had been before God, and I had meant every word of them. I realized it was not the sex with other women that caused my mental anguish once Jack admitted his extramarital relationships; it was the sense of betrayal. Moreover, I felt an idiot, because so many of our friends had known that he had been having affairs, and I had been blind.

After we had reorganized our home and the family was settling down once more, I was asked to lecture at a major conference on child abuse. I was standing alone on the edge of a crowd of people who all seemed to know each other when a very dignified woman came up and touched my elbow. 'Her Royal Highness would like to speak to you,' she said, guiding me towards a table.

I saw a tiny, elegant woman waving a long cigarette-holder in my direction and sipping what looked like a gin and tonic. I recognized Princess Margaret straight away. 'Read about you in the *Observer*,' she said cheerfully. 'It's bad enough when they sneak out of the house to other women, but it's even worse when they're after men as well!' We laughed, and I reflected that betrayal happens to most of us at one time or another, whatever our background.

Our family in Goldhawk Road was immensely blessed by the presence of young Trevor Shillingford. He came into our lives in 1968 when he was seven years old. Cleo was the same age, and Amos was one. His father had left his mother and was in the process of emigrating to Canada. Trevor lived with his mother down the road in Shepherd's Bush but soon adopted us as a surrogate family. He often stayed with us during the years I owned a caravan in Pevensey Bay, near Eastbourne in Sussex.

Buying the caravan in 1969 was probably the beginning of my rebellion against our staid middle-class lifestyle in Hammersmith. For a few years we would drag the children off to a villa in Spain with an au pair for two weeks every summer. There I would end up spending most of my time cooking, cleaning and taking care of the children in someone else's immaculate house. The au pairs inevitably discovered sex and alcohol on these trips and were useless at helping out with housework and child care. I didn't much enjoy these holidays, despite the sun. I decided that the children and I would be happier if we had a caravan on the south coast and I could take Cleo and Amos and their friends down for weekends and holidays.

I found the perfect beach at Pevensey, and the caravan had room for five adults – which meant at least eight children plus me. I protected the seats with bright-orange washable plastic and had orange PVC blinds made to fit the windows. I bought pretty little glass lamps and a butane stove to cook on. The dining-table became my double bed, and the children piled on top of one another in sleeping bags. Suddenly the dreary weekends when Jack was away and we were on our own in London were over. on Friday nights I would pack the car with children and dogs, and together we would drive down to the Sussex coast.

Trevor usually accompanied us, and the children invited a number of other friends. Two who often stayed in Goldhawk Road over the years were Annie Ruddock and Caron Ramsingh, good friends with Trevor as well as Mark Ashby, Ann's son.

The children roamed round the campsite, hung out in the nearby arcade with its games machines and zoomed around in go-carts on the paths. There was a fishing hut at the end of the beach where I could buy crabs. In those days almost no one in Britain ate squid. The fishermen would throw them on the pebbles, and I would rescue them to make delicious stews. At night I cooked up big meals, and then the children would watch television on a tiny bright-red set in the main room while I made up my bed and read.

During the day I drove everyone around the countryside in our Ford van visiting castles and other interesting sites. We had picnics in the car if it rained and picnics on any available patch of grass if the sun shone. I was much happier in my caravan than I had ever been in the trendy houses in Spain. I have never enjoyed lying in the sun and doing nothing. Roaming around with a band of children exploring the lesser-known nooks and crannies of the south of England kept me happy and entertained. Occasionally Jack would join us, but this was never really a success. Looking back, I think the end of our annual Spanish holidays also contributed to the rift in our marriage.

There came the parting of the ways when Jack was going to spend his first night downstairs in the basement flat, and we decided to invite some close friends over for dinner to mark the occasion. The builder we appointed to undertake the necessary alterations in the house, however, announced at the last minute that he needed to work late to finish the partition. Our friends sat in the dining area of the sitting-room chatting away while he banged and hacked and sawed all though the meal. I sat in my chair drinking vast quantities of red wine, and no one mentioned the mayhem that was going on behind us. Thank God, I thought at the end of the night, I would never have to give a formal dinner party again!

Once the builder had finally finished the partition work he put up the most beautiful wallpaper. It was very pale green with peacocks and palm fronds picked out in gold. I had a bed on the floor with satin sheets, and I cultivated a garden of ferns and palm trees in the room. I used a white marble washstand for a dressing-table. Tall Biba fringed floor lamps lit the room with a soft yellow light. It made a restful space.

Even if the separation was hard on everyone, on the whole I think it was for the best. And the children were able to move between the two households for several years before the divorce was finalized two years later in February 1979 and Jack moved into a flat in Shepherd's Bush. Amos said to me once when he was around nine, 'I don't care what happened between you two. I just want you to be married like everyone else.' I could hear the anguish in his voice, and I ached for him, but really there was no going back.

Trevor moved in permanently around this time, sleeping in the tiny room that doubled up as my office. By this time he was fourteen. Very soon he introduced one of his best friends, Mikey Craig, to us, and he, too, began to spend a considerable amount of time in our home. One day I got up half asleep to prepare a morning cup of coffee and nearly tripped over a large youth sprawled on the dining-room floor fast asleep, I stepped over him and carried on into the kitchen. This is how Richard Lewis, nicknamed Cass, first joined us. He would in due course become another much-loved member of our household.

It was perfectly natural for children to turn up at our house. I was brought up among large numbers of children, and I felt at home however many friends Amos and Cleo invited into their home.

Fortunately I enjoyed cooking, and if I wasn't preparing meals I was writing. I decided not to ask Jack for alimony but to get him to agree that once he moved out he would hand over the deeds of the house. I also kept the small amount of rent from the tenants who lived in our first house at 9 Coulter Road in Hammersmith. They couldn't afford to pay much, but the money helped feed and clothe all the children.

One morning when reading the *Guardian* letters page I came across one from Barbara Cartland, famous for her romantic novels. She was lamenting the lack of 'real men' in her life. I wrote a jokey letter in response to say that all the real men I met usually turned out to be six-foot six-year-olds! My lament was picked up by Deirdre McSharry, the editor of *Cosmopolitan* magazine. Could I write an article about the men in my life? she enquired.

Deirdre liked what I wrote, and very soon I was writing a monthly column for her magazine. With the money from this and the odd commission from newspapers I was able to survive. The mothers at the refuge held back any large-sized clothes donated to the refuge for me, and the mothers in the Bristol house made me several dresses.

Around this time Cass and Mikey were expelled from St Clement Danes Grammar School in Shepherd's Bush. They were upset because they felt their expulsion was unfair. Both were very bright, and they were due to take their O-levels. I had a massive fight with the school, with the support of the Race Relations Board, and finally both boys returned to school and passed their examinations. The two subsequently decided they wanted to become musicians, and I bought Mikey his first guitar.

I had studied the violin at school and got as far as playing with the National Youth Orchestra at their summer schools, so our house would reverberate with classical music emanating from the stereo in one room and hard rock, reggae and drumming from another.

My life had changed dramatically from the days when I was living in Goldhawk Road with Jack. We now lived in the upper part of the house as bohemians. Cleo had loved being at Unicorn, but Amos had become a misfit there by the age of ten. I had a very difficult time convincing his school that he was dyslexic – a condition not then widely recognized by teachers and educationists – but I remembered the struggles I myself had experienced learning to read and write as a child. I was told by the head teacher at Unicorn that Amos might be 'backward'. In the light of this assessment I took him to a newly formed organization that could test for dyslexia, and, as I suspected, like me he had the condition. He spent two days undergoing tests and came out with a piece of paper that said he had an IQ of 170. I took the findings back to the head teacher, but it made no difference.

She couldn't make him out at all. One day I had an angry telephone call demanding that I come over to the school straight away. She was furious because she had been inundated with telephone calls from mothers saying that Amos had told their children that he was allowed to smoke at home. That morning he had mischievously scattered cigarette butts on the floor outside his classroom, and now he was sitting penitently on a chair outside her office. I took him home for the rest of the day. A few weeks later he arrived on his own at the refuge and demanded, 'What has Paddington Bear got to do with my life? Why do I have to read about him?' I knew he must have been very upset to make the long journey on foot to find me. Unicorn was not the school for Amos, and I genuinely feared that he would be put off learning for life.

I personally had been relieved when the time came for Cleo to move to Chiswick Comprehensive. By the early 1970s Unicorn was attracting a sophisticated group of powerful women with husbands working in the media. I found them intimidating. On one occasion Jack and I were invited to a party that looked like turning into an orgy when after dinner we were herded around the swimming-pool and the hostess stripped naked. I struggled not to laugh. Nobody joined her for a few moments, as the guests stared at one other sheepishly to see who would go first. Then a ginger-haired man cast off his clothes and plunged into the brightly lit pool. I could see his tiny penis bobbing about, and it was too much for me. I ended up sobbing with laughter. Very slowly the pool room emptied, and the hostess never forgave me.

Another evening one of the Unicorn fathers rushed up and down the stairs, unkempt and sweaty, lugging reels of film and frantically setting up a projector in his living-room. After dinner the guests, including Jack and me, were asked to file into room and the lights were turned out. It was not, as I expected, a family holiday film; instead it featured a very large naked Japanese man attempting to crack a vase with his huge erection. We sat in silence broken only by the whirr of the film projector. After that I gave up on socializing with the school's parents and took solace in the fact that the women in the refuge seemed a good deal saner than those supposedly 'normal' families.

I discussed Amos's educational problems with Jack and suggested that our son might do better if he could be home-tutored. I felt that if he could choose his own tutor and create his own educational programme he was less likely to abandon his education. Jack agreed, and Amos was enthusiastic.

With the help of the Gabbitas agency we selected his first private tutor and his new regime began. I would leave the house to take Cleo to school, while Trevor caught the bus to Holland Park Comprehensive. Later on the rest of the children would awake, and Amos would start his lessons and Mikey and Cass would get on with their music. Annie and Caron were often around as well. Annie would, in years to come, play with the children in the refuge and became a mother figure to them as well as to Amos. Like Mikey and Cass, she would go on to develop a professional career in music. I loved coming back to the house. There was a warm, friendly atmosphere, and we all sat around the dining-room table and tucked into sociable meals.

Trevor's school experiences epitomized my concerns about what was happening in education in the 1970s. Holland Park, like the rest of the state schools in our area, was quickly overrun by the same middle-class left-wing parents that I had seen at the favoured primary schools when I was looking for a suitable one for Cleo. Soon after Trevor arrived at the comprehensive I telephoned the music department to tell them he had a beautiful voice and was anxious to join the school choir; he also wanted singing lessons. No one contacted him about this, so I decided to go to the school in person and talk to a teacher in the music department.

Trevor and his friends often regaled me with stories about the school. There was little attempt made to enforce the wearing of school uniform. The teachers did very little teaching, and many of them seemed to spend more time preaching radical politics. Trevor brought home a copy of Chairman Mao's *Little Red Book* and explained that the children in his class had been asked to 'sneak' on their parents if they were considered to be 'bourgeois capitalists' or to have dubious political views. I was horrified, but, as I was later to discover, Trevor and his friends mostly bunked off school and spent their time in the local parks and cinemas.

My personal visit to the school did nothing to change my low opinion of the place. In the 1960s there was much trumpeting from Anthony Crosland, Labour's Education Secretary, of the benefits of the comprehensive-school system and a promise to 'destroy every fucking grammar school in England. And Wales and Northern Ireland'. Shirley Williams was another architect of the destruction of the grammar schools. I was outraged. My father and his brothers had passed their Eleven Plus examinations and obtained an excellent education at Brentford Grammar School. For children from poor families, it was the one avenue of opportunity, of escape from a future of manual labour, offered to academically gifted children in Britain, while those who failed the Eleven Plus mostly went on to learn trade skills at the secondary modern schools. Now, in this age of socialist tyranny, bright children were to be sacrificed on the altar of revolutionary ideology by being placed in mixed-ability classes; there was to be no streaming to enable them to progress at their own pace. Cynically, I always thought that one reason why the left-wing middle classes were so keen to see the grammar schools abolished was that some of their sons and daughters would have failed the Eleven Plus and would thus have been relegated to the secondary moderns. Their parents were not going to allow that to happen.

I wandered through the circus of extracurricular activity that was Holland Park Comprehensive, and eventually, as there were no staff in evidence, I made my way to the modern block that housed the music department. Most of the pupils I spotted were white and looked and sounded middle class. I finally approached someone who seemed to be a teacher draped in a loose bright kaftan. I explained my desire for Trevor to be encouraged to develop his aptitude for music, and she nodded, but I perceived that she was not taking much in. Her eyes were bloodshot, and her look was unfocused. I assumed she had been smoking dope.

I told Trevor of my visit, and he cheerfully agreed that many of the teachers smoked with the students. Some of his lessons consisted of readings from *The Little Red Schoolbook* and other revolutionary literature, but he tended to bunk off most of these classes because he found them boring and dogmatic. Although it was a shame that he wasn't getting a proper education I wasn't surprised. At any rate, while he was able to ignore his teachers and do exactly as he pleased at school, when he was home with me he had to behave himself, respect me and my property and put up with my nagging him about his table manners.

From the early 1970s on thousands of young people were emerging from the universities to spread the revolutionary gospel according to whichever branch of left-wing ideology they espoused. They flooded into the caring agencies and particularly into social work, the state schools and the Civil Service. Many had little vocation for these jobs. They were high on being placed in positions of power in which they could tear down institutions, radically influence school education and destabilize formerly happy communities. I was depressed at what I saw. I suspected that many of the new inner-city comprehensives were creating illiterate, unemployable adults. Encouraged to have sex with no responsibility, they would inevitably multiply to form a group that could be described only as feral. When I spoke out in public against the erosion of educational standards and the dangers of dogma I was branded a 'running-dog lackey of capitalist imperialism'. I suppose it had a certain ring to it.

19

SISTERS UNDER THE SKIN

My idea of a happy family life was probably most influenced by my reading as a child. I have always been addicted to books, and Louisa May Alcott's books had a big influence on me. I was passionately attached to Jo Marsh in *Little Women*, who was the tomboy in her family. She went on to become a journalist and gather a collection of boys around her. Now I was a journalist surrounded by boys.

Although my mother and father fought incessantly, my siblings and I were rarely stuck alone at home with them, because when we lived abroad there was always a retinue of servants to hide behind. The safest place was the kitchen with the cooks and the serving staff. Maybe that is where I learned my love of cooking. Most of the staff knew and disapproved of my mother's violence and animosity towards me, and I can remember many times when a sympathetic servant wiped my tears or gave me something comforting to eat.

St Mary's, the caring holiday home run by Miss Williams, also influenced my idea of a happy domestic life, and I grew to find the idea of a house in which two adults lived with just a few children unappealing. I preferred extended families, such as I had observed in the Middle East in my childhood. The early years in Hammersmith, during which I lived at home with just Cleo and Amos for company, had been lonely ones for us all. Now our lives were full and creative. Books tumbled off the shelves; musical instruments lay ready to play in every room, and the children would invite their friends to fill the house and play ping-pong in the garden.

Even though I was now a single mother I still regarded family as the backbone of society. I was aware that marriage as an institution was under attack. But I had survived the radical feminist onslaught against me, and even while they attempted to brainwash the women and children entering their refuges I was convinced that most women were immune to their fanaticism.

Many of these refuges were spewing out statistics that bore little relationship to the reality of domestic violence in Britain. Their administrators collected information from the those entering their refuges, just like I did, but instead of asking a woman to discuss all aspects of her life, including her own potential for aggression, the feminists failed to ask a single question that might contradict their belief that all violence was perpetrated by men. Thus the research was inevitably skewed.

I received an invitation from a large conference to be held on the subject of child health and welfare. I often accepted such invitations and thought little about the event until I checked the refuge diary to discover that it was almost upon me. On this occasion I checked the diary in the office and found I was meant to be speaking after lunch that day. Grabbing Becky, the two of us leaped into a taxi and headed off.

We arrived mid-afternoon at an imposing building to find an enormous number of people gathered in a vast room. The walls were lined with golden plates, and dark, sombre portraits of men in glowing uniforms stared down at us. I had almost no time to prepare my speech. Becky shoved me on to the stage and sat behind the curtain to make sure I didn't run away. I was shaking with nerves. This was the biggest audience I had ever seen in my life. I don't remember what I said, but it seemed to be well received. We had no time for lunch, so at the end of the day we stayed on for what I hoped would be an evening meal.

We got stuck into what I assumed were pre-dinner drinks. Both of us drank quantities of red wine, while all there was to consume was little squares of cheddar on cocktail sticks. Soon I was finding it difficult to stand without swaying, and Becky wasn't doing much better. Just as I was about to suggest that we make our way out I saw to my surprise a swathe of women curtsying low to the ground. I crossed my hands behind my back and held on to Becky's. To my consternation the Queen stood in front of me. There was no question of either of us curtsying; any attempt would have found us sprawled at Her Majesty's feet.

The Queen and I conversed for what seemed like a long time. She was well informed and very concerned about the conditions at the refuge and the fate of the children. At last she moved on, and

Becky and I escaped outside and fell into a taxi. As I sighed with relief, I thought about my mother's long-held desire for her daughters to be presented to the monarch – and here I was drunk and incapable of even a low bow when the moment had come!

At the refuge I worked mainly with women and children who grew up on our worst housing estates. Like my father, they came from generations of disadvantaged and impoverished families. However, I was aware that among the very wealthy who had no material disadvantages the same violent and sexually abusive behaviour could also be found. Women from aristocratic or famous families would sometimes contact me privately. I understood that they felt unable to visit the refuge in person. Too often we had journalists visiting the house, or else idle chatter might cause their names to be splashed across newspapers.

One time I was faced with a woman from a very wealthy farming family. She had broken ribs and black eyes. Her husband ran an enormous estate, and he beat her regularly. She was desperate to get away from him, and I offered her the safety of the refuge. She stayed for a few days, but she was racked with guilt about the welfare of her children. Her brother-in-law was a Member of Parliament, and she wanted to confide in him and see whether he might ask her husband to seek professional help for his violent behaviour.

She returned from her meeting with him at the House of Commons in tears. On seeing her blackened eyes her brother-in-law had hissed across the lunch table, 'You go back to my brother – and don't you dare tell anybody about this!'

I begged her to fight her husband in court, but she was resolutely opposed to this course of action. She said that she would never get any justice in the courts in the Devon countryside in which she lived. Her husband was a Master of Hounds and known as a 'jolly good chap'. He had friends across the county, and no judge would find against him.

I knew of a very famous actress who was married to a British film star who not only battered her but who would strip her naked and throw her out of the house. She was forced to spend the night in the back seat of her car until he allowed her back in the next morning – usually after he had sobered up. Mother of two children, she, too, was disinclined to publicize her plight. The mother from Devon went back to her husband and children. Like her, the actress was not willing to face a lonely and uncertain future without the trappings of marriage. No doubt she was also afraid of the publicity caused by a public separation and what her partner might do in retaliation if she left him.

I was well aware of the isolation such women experienced from my own experiences. Now I was separated I was no longer invited along to dinner parties. Jack, however, was viewed differently – he was now an eligible bachelor on the dinner-party circuit. I didn't mind the lack of social invitations, as I had always regarded such parties as pretentious and tedious. In my house it was different. Informality was the rule: anyone who came to my home was very welcome to join my family at the table for whatever food I was preparing and for an evening of good humour and laughter.

One woman who arrived at the refuge and who proved an exception to my experiences with middle-class women was the wife of the literary agent Paul Scott who in the late 1970s became famous for writing *The Jewel in the Crown*. One day I saw an old Volvo hurtle up Chiswick High Road and screech to a halt outside the house. The back of the car was packed with stuff, and a shabby old suitcase was tied to the roof rack.

Penny dashed into the refuge with a mountain of belongings, sat down in the sitting-room and began talking a mile a minute. We gathered round to hear what she had to say. She told us that her husband had been threatening her with an axe. She was terrified of him, and although he had never hit her he constantly bullied and verbally abused her. If he had been drinking heavily he would smash things up in the house, and she felt she could no longer put up with his behaviour. She had heard about the refuge and wanted to start her life again.

In our morning meetings we had often talked about the difference between physical and mental violence. I had experienced both, because my mother used to beat me but my father terrorized us all with his violent rages. He reserved his most vitriolic comments for my brother whom he constantly humiliated; he warned him that he was going to be a total failure in life. The majority of the women felt as I did and agreed that bruises can fade and bones heal but harsh words remain with one for life.

We were all glad that Penny had sought our help. I was, however, concerned about how she would fit into the community. I need not have worried. Within a few days she had made new friends. She told me that living in the refuge was like being at boarding-school. Even the dormitory accommodation was not so different. She was much loved by the mothers and children, and she was a wise and gentle influence. Eventually she was offered accommodation in north London and began a new life there. I heard many years later that after hearing that Paul was dying of cancer she returned to nurse him until he died.

There was a much less happy ending after the pianist Hephzibah Menuhin contacted me and asked me to visit her at home. I had long admired her violinist brother Yehudi Menuhin. I had played the violin, and to me he was a god. I took a member of staff, Tina, along, and we were met at the door by a very pretty dark-haired woman who led us into a small room in which a man sat in an armchair. Without introducing us Hephzibah crouched down at his feet and picked up a notebook. This was her husband, the Austrian sociologist Richard Hauser. For the next hour and a half he regaled us with his life story. Tina and I were astounded. Here was one of the most lauded pianists in the world taking down every word this pompous, boring man uttered.

Richard Hauser considered himself a genius, and Hephzibah plainly cast herself into the role of his slave. I could see there was a degree of complicity in their relationship and that she was unable to break away. As far as I was concerned, this man was charlatan as well as a tyrant, but his hold over Hephzibah was soon explained.

On a subsequent visit, when Richard was out of the house, Hephzibah told us about her violent bully of a mother; how she and her brother were made to practise duets at the piano and if they got off the piano stool they were beaten. She told us with tears in her eyes that if she was left alone for a moment she used to pull back the carpet and pee, then quickly replace the rug because she was too afraid to ask to go to the lavatory. Richard not only bullied Hephzibah emotionally but physically pushed her around. It was obvious to me that she had replaced one abusive relationship with another.

I was convinced that once she was made aware of her dependence on him and had his violent tendencies pointed out by another she could begin to contemplate a future without him, but the only way I could get Hephzibah away from him for any length of time was to ask her to join a women-only meeting in my home. I arranged for a number of women friends to attend, but it was a waste of time. Hephzibah, like any addict with her drug, simply replaced Richard's physical presence by talking obsessively about her love for him. I decided that since the refuge was full of women who did want to break free from their violent if addictive relationships my time was better spent with them.

Several years later I got a call from her asking me to pay her a visit. She had cancer of the throat and wanted to see me. Again I went with Tina, and Hephzibah sat as usual on the floor beneath Richard. In between writing down his every utterance she rushed about getting cups of tea. Nothing had changed, and I had no idea why she had wanted to see me. As she let us out of the house I took her to one side and explained gently that, in my opinion, malignant relationships could trigger malignant cells. There was a flash of understanding in her beautiful brown eyes, but I knew there was no hope of her acting on what I said. In due course the cancer killed her, and I heard from a member of the family that as she lay dying she could hear Richard making love to one of his mistresses in the next room. I mourned the death of such a wonderful and gifted woman. To me, it seemed that violent and abusive relationships could be as addictive as drugs or alcohol. I was coming to the conclusion that chemicals in the human brain could trigger an addictive personality, but it would be years before scientists would start to prove me right.

20
THE BAM BAM CLUB

One morning I came into the refuge to discover a large party of German women standing in our scruffy sitting-room. The room looked especially dilapidated by contrast with the beautifully dressed visitors. It turned out that the large blonde who seemed to be in charge was a West German Minister who had made an appointment to visit the refuge with a retinue of her colleagues. I had entirely forgotten about their appointment. Becky volunteered to show them round the building, and I headed off to the cubby-hole for a cigarette and strong cup of coffee.

They looked surprisingly shaken by the time they returned to the sitting-room, and I was in the middle of an impassioned speech when I noticed white balloon-like objects floating past the window and noisily exploding below. Some of the mothers had found a new use for the hundreds of condoms we had requested from the London Rubber Company. Our housemother JoJo, practical as ever, had decided to offer family-planning advice since, according to our questionnaires, very few of the women entering the refuge used any sort of contraception. The preferred method of family planning seemed to be abortion, and we had spent many hours discussing the issue.

As the balloons continued to rain down my guests asked me to explain. Trying not to laugh, I explained that some of the women were taking part in a therapeutic exercise. I thought it best not to elaborate.

Before she left the Minister expressed a desire that I should take our television film to Berlin and show it as publicity for the setting up of similar refuges in West Germany. I didn't give the matter much thought, but I must have said yes, because before long I received an official invitation, and I agreed to go provided that I could take one of the refuge's mothers along together with the film-maker Michael Whyte.

In the event I managed to combine the trip to Berlin with an invitation from my German publishers who wanted me to attend the Frankfurt Book Fair to publicize their edition of my book *Scream Quietly or the Neighbours Will Hear*. We flew to Frankfurt, and a car took the three of us to a hotel. Early the next morning a car collected us and dropped us off to what seemed like an enormous abattoir, the site of the book fair.

On the stand, at which we were to spend the next two days, we did, indeed, feel like meat on a slab. People from the publishing house rushed about, but nobody bothered to talk to us. I discovered that we could freely order drinks and decided the only way I was going to get through the experience was to get mildly plastered. Christine, who had accompanied us as a representative of the mothers, was much better behaved, but Michael and I drank as much as we could while tolerating the occasional camera intruding on our rambling conversations. We were generally left to our own devices by the publishing staff until the evening when we were informed that we were invited to join the company for dinner.

We duly found ourselves in an impressive restaurant in the centre of town, but instead of sitting with the other invited guests the three of us were allocated a separate table. We consumed a dreary meal of meat and vegetables served with a pile of potatoes. Fortunately the wine was excellent, but we were studiously ignored throughout the evening.

The second night I was told that the three of us could go out to dinner at the publisher's expense, and I was given the address of an excellent restaurant in the city. No one bothered to accompany us or suggest a brief tour of the city. We took a taxi, and when we arrived at the restaurant I was delighted to see lobster on the menu. Christine decided to share one with me, but when it arrived on her plate she took one look and sent it back. She would have fish and chips, she told the waiters.

I was still annoyed at the offhand way we had been treated by my publishers, and when we got back to the hotel I decided to throw a private party. I have a vague memory of bottles of champagne littering the floor and Christine and I singing raucous songs. We flew off to Berlin the next day, and I left behind an enormous bill. I have no doubt that this sort of behaviour did nothing to further good relations with the publishers, but I was infuriated that no one had bothered sitting down with us to discuss the book or even take an interest in our work in Chiswick. Nor had we been introduced to journalists or any kindred spirits. We had just been curiosities camped at the stand.

There was tension of a different kind once we reached Berlin. It started badly when we found ourselves seemingly miles out of the city deposited in a dormitory at the university. I was outraged. After the wasteland of Frankfurt, we had been looking forward to staying in central Berlin where Michael had friends. Our kindly German escort was preparing to leave when I decided to kick up a fuss. The last two days in Frankfurt, I told her, had been awful, and now we were stuck in the middle of nowhere. All we would get to see was the inside of a meeting-room that evening, while the next day I was scheduled to give a speech at the university in an adjacent building. 'Take us back to the airport!' I demanded imperiously. 'We will not stay here!' The poor woman looked astonished and scurried away.

Eventually she returned and told us to get back into the car with her. Her jaw was set, but I didn't care. We were taken to a delapidated hotel in central Berlin. We were allocated two rooms, and Christine and I had to bunk up in a double bed. We had a meeting with the Minister and her associates where I was due to speak and Michael was to introduce his film. I was surprised to see that he was the only man in the room. There were a lot of very grim women in attendance, and I had a nightmarish flashback. I felt I was was back in the dark days of the emerging feminist movement when crowds of belligerent and drably dressed women would gather to pledge the destruction of men and the family.

The lights went out, and the opening chords of the film's music filled the hall. The Minister watched for all of ten minutes and then gestured to have the film turned off. I couldn't decide whether she was deeply moved or just bored. The lights came on, and the women in the room began to talk among themselves in German. A small group came over to where we were sitting, and one of them invited Christine and I to a party. 'No men allowed,' another added impassively. Michael, ever good-natured, jokingly offered to put on a skirt, but no one laughed. We politely told them no thanks and promised to meet up with some of them the next morning to discuss the setting up of their refuge.

Michael invited one of his Berlin friends to join us for dinner, and we went off to meet him at a restaurant that took my breath away. All around the walls were huge pictures of penises and vaginas. The person serving us might have been male or female; it was impossible to tell. Christine and I were in shock. Michael's friend was a tiny elf from the Far East, and he howled with laughter at our confounded faces. After dinner we ended up a place called the Bam Bam Club. We pushed our way into the middle of a heaving throng of people. I was amazed to see they were all women.

They bore no resemblance to the ones we had been with a few hours earlier. All were beautifully dressed and made up. With a shock I realized that they were not women but men. I looked around for the others, but they had melted away. I burst into tears, confused and alarmed. A very tall individual with long brunette hair took my hand. 'Don't cry,' he said kindly. 'Come with me and I'll introduce you to the Queen of Berlin.' He led me across the floor to a small alcove where a Buddha-like man was holding court. The Queen of Berlin could see I was upset, but within minutes he made me forget my surroundings with his entertaining chat, and I soon began to enjoy myself enormously.

Christine and I awoke the next morning, aware that we had another grim day ahead of us but glad to be flying home that evening. We agreed that we had spent a great night in the Bam Bam Club and that maybe if all feminists were transsexuals we could have a women's movement that would work.

Michael was not invited to our meeting, so Christine and I made our way to the offices of the women who were planning to open refuges similar to ours. We were ushered into a brown room and asked to sit down at a large table. Around us was the sisterhood. The mood was sour, because by now it had dawned on them that we were renegades. The meeting began courteously enough with an invitation for us to talk about the refuge and our roles there. Christine told them how she had been given a slip of paper by a social worker with our address on it when she had needed help.

She explained that she had managed to get the money together for a taxi to drive her and three children to the refuge. She told them about the crush of the mothers and children already in residence and how it had taken her nearly two weeks before she found the courage to leave the sitting-room sofa and go upstairs to a dormitory where she and her family had been allocated bunk beds. She explained how grateful she felt that no one ever made her feel stupid but were sympathetic to her trepidation and fear. I, too, remembered those first two weeks after her arrival and how her little family were like frightened rabbits crouching in the one spot where they felt safe.

'You go home at night?' an incredulous woman asked me. She had a massive bunch of keys hanging off her belt. 'Don't you lock them in?'

'Just because you get into a violent relationship doesn't mean you're incompetent or an idiot. Why shouldn't I go home? The women in the refuge run the place. It's their home, and they can do anything I can do.' I could sense the disapproval around the table, and inwardly I sighed. Years before I had been given a book by Franz Fanon, a black revolutionary poet. In it he explains how the oppressed can, after they have thrown off the bonds of their oppressors, begin to ape the behaviour of the people they have overthrown. I saw women in Britain accuse men of being oppressors and then exhibit the worst attributes of oppressive behaviour. The women in Berlin seemed to want power and control over the women entering their refuges. What sort of liberation was that?

I explained my theory that not only men were violent; that women, too, could develop violent tendencies from a young age. I expounded our findings that what we had learned was that the best way of caring for women escaping abusive relationships was to enable them to become resilient survivors – not simply rescue them as 'victims' and deny them their right to become competent human beings. I looked at the faces around me and realized I was talking to deaf ears. We had nothing to say they wanted to hear. Christine and I left for our flight that night feeling defeated. But after several stiff gin and tonics we remembered the fun we had at the Bam Bam Club. We now knew the city had another side.

21
PLEASURE OR PAIN?

I was invited by my French publishers to spend a couple of days in Paris to do interviews for the French edition of *Scream Quietly or the Neighbours Will Hear*. I asked Jane to accompany me, as she was a feisty woman albeit with a powerful temper. I thought we could spend some time wandering around the Louvre and hanging out in cafés. I figured she needed a break, and with her raucous sense of humour she made me laugh. After she had been in the refuge for a short while she came into the cubby-hole to talk to me. She had fallen pregnant very young and was told by her family that there would be no support if she decided to keep her baby. The father of the child abandoned her as soon as he heard about her pregnancy, and she was left in a mother-and-baby home until the infant was born.

As soon as Jane held her baby daughter in her arms she knew she wanted to keep her, but she was given no choice. Her baby was taken from her, and she left the home bereft, angry and full of vengeance. I found the idea that either of my two children could ever have been snatched out of my arms unimaginable. Jane wasn't the first or last woman to come into my tiny office to tell me of such a devastating loss. As a result of losing her daughter, she threw herself into a destructive lifestyle. She ended up replacing her first child with several others and ricocheted from one abusive partner to the next.

I walked into the sitting-room in the refuge one morning in time to see Jane and her friend Millie giving a young woman very graphic instructions, with mimed demonstration, on how to give a 'deep throat' blow job.

'How could you', I said, deeply offended, 'encourage women to do that?'

Millie glared at me. 'She's on the game, and if she doesn't get it right she could break her neck.'

That silenced me, and after a strong cup of Nescafé and a cigarette I realized that I had a lot to learn.

Later on we sat around and listened to Millie's life-story. She had
been sexually abused by an uncle over a long period of time, and her
mother had refused to believe her when she tried to tell her about it.
Finally, after one particularly brutal attack when she was fifteen,
she engineered events so that her uncle was found by her mother in
her bedroom. The uncle made an unconvincing attempt to assure
his sister that nothing had happened. Her mother could no longer
deny the evidence in front of her eyes but hissed at her daughter,
'And what did you do to encourage him?' From that moment Millie
was estranged from her mother, so when she became pregnant by
one of her many boyfriends her parent's lack of support came as no
surprise.

In my experience I had noticed that happy girls from warm,
loving families rarely got pregnant as young unmarried teenagers.
I suspected that most young girls were not looking for straight-
forward sexual or erotic kicks when they engaged in under-age
sexual activity. The majority were seeking to find a substitute for
the love and affection they had failed to find in their relationships
with their parents.

I asked Millie to explain what satisfaction she got out of her
sexual encounters with men, since she had been a prostitute since
her early teens. 'It's the moment when he puts the money in my
hand,' she said. 'That's the buzz.' She went on to explain that while
she was having sex with a punter she felt in control and that when
he gave her the money sex and power fused. She also said that, as
much as she had hated having sex with her uncle, she did enjoy the
power to blackmail him for presents, and she had felt empowered,
too, when she was able to threaten him with the police. These are
powerful emotions for a young child to feel, and several of the other
mothers listening recounted their own early experiences of sexual
abuse.

Several of the prostitutes in the room told of times when they
had put themselves in dangerous situations resulting in rape. One
of these women, Laura, was a particular favourite of mine. The first
time she came into the refuge she was on the run from a pimp who
was coming out of prison. She was a big, bulky woman with a grim

expression, but she soon she settled into the refuge and proved to be excellent with children. Her own had been all taken into care, one after the other. She showed me a scar running from just below her breasts down to her thighs. ''E did that,' she said, referring to her pimp, when she saw me wince.

Her probation officer was frightened of her, and she knew it. ''E's afraid I'll kill 'im,' she said cheerfully.

'What do you do that makes him so scared,' I asked her.

'I just knock 'is filing cabinets around a bit and 'e calls security.'

Actually she did look terrifying, because she was so big and she glowered at everyone, but seeing her engaging with children in the sitting-room I could perceive the sweet, gentle side of her.

Laura went back on the streets, and the next time I saw her she came flying in because she had been gang-raped and beaten up by a group of men on the docks in Southampton. 'What were you doing by yourself in a godown in the docks at that hour of the morning? You know how dangerous that is!' I exclaimed. I wasn't condoning the rape. I just wanted Laura to consider her behaviour. She was back with her pimp and getting physically abused by her punters.

I told Laura about a time when the police had arrived at the refuge with a photograph of a woman's head. They never found the body, but it was said that she had died in a 'snuff' game. I knew about such games, because when I lived in Hong Kong I had a Chinese girl-friend who was an 'escort girl'. We were passing some pretty little sampans one day when I saw a group of men and some very beautiful women getting into one of these precarious boats, and she shook her head as the boat was carried out to sea. 'This is a dangerous game,' she said. 'Some of those girls won't come back.'

She explained that the attractive young women were prosti-tutes who would have accepted very large sums of money to be bent over backwards with their heads in the sea while the men reached orgasm. If the man failed to reach an orgasm in time, the woman drowned. 'Those young women don't need to play that sick game,' I said. 'They're attractive enough to find work that isn't so dangerous.'

My friend looked at me and said sadly, 'Some people have bad needs, and they choose to risk their lives. It is like living on a razor's edge.' At the time I was horrified and didn't want to discuss the matter further, but now I could begin to see a connection between pleasure and pain.

Another mother who had been a prostitute told a story of how she had been asked to give evidence at a London inquest when one of her friends had been found dead in a home-made dungeon owned by a policeman. 'The only way they identified her', she said, 'was by a little bluebird tattooed on her left shoulder.'

'But why would she go with a man like that?' I asked, genuinely puzzled.

Because, the mother explained, she liked rough, violent sex. 'She got off on it.'

The idea that some chose pain to achieve pleasure shocked and upset me, and I felt helpless because I found it so difficult to understand.

It was time to go to Paris with Jane to visit my feminist publishers. I had learned to speak French when my father was posted to West Africa, so I wasn't too worried about language problems – unlike my experience in West Germany when I had to rely on the assistance of a translator. We were to meet my French editor at the publishers' bookshop, and when we arrived I realized that men were not allowed into the store to buy books. I looked at Jane who gazed back blankly. The women we met were very friendly and a lot less intimidating than those organizing the West German refuges. However, we nearly came unstuck when during a convivial lunch where we all drank litres of wine my editor spoke directly to Jane and left me to help with translation. 'Since you live in a refuge and you sleep in dormitories', she asked, 'what do you do for sex?' I translated, and Jane replied, 'Those of us who have boyfriends arrange to meet them outside.'

'But you have nowhere to have sex with each other,' the editor persevered.

I translated with one hand on Jane's arm. She was about to get very angry. 'We aren't lezzies!' she declared.

There again was a clash of realities. We did have lesbians coming into the refuge. One young woman was the daughter of a vicar, and she had been battered for most of her childhood. She took refuge with a woman lover, and she received some of the worst beatings I had ever seen. She never stayed any length of time in Chiswick. She was completely addicted to violence, so, as with so many of the women who went back to brutal partners time and time again, I feared for her life.

The chill that descended over our previously friendly group meant that Jane and I wandered off soon afterwards and disappeared into a shop overflowing with cheese and wine to stock up with presents for the community.

One of the most memorable lesbians I encountered at the refuge arrived on our forecourt dressed in black leathers on a huge motorbike. She introduced herself as Boots and settled in quickly. She had walked out on eight children and her husband and said that she was going to discover her true sexual nature. To this end she taped up several large pictures of naked women with their legs spread wide on the wall above her bed. This prompted a heated discussion the next morning at our house meeting. She eventually saw our point that the heterosexual women in the community would not put up pictures of men's genitalia – so why should she be allowed to display pictures of women's? She soon became a much-loved member of the community. In time I tracked down a group of like-minded lesbians who called themselves Ice Breakers, and before long Boots found the friends she needed and roared off our forecourt for the last time.

I was always puzzled by the fact that gay men seemed perfectly comfortable in the company of heterosexual woman but that the lesbian community were generally so dismissive of their heterosexual sisters. In the early days of the feminist movement those of us who were heterosexual and who lived with husbands were accused of 'sleeping with the enemy'. In spite of figures that proved beyond doubt that same-sex partners were as likely to hit one another as heterosexuals, the lesbian movement continued to deny that women could ever be violent towards each other.

Jane and I decided that we could not be accused of homophobia, but my French publishers were definitely heterophobic. As far as I am concerned, my God doesn't care who you love; it is how you love that matters. To be able to love another human being more than yourself and to be rewarded with a reciprocal love brings the greatest happiness to anyone.

The time that Jane and I spent together in Paris cemented our friendship. I knew that I was woefully ignorant of all aspects of deviant sexuality. I needed her to help me understand why so many of the women coming to the refuge were bonded to men who sexually abused them. I was particularly bewildered by the women who explained that they got sexual gratification through pain. It was through talking to Jane that I began to understand. She explained that she had many friends who were prostitutes who specialized in beating their punters and that some of these women also enjoyed rough, violent sex; indeed it was the only way they could reach orgasm.

Millie, too, more worldly-wise than most, opened up a whole new way of thinking for me by explaining how a prostitute might relate to her punter and how her childhood experiences could impinge on present behaviour. I owed her a debt of gratitude, because had she not shared her knowledge with me I would not have been able to understand many of the confused stories that women told me. Their accounts were confused because so many people who have been violently and sexually damaged in childhood find themselves driven into dangerous relationships and have no idea why. And because they are women they are assumed to be 'victims' and therefore unable to admit that they are complicit in the sexual violence they subsequently experience.

Sally, a prim and devout Catholic, arrived at the refuge with two small girls. She was running from her husband, she said, a sadist who forced her to have anal sex. He caused her anus to split on several occasions, and she had ended up in the emergency ward of her local hospital. We were horrified.

The next morning I got a telephone call from the landlord of the pub across the road complaining about one of the refuge's mothers who had danced on a table the previous night with no knickers on. During our house meeting I brought up the subject. The mothers told me that it was Sally who had danced drunkenly. She, however, was adamant that this was a lie, and she seemed so outraged I decided to suspend judgement.

A large bunch of flowers arrived at the refuge addressed to her from her husband, so I knew she had given him our address. She was on the phone to him continually. And her two girls couldn't wait to talk to him. The flowers were followed by boxes of chocolates and toys for the children. Sally was adamant that he was a sexual pervert. After another rowdy night at the pub she was in trouble once more, because the other mothers feared they would be banned from their favourite drinking hole. I lent one of them my Polaroid camera, and she said that the next time Sally got drunk she would take pictures of her exploits so that she would have to take responsibility for her behaviour.

Before long we had the visual evidence, and at a house meeting I handed Sally a photograph of herself wound around a man and kissing him passionately. There were more pictures of her dancing wildly in front of the men in the pub. Obviously Sally when drunk was a different person to the woman we knew during the day. Daytime she was a rather priggish mother of two. She would ram her religious beliefs down everyone's throats and boast about her virtues as a housewife and mother. Now she had to face the truth.

She was horrified by the photographs and asked me if I would talk to her husband with her. He turned out to be a very warm, caring man, and he wept as he hugged his wife and told her how much he missed her and his girls. I decided I would have to talk to the two of them together about her allegations that he forced her into rough anal sex.

Once I put the question to him he looked deeply embarrassed and upset. He said he didn't want to have anal sex with his wife, but when Sally was drunk she insisted that he penetrate her so roughly that sometimes he knew that he had hurt her. He had told his wife that he didn't know how to cope with her wild behaviour when she was drunk. And he also didn't know what to do about the fact that the next day she would act as if nothing at all had happened – except when he had to drive her to the hospital and face the angry faces of doctors and nurses who regarded him as a sexual monster. No one at the hospital had ever tried to talk to the couple about Sally's injuries. And she never told her husband about her abusive childhood. Until she was faced with the evidence of her Jekyll and Hyde nature she had repressed a great many unpleasant memories. It seemed the only way she could deal with them was to bury them deep in her unconscious.

I could tell that Sally's husband was telling the truth, and now that she felt able to confide in him about her father's sexual abuse he hoped he could begin to have a better relationship with her. The three of us talked for a long time about Sally's abused childhood. I told them that I could put them in touch with a counsellor who could explore ways of helping her. The family went home. Every so often I would hear from Sally. The news was good. The family was happy, and she had greatly benefited from professional counselling.

22

ACTON MAGISTRATES' COURT

The court case against me finally took place in April 1976. I had been dreading this, and my only consolation was that a very kindly health inspector scoured the local by-laws and discovered that if I claimed to run an Elizabethan coaching-house that merely provided a place to sleep there were no laws covering the overcrowding. In order to help me petition along these lines he introduced me to a young left-wing barrister called Stephen Sedley who was willing to take on my case for free.

I was fairly battle-scarred by now, because if you were not particularly left wing in the 1970s and hadn't succumbed to the proselytizing of the left splinter groups you tended to be demonized and denounced. I was no doubt slightly paranoid by this stage because of the ferocious antipathy I had experienced whenever I came across individuals who had adopted the revolutions in China and Russia as their new religion.

I was therefore glad to discover that whatever Stephen felt about me he didn't demonstrate any animosity, and I will be eternally grateful to him for his concern for the desperate mothers and children who made up their beds nightly all over the floors of every room in the house.

Around this time I had a received a phone call asking me if I would like to attend a one-day seminar arranged by Robert Maxwell at Headington Hill Hall in Oxford. The caller told me that Mr Maxwell particularly wanted me to attend because he admired my work. I would be picked up from Oxford Station by a chauffeur in his Rolls-Royce. I decided to go to see what the meeting was all about, because as far as I knew Robert Maxwell, despite having been a Labour MP in the 1960s, was a multimillionaire without a left-wing bone in his body.

I duly arrived and was ushered into a palatial building to discover

that almost the entire flotilla of dissident dissatisfaction from anywhere in the British Isles was awaiting the outcome of this meeting.
Present were a motley assortment of left-wingers, feminists, aid
workers and general mavericks. We were not disappointed. Robert
Maxwell joined us in a large theatre and harangued us from the
stage. He had invited us, he said, because he wanted to help us in
our work. He promised that all our organizations – whether left-
wing groups or charities – would benefit from his largesse. I felt
hopeful and went back to London to give the mothers the good
news. We never received any actual money from him, but I was to
recall his offer many years later.

We amused ourselves while waiting for the trial by threatening
Hounslow Council with a sit-in in Chiswick High Road. When I was
dragging my children around shopping I had felt a sense of outrage
that there were so many shops with no facilties for members of the
public. What we needed was a public toilet. In seeking a loophole in
the by-laws to save me from gaol my friendly health inspector had
found one stating that pregnant women should be shielded by a
police cloak if they found themselves taken short on the Queen's
highway. This became the subject of a lively debate between us and
Hounslow Council. We demanded on behalf of all women in our
streets that a public toilet should be erected somewhere along
Chiswick High Road. If the council demurred we threatened to con-
vene and demand that the local constabulary provide us with
sufficient numbers of policemen wearing capes to protect our naked
bottoms from the view of the horrified public. We were slightly disappointed when Hounslow caved in straight away and erected a
public convenience along the street.

We wore our best clothes to attend the hearing at Acton Magistrates' Court. I was pleased to see Spike Milligan sitting on one of
the long polished wooden benches. The court was full of mothers
and our supporters. Outside there was a forest of placards painted
with our slogans 'BATTERED WOMEN NEED A REFUGE' and
'DON'T GAOL ERIN PIZZEY'. I very much hoped they wouldn't, but
I was very frightened – less for myself, because in prison I would
doubtless come across many women who had been in the refuge,
but for my children, as I could not see how they would manage
without me.

Stephen Sedley explained to some very bewildered magistrates that Chiswick Women's Aid was not a common hostel – it was an Elizabethan coaching-house and under the by-laws (he quoted chapter and verse) there were no regulations as to the numbers of clients who could seek accommodation there. This by-law had never been repealed, thus there was no case to answer. When it was my turn to take the stand I assured the magistrates that I provided no food for the occupants. At this point the defence barrister interrupted and asked why there were fitted cupboards in the kitchen. I replied that I kept doughnuts and my coffee in them. At that point the barrister put his hands up in defeat, walked back to his chair and sat down. The magistrates filed out of court to deliberate. After a very long time they returned and acknowledged that that we had won. I was able to walk out of the court a free woman. We went back to the refuge to celebrate – although not for long because Hounslow immediately applied to appeal at the High Court in London's Strand.

The strain of the fighting on all fronts meant that by 1976 my blood pressure was far too high. I was on heavy doses of beta-blockers, and my weight and habit of drinking too much wine didn't help. I generally slept very little, and sometimes at around five in the morning when the newspapers arrived on my doorstep I would get up, drag out my copy of *Who's Who* and telephone my enemies at home. I discovered this method of communicating with the so-called great and good after finding that I could never talk to them in person in their offices, so defended were they by a phalanx of minders. Half asleep, they would answer their phones themselves, and I was able to threaten them with my wrath.

Soon after the court case a journalist was sent by the *Observer* newspaper to write an in-depth article about life at the refuge. The mothers were always happy to talk to journalists because we felt the more we talked about violence in the family the more likely it was that victims could find sanctuary.

I was conscious of the failure of the men's house we had tried to establish, but as far as we could we tried to help male victims of a partner's violence; we had people who were willing to visit them or to supervise access to their children. Often we were able to work with a couple together to resolve their violent behaviour. I was desperate for the judiciary and the lawyers to recognize that in most cases mediation was the way forward. Once lawyers became involved the adversarial nature of the law made a very volatile and dangerous situation far worse.

I used to ask the Law Society for a waiver so that solicitors could come to the refuge. I did this for two reasons. The first was a necessary precaution so that a violent partner could not track a woman down by following her from the solicitor's office. The second was that the solicitor involved could get to know the client personally. Meeting the woman and seeing the refuge for themselves was important in the training of the solicitors. This was partly because we were aware that periodically a woman coming into a refuge would falsely accuse her partner of acts of violence just to get him expelled from the family home. Others would make false claims of sexual abuse. It was important that the refuge was not used as a weapon against an innocent man, and legal discussions frequently took place, with the mother's permission, with workers from the refuge present.

The journalist from the *Observer* duly arrived and spent several days talking to the women in the house. To our dismay she decided to write a trivial article foregrounding the fact that many of the women in the refuge enjoyed dancing at the Hammersmith Palais. I was furious because the tone of the piece was condescending and frivolous. She was incapable of appreciating that we thought it an excellent idea for women who had been battered and abused to feel that they could go out together and have a good time dancing with men without fear for their safety. Our one house rule was that anyone going out for the evening should make babysitting arrangements; how often a woman went out at night was entirely her business. I sat down and wrote an angry letter to the editor of the *Observer*.

I got a letter back asking me to write my own article, which I did. I explained that I believed that part of the problem with the genuine efforts made by well-intentioned people to help was that they tried to impose unnecessary rules and structures on the people they hoped to support. An example was that I had frequently had arguments with the Health Department whose staff wanted mothers and their children put together in a room on their own when they first arrived. I argued that many of the women feared that their partners would follow them and kill them. Their first nights in a dormitory thus provided the best sleep they might have had in years. I said it was hard to get anyone to understand if they had never been genuinely frightened for their life. The article was duly published, but we learned not to be naïve or too trusting around journalists.

I felt that those of us who entered the refuge as staff and volunteers had no right to impose unnecessary rules on those who were running the house and paying the rent. I knew from my own rebellious background that the power had to rest in the mothers' hands. If they made the rules themselves they would see that they were obeyed. The mothers created the rotas that kept the house running smoothly. They also organized their own cooking rotas. We generations of British public-school graduates knew the value of the prefect system. This worked perfectly in the refuge, and many of the women subsequently became highly capable and reliable organizers and members of staff, and those who moved on often came back later to volunteer or work in their own communities.

Many of the mothers had been in care for much of their lives. In a way so had I. I had spent much of my childhood in a boarding-school, so I, too, knew what it was like to be ruled by a bell, threat of punishment and endless regulations. Many of the women had been ruled by the boot and the fist as children and when they lived with partners. They needed to determine their own structures among themselves. If I ran the refuge like a hostel with a strict set of rules and regulations I would have prevented the mothers from taking control of their lives. I viewed the refuge as a big rumbustious family with its own coherent history. The older mothers passed the history on to the newcomers, and the rules that the mothers created were fluid and could be amended as circumstances changed.

At a house meeting after the court case I was astounded to witness a member of staff scream at a young mother across the room, 'You're a filthy woman! I've asked you time and time again to tidy round your bunk bed, and you've done nothing!' I could see the young woman's eyes fill with tears. There was a shocked silence as we sat staring at the red-faced member of staff.

'What gives you the right to scream at her like that?' I asked.

'Your own house is so dirty I don't even like to drink a cup of coffee in your kitchen!'

After the meeting the angry staff member came into the cubby-hole and asked, 'How could you do that to me in front of everyone?'

'How could I not?' I replied. 'You were being a hypocrite. Your house is filthy – and you know it. How could you think you have the right to shout at anyone here?'

She didn't last long after that.

I found it a struggle to get well-meaning people to realize that they could not come into the refuge to work and think they were in a position of power. It was important that the mothers held the reins of power. This is why we staff had just a tiny cubby-hole to talk privately to one another. The main office was the big sitting-room, where the mothers decided who should run the telephones and fill in the daily diary and make appointments. All house meetings were held here, and it was here that all major decisions were made. It certainly sorted out those people who came along feeling that they were on a mission to help and those who came to the refuge because they knew they had much to learn about themselves.

23

THERE ARE NO TIDY
SOLUTIONS

I was feeling even more desperate than usual because I was facing the appeal by Hounslow Council to the High Court in the Strand. Jack was living in the downstairs flat, and the pressure of being a single parent was beginning to tell on me. I was immensely grateful to the mothers in the Bristol house who welcomed me on Friday nights when I arrived exhausted with my children and delighted to find a meal on the table. The mothers and children would crowd around while I recounted the week's events from the Big House.

I think you have to be a single parent, widow or widower to understand the sense of isolation that descends on your shoulders once your children are in bed. Even if a marriage has been moribund for many years there is still the presence of A.N. Other in the house and someone else to share decisions. I was busy at night writing for newspapers and magazines, but, more importantly, I was preoccupied in thinking of ways to protect the mothers and children who were by now living in the many properties springing up around the country designated for their use.

What had become known as second-stage housing ran smoothly. Families would leave the Chiswick crisis centre to move into these buildings. Those mothers who wanted to work had on-tap reciprocal babysitting, and the majority of the women who opted to move to shared housing were happy to remain there for some time; most stayed for the three or four years it could take to get rehoused permanently by a council. The idea of shared housing arose when a number of us discussed the problem that some of the mothers returned to violent partners because they were too vulnerable to begin life again once they were rehoused or else they ended up taking in predatory violent men who preyed on their sense of isolation.

Rowena came to our refuge accompanied by her social worker and young son. She had a large disfiguring scar that ran from her brow down to her chin. She told me that she had been in a car accident. She had not been wearing a seatbelt and was thrown out of the front window. Her face almost disintegrated, and it took many operations to restore it. The traumatic effect of the crash and the injury sent her spiralling into depression. She was moved to a mental hospital for treatment where she met James, a fellow patient. She was soon pregnant with baby John, and she left the hospital with her lover.

It didn't take long for Rowena to discover that her partner was very violent. Before her accident she had nursed ambitions to be a model, and she could have been successful; she was certainly a beautiful young woman. I suspected that her choice of James was made in desperation – because she could not believe that any man would love her with her dramatically disfigured face.

I found myself in a tug-of-war with her social worker. The woman despised our refuge and complained that Rowena had to share a dormitory with others. I argued that her client suffered from very severe depression and that she and her son were safest surrounded by people happy to support her. John went to playschool during the day, so Rowena had time to talk to other mothers in the house. She also spent periods with me.

The social worker was adamant that she would find Rowena somewhere that was 'properly' run. She duly found a place in an organization that ran rigidly regulated community homes. I wasn't at all happy about the move and expressed my doubts to the care professional. Most social workers could see only chaos and anarchy when they visited our refuge. They wanted neat and tidy solutions to their clients' dysfunctional behaviour and problems. They believed that if they could impose rigid discipline on their clients somehow they would miraculously change overnight into contented and law-abiding citizens. A new flat or house was a prize to be offered clients – as if a roof and four walls was a panacea for every ill.

I knew Rowena was still very depressed and drinking far too much. She was ambivalent in her feelings towards John. He looked very like his father who had disappeared off the scene as soon as Rowena came into the refuge. I begged the social worker to wait, but she was hell-bent on telling her client that she would have to be in the community home only for a few months and then she would be offered her own flat. Rowena was excited at the prospect of having her own place. I knew she needed people around her, and while I accepted that she was going to leave us I was concerned that she should end up isolated with her small child.

I was surprised to discover that she was to be moved to her own accommodation within a few weeks of being transferred to the new community. Rowena telephoned me to say that she had some friends who were helping her decorate her flat before she moved in. Then there was silence for a few weeks. One morning I got a call to say that a few days after she had moved in she had killed herself. John had been found in his cot and was subsequently put into care. Whether depression had overwhelmed her or life on her own was too much for her I will never know. We all mourned her death and feared for the future of her young child.

For a long time I had been aware that many of our mothers benefited from living together in groups, whether in squats or in donated houses where they could support one another. Our shared housing projects grew organically as new mothers, seeing other communities, made their decisions, and many opted to continue on to shared housing. Sometimes if we had a young mother who found it difficult to look after her children I would ask when a place came vacant – for instance, in our Bristol community – if some of the older mothers were willing to take her in and give her a hand. They never failed to offer help when needed, and the occupants of the Bristol house had a proud record of rehabilitating women who otherwise might have lost their children into care.

I tried on many occasions to talk to agencies about the fact that we needed to agree that removing children from their mothers should only happen as a last resort. Everyone knew that children who grew up in the care of the state were far more likely to fail academically and socially than children from homes with parents.

As a child, when I stayed with my schoolfriends at their homes I would observe parents kissing and hugging their children. Our house was always silent and without overt expressions of affection. My mother stayed in her room if there were no guests to for her to impress, and any noise or sudden laughter would make her fly out of her bedroom looking for the culprit. We never had happy family meals together. My father brooded at one end of the table, while my mother picked at her food; we children were not allowed to speak unless an adult addressed us directly. I yearned for normal family life. With our shared housing programmes, women like my mother could learn parenting skills.

I had many invitations to go across the Channel and speak to groups opening refuges in Europe. I was invited me to speak in Amsterdam. I coupled that invitation with others from Bonn, Brussels and Paris. As a reward for all the hard work the mothers did in Bristol I decided that, rather than go by myself and stay in hotels, I would hire three motor homes and take some of them and their children along. Tina and two of our playstaff were going to drive. We designed posters introducing ourselves and highlighting the need for refuges across the world for victims of domestic violence.

I was still impatient and angry with the British government. During the years of opposition to our refuges no attempt was made to address the fact that the cycle of violence was one of our most significant family problems. I wrote regularly to Members of Parliament, to civil servants and to anyone that I thought might help. We wrote case histories of 129 women with their children who had arrived at the refuge between May and July 1976 and sent our findings off. The majority of the women had been born into violent homes and were themselves violent. There was no acknowledgement from anyone that they had received the report. The prevailing wisdom was that men were the perpetrators of aggressive behaviour, and the only remedy was to banish them from the family.

We set off for Amsterdam on a bright, blustery spring morning. Local newspaper photographs showed our vans covered with posters and children hanging out of the windows waving. We were amazed when we got to the other side of the Channel to find that we attracted big crowds everywhere we stopped. Our first night was spent in a spotless camp site in Amsterdam. We unpacked the vans, and the volunteer male playstaff and the boys set up a camp fire while I got on with the cooking. We sat round the glowing embers and sang songs; later I told ghost stories. I went back to my van with Amos and several of the children and slept on a dining-table that converted into a bed.

In the morning I woke up and made myself a cup of coffee with a slug of brandy and a large dollop of condensed milk. Fortified, I made breakfast for the children in the van and went off to the shower block. I could see the children running about the camp site, and very soon a small crowd of people were standing around our vans. It wasn't until we got to the community centre in central Amsterdam that one of our hosts explained the reason why we had attracted so much attention. The person who had translated our poster into Dutch had mistranslated the term 'battered woman' as 'prostitute'. After that we spent several hours changing the word on our literature.

None of the mothers and children had been across the Channel before. The community centre in Amsterdam made us very welcome. Jeannie, Maureen and I made speeches, and then we were taken to the big Dutch refuge on the banks of a canal. The playstaff took the children off to the museum to see the Van Gogh paintings. There was a near mutiny when I said the word 'museum', but they came back full of enthusiasm. Meanwhile we were taken on a tour of the very comfortable refuge. The Dutch workers told us anxiously about a couple of women who had camped upstairs in one of the bedrooms and who were refusing to come down.

The three of us went up to the bedroom and pushed open the door. Sitting on the bed were two very truculent Dutch women. We folded our arms, and I indicated my thumb towards the stairs. "Op it,' said Maureen. There was a moment's silence and the women got to their feet and shuffled out of the room. We spent the rest of the visit explaining that not all the women coming to the refuge were pathetic victims of their partner's violence and that many gave as good as they got.

We spent two nights camping on the Rhine on our visit to Bonn. Those evenings were magic. In the light of a large bonfire we could see the water of the river glinting, and running down the spine of the mountains were silhouettes of castles and thick clumps of pine trees stretching down to the bank. While I made my speeches the rest of the group enjoyed seeing as much as they could of the cities we visited. Finally, on the last leg of our trip, we ended up in the Bois de Boulogne, not far from the Champs-Elysées in Paris.

One of the purposes of our visit to Paris was to see a senior British official about the possibility of obtaining a European

Economic Community grant for training people into work. I think the Parisian who had issued the invitation for me to visit him was quite surprised to find a gang of women, children and playstaff invading his pristine office. However, I felt that Maureen and Jeannie would put their case far better than I could, and we were delighted to be told that we could look forward to some funding.

We drove back to London to a rapturous welcome from the refuge and a very ill-tempered discussion in the House of Commons. Someone had raised a Private Member's Bill in the House to enquire why 'Erin Pizzey was doing our dirty laundry in public'. At least for a few minutes we had their attention.

24

THE GREAT AND THE GOOD
COME ON BOARD

Once I arrived at the refuge in the morning most of my day was spent sitting down and talking to any of the mothers and children who wanted to talk to me. There was rarely a break, and often I moved only to go to the toilet. Once I got home I went straight upstairs with a copy of the *Evening Standard* and a cup of coffee. I had a bath, drank the coffee, read my paper, cooked a meal, and then I was mother to a house full of teenagers. I had no time to myself, and I sometimes felt like a roving resource centre.

Cleo was a gregarious girl, and she often invited her friends over for supper. Usually there would be at least seven or eight of us at the table. Mikey had fallen in love with Cleo and was with us most of the time. Trevor lived with us full time, and Cass could usually be found sleeping somewhere or other. Sitting with the children around the table I felt a great sense of consolation. There were children in the refuge that I knew would only stay for a short while before they were dragged back to their warring homes. While they were with us we put all our resources into taking care of them. But the teenagers in my own household could make their own choices – and often they went back to their own homes and then returned. Our house was a safe and secure home when they needed us, and I knew that our relationships were long-term and rewarding ones.

I often took children from the refuge with me during the day if I had to go out. If the weather was bad, I might fill the car with boys and girls and drive to Harrods. I would take a book, and after leaving them in the toy department with a member of staff I would sit in the banking section and wait until they were bored with playing with the toys. We would then head down to the food department and peruse the fantastic fish counter. The children saw as many of the historical sites of London as we could afford. Whatever their future, while they were with us they were treated with love. During the school holidays the Goldhawk Road children accompanied me to the refuge and hung out with the teenagers. They developed a rapport with some of the most disturbed teenagers far more effectively than most of the adults.

One morning in 1976 JoJo met me at the door and said there was a man waiting for me in the cubby-hole. I assumed it was a reporter or someone with a complaint about the noise the refuge created in the high street. Those who lived around us were right: we were disruptive and noisy, and I felt guilty about the chaos we brought their lives. We did our best to keep order, but with so many children in the house and garden it was difficult to keep the noise down at all times.

On entering the cubby-hole I saw a tall man sitting beside the sewing-machine that made do as a table. He had fair, silvery hair and a damaged smile. I sat down and lit a cigarette and waited for the complaints to start. Instead he surprised me by asking me to tell him what I wanted and needed. I talked to him at great length about the difficulties we faced – not least the appeal by Hounslow Council that was now pending at the High Court. Whatever the sentence, I could never agree to limit the numbers of women and children who arrived at the refuge, so I was facing a custodial sentence for contempt for disobeying the court. I felt wretched for my children and those who relied on me. I think the man sensed my despair.

JoJo returned, her eyes alight with curiosity. 'I gather you've just left the *Observer*,' she said with a meaningful glance at me. Finally the penny dropped that it was David Astor, until recently proprietor of the Sunday newspaper. I was surprised that he, of all people, would bother to visit someone like me, but I was grateful that he took the time. I was the one usually dishing out advice and comfort to everyone else.

Just before he left he asked again what he could do to help. I think he expected me to ask him for money. I said that the next time I was confronted by television cameras about the court case I would be grateful if he could tell the press that he was willing to go to prison in my place. Hounslow Council had no problem with gaoling me, but imprisoning David Astor would make them stop and think. He seemed quite amused at this. He shook my hand and said he would be back in touch soon.

Ruth and Cyril Carney with their twin daughters
Erin and Rosaleen, Tsingtao, China, 1939

Right: Erin in
Shanghai, 1940

Erin's paternal grandfather in
police uniform, Hounslow,
London

Erin aged eleven at St Antony's convent
school, Leweston Manor, Sherborne, Dorset

Right and below right: Erin with husband Jack during a visit to Macau, 1963

Above: Erin in 1964

Erin with Jack and daughter Cleo, 1965

women's
liberation
workshop

12/13 Little Newport St.,
W.1.

734-9541

Dear Erin,

I'm including, with this letter, some Newsletters
for your group. At the same time I want to tx tell you about
what happened at the Office Collective. It was very surprising
xx that there was nobody there from your group, since you had
promised to ensure that somebody would come. XxxxxxxxxxxX
Jenny brought up the problems arising from what you told us in
general terms, and the collective decided that until the whole
matter was sorted out, and you had given a statement of the
position to a woman lawyer, or someone in the N.C.C.L., you
should no longer work in the office or attend meetings of any
of the collectives. This means, immediately, that you can
no longer be regarded as the office representative of the Goldhawk Rd. group. So could you or your group let us know the
name, address, and phone number of your new office rep.? I xk
should add that no names were given at the meeting, so that x
you could be given some protection,

Yours,

███████████████

SHREW

Letter to Erin Pizzey from the Women's Liberation Workshop, c. 1970,
informing her that she was no longer welcome at its headquarters

The original 1971 poster with
Erin's famous slogan

Erin with Ann Ashby and Spike Milligan outside Acton Magistrates'
Court, 1976 *(photograph courtesy of Mark Ashby)*

The refuge at the time of the 1976 hearing at Acton Magistrates' Court
to get the house closed down

Office by day, dormitory by night *(All interior refuge pictures courtesy of Christine Voge, 1978)*

Left to right: Male staff, Russ, Trevor, Dave and Nick, at Chiswick Womens' Aid with three of the children

Right and below:
Mothers and children in
the overcrowded refuge

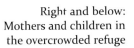

Erin (second from right) meeting the Queen in London, c. 1972

Erin at work in the
cubby-hole at the refuge

Erin comforting one of the children, 1978

Erin with some members of the refuge community in the back garden

Singer Roger Daltry
and drummer
Kenny Jones of The
Who with Erin and
children during
a visit to the
refuge, c. 1977

Erin sharing a secret with Phyllis, one of the housemothers

A dormitory with its bunk beds

A mother with her children

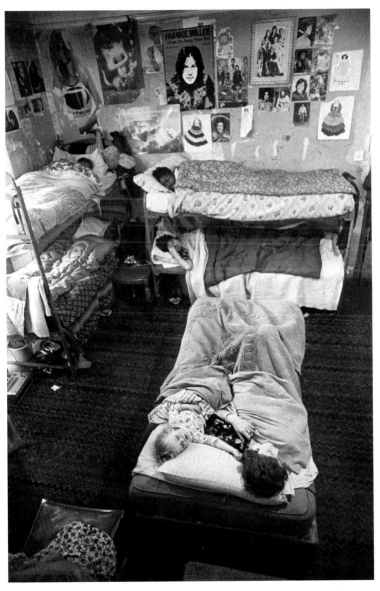

Conditions in a refuge dormitory

Watching fireworks   Fighting closure

The original boys' accommodation in a shed at the back of the house

Young mother with personal effects

Mother-to-be and child

Children at play in one of the dormitories

One of the younger
residents

The girl with one of the 'skippers' (a woman living rough) and mother

Three of the refuge teenagers

Erin camping in France while on the run
from the law during Glenda's court case to
retain custody of her children

Lord Goodman
in the 1970s

Trog's Observer cartoon to mark the Greater London Council's offer to the refuge, 1981

Front cover of *The Slut's Cook Book*, published in 1981

Left to right: Mikey, Erin's daughter Cleo, Annie Ruddock, another friend, grandson Keita and son Amos modelling Boy George's fashions, 1980

We had another meeting at the Department of Health and Social Security within a week of David Astor's visit. By then I had learned how influential he was. His mother Nancy Astor had been the first woman to take a seat in Parliament, and his family were immensely rich. As proprietor of the *Observer* he could be a powerful ally in my battle against Hounslow Council and the civil servants determined to close us down. I telephoned him to say that we were facing a very serious threat at the meeting, and I knew the press would be awaiting the outcome. I asked him to join us, and he said he would.

Ann came with me, and the four of us made our way to the Department of Health and Social Security. My chief tormentor, the granite-faced civil servant, restrained herself in the presence of the two men. I don't know if she recognized David, but we left without too many bloodcurdling threats.

The impending case in the High Court was mentioned. I explained that I would not be around to attend because I had recently accepted an invitation to undertake a tour of the United States to help American women set up refuges there; this was to culminate with a lunch of honour on Capitol Hill. I looked at the impassive faces sitting in a ring around the horseshoe table and wondered whether they could see the irony that when I should be standing in the dock facing gaol I would be receiving an honour in Washington. If any of them saw the absurdity of the situation they didn't let on.

As we came out of the building we faced journalists and television cameras. David, true to his word, stepped forward and stated that he intended to go to gaol instead of me if it came to the crunch. I was quite surprised to find that David was so succinct and assertive in public, because he usually spoke very quietly. He had a tendency to put his head down and mumble, but on this occasion he was defiant and forthright. His speech was picked up by the press, and he telephoned me the next afternoon to say that his good friend Lord Goodman was in the London Clinic and would like to meet me. He hoped I would agree to the meeting. I said yes straight away without giving the matter much thought, took off my pinafore, dabbed with a damp flannel at the sticky hand marks on my skirt and headed off to see David's sick friend.

At the hospital I was immediately taken back by the hostility in Lord Goodman's voice. He was lying prone on a bed in a private room. He turned his massive head to where I was standing and fixed me with an intense, angry glare. It seemed obvious that he didn't like me, and I didn't take to him. David stood on the other side of the bed and said nothing. Goodman told me to stop being a silly woman and to bring myself and my project within the law. I could tell he was furious because David had committed himself to helping me. He roared at me until I shrugged and said that I wasn't really interested in his opinions. I told him our shelter would stay open for all until there were sufficient numbers of refuges across the country to make our open-door policy redundant. There was a frosty silence in the room. I stared at his enormous bulk and waited. I could hear his laboured breathing, and suddenly his tone changed completely. He asked for details about the upcoming court case – and suddenly he was acting like my new best friend.

I left the clinic wary and convinced that I had a dangerous enemy. On the way back to the refuge I stopped by at our local library and checked out *Who's Who*. I found his name next to a long list of his financial interests. He was, according to another source I checked, 'the most powerful non-elected figure in great Britain', and he would become my most powerful opponent in the years to come.

I was momentarily taken aback when David telephoned me at home to tell me that Goodman had suggested that they form a committee with the two of them jointly acting as chairmen. I said I would have to ask the mothers at our next meeting if they approved – I wasn't actually sure that any of us wanted one.

In bed that night I thought about the implications of the changes that faced us. Actually we had no choice. We had been living from hand to mouth since we had opened the first refuge, and at times we collected money from sympathetic members of the public. However, support was sporadic, and I had little time to go out and raise funds. Moreover, I wasn't good at formal meetings. Ann Ashby was a much better negotiator than I, and if there were meetings to attend she usually went off cheerfully with some of the mothers. I preferred to stay at the refuge and spend time with the mothers and children.

Now and then I did go out to speak publicly, driven by the need to educate people about the devastating effects of domestic violence on children. I was, however, disturbed by the number of awe-struck individuals who would come up to me afterwards; one or two of them even touched my clothes. One day a bunch of such women volunteered the information that they followed me around as a group whenever they saw I was speaking. This panicked me, not least because I was sure that I used to repeat myself when giving talks. 'We think you're like Mother Teresa,' one of the woman breathed reverentially.

'Mother Teresa doesn't have a drink problem!' I said and fled. I didn't speak in public for some time after that.

I realized that Goodman had made a very clever move and was now in a position to influence David at every turn. I trusted David, and I believed him when he promised he would never allow anyone to interfere with the running of the refuge or try to close our door. I could see the value in having these two powerful men take up the cudgels against the civil servants who were determined to support Hounslow Council in getting us shut down. Our supporter on the council, Jim Duffy, would finally have some formidable allies, and for at least a while I could sit between the crab claws quite safely. I felt intuitively, however, that a time would come when the two antagonists would join forces and the claws would snap shut. The timing of that event would depend on just how long it took Lord Goodman to negotiate a settlement between ourselves and the opposite side – but for now we were safe.

25

'THE MORE YOU BEAT THEM
THE BETTER THEY BE'

As I had told the Department of Health and Social Security, I had
been invited to go to the United States for a two-week speaking
tour. Michael Whyte's film of the refuge was to be broadcast on the
USA's public service television channel shortly before I arrived. I
had been taken aback to be approached by the feminist Gloria
Steinem who said she had been asked to introduce the documentary. She and the broadcasters reasoned that I was unknown in the
United States and that an American was needed to put the film into
a national context. I was not especially happy about this because I
feared she would put a hardline feminist spin on the aims of the
Chiswick refuge. Still, I knew that shelters were needed across the
world, and I felt helpless to challenge the decision because the film
would inevitably stimulate interest and outrage which would lead
to refuges being established across the United States.

I selected three women who worked with me at the refuge to
accompany me. Eventually the day came in March 1976 when we were
to fly to New York to begin our tour, mostly of the east coast. I was
wearing an ancient mink coat that David had given me because I had
nothing warm to wear and it was freezing in New York. Although I
had occasionally donned my antique fox furs in the past, I was disinclined to wear fur as a fashion item, but the coat had belonged to his
mother Nancy, and I figured the animals were long dead.

In New York we stayed with a very kind woman called Diana in
her loft in Greenwich Village. Her home was just around the corner
from Bleecker Street, with all its music clubs. Her loft was a magical
place. It seemed to stretch for miles, and at one end small owls
hooted softly. I was only too grateful for her immense hospitality.

That first night in New York was spent with the four of us dropping in and out of various small clubs in Bleecker Street. We had a
wonderful evening. Although I had been in New York as a child with

my parents I had no memory of it except when our ship had passed the Statue of Liberty – I recalled hanging on to the railings of the ship and looking up at her crown illuminated against the night sky. Now I was to speak at the House of Representatives on Capitol Hill. Had my mother still been alive I felt she still would not have been proud of me. She always disapproved of me and said I was 'born to be hanged'.

Soon after our arrival in New York we met up with Murray Straus, Richard Gelles and Suzanne Steinmetz. These three had been the first to undertake research into domestic violence in the United States. By this time they, too, were coming to the conclusion that domestic violence was not really a gender issue. They recognized that boys and girls exposed to violence and sexual abuse were likely to continue these patterns in their own lives. They also had suffered threats from the feminist movement, and Suzanne Steinmetz, who had written a book on battered men, had received death threats. It was a great relief to sit down and talk to people who understood the uphill battle that lay ahead.

We were scheduled to have lunch with Gloria Steinem at the offices of *Ms* magazine, where she was editor, and I hoped to discuss with her our findings about violence in the home.

By this time I wasn't sure I felt at home in New York. Steam gushed from the gratings in the streets. Commuters charged along the pavements, elbows jutting out as they jostled their way past each other, seemingly in a perpetual rush. Their faces were tight and angry. I saw a great many homeless men and women lurking in shop doorways. There was a brooding sense of violence in the air, and I was glad to reach the gigantic mausoleum that was *Ms* magazine's offices.

I was very disappointed to discover on arrival there that Steinem had decided not to accompany us for lunch. In fact, I was not to meet her at all. I had wanted to discuss her film commentary. I understood that she had said on television that people regarded women as lesser creatures, while men were regarded as 'full human beings with some right to rule or possess them'. I was unhappy about her hardline feminist angle on the refuge, but it seemed that my views would be sidelined in the movement to end domestic violence. It was, however, apparent from talking to Murray Straus and his colleagues that the women's movement in the United States was much better organized than that in Britain. Even if they had no shelters already established, funding would soon pour in – much of it as a result of Michael Whyte's film. I couldn't risk rocking the boat, because in the discussions we had in the refuge there was general agreement that any refuge was better than none.

Once inside the *Ms* building we noticed there were no men around. The interior was glossy and white, and I spotted on a wall the slogan 'A woman needs a man like a fish needs a bicycle'. Gloria Steinem came up with that, we were told. The four of us looked somewhat incongruous in our least-shabby clothes. We all wore makeup, and I for one was wearing perfume. The women at *Ms* wore dungarees and boiler-suits and looked like plumbers or building-site workers. It felt odd to be walking around a building devoid of men. I liked male company; I enjoyed the laughter and the flirting. Working for *Ms* magazine would be grim, we agreed later.

We were taken for lunch at a very expensive restaurant that looked out over the New York skyline. Our hosts ordered us Tom Collinses. I had never had this cocktail before – it was delicious. The meal itself was sumptuous. I spent some of the time at the restaurant reading the press hand-out for our film. I saw on the front that the Corporation for Public Broadcasting had provided a grant. I asked our hosts if we could have any of the money since our film had made up the bulk of the television programme, but I was told that the CPB never offered money for film footage. I saw Steinem's staff exchange glances, and I suspected they were telling an untruth. The four of us drank far too many Tom Collinses and crawled back to our refuge in Diana's loft.

All I can remember of the rest of that evening is collecting ice from the huge fridge in the kitchen and making myself an enormous gin and tonic. There was a moment when I thought I must be really drunk as I peered dimly at a tiny pair of pink feet floating on top of my drink. Diana laughed. She briskly took the glass off me and assured me they were no hallucination – they belonged to a tiny mouse she had frozen in an ice cube. She kept a stash of dead mice in a corner of the freezer to feed her owls!

26
LUNCH ON CAPITOL HILL

Harvey Taschman was a tall, gentle man. We stayed with him and his very hospitable wife in Washington. I watched him smile at his wife across the dinner table, and I felt a pang of regret that my own marriage had failed so miserably. The couple plainly shared a deep bond of love and affection. As soon as dinner was over Harvey disappeared into the kitchen to help his wife with the washing-up, and I went to bed. We had two appointments the following day. We were to show our film at the National Institute of Mental Health and have lunch at the House of Representatives hosted by Congresswoman Lindy Boggs and Congressman Newton Steers.

I suspected that our lunch of honour on Capitol Hill might cause a degree of awkwardness for the British Embassy in Washington. I didn't think the British Ambassador would want to throw a party for us.

The Embassy got round this by inviting the four of us to morning coffee with the Ambassador's wife. I was very thankful for Nancy Astor's mink, which concealed my shabby clothes underneath, and after coffee and tiny cakes she offered to show us the dining-table that was being dressed for a formal dinner that night. We followed her into a magnificent chandeliered dining-room, and I stared at the opulent gold plates neatly laid out on the table. For a moment I had to struggle with a sense of outrage at the ostentatious affluence before us. At home the refuge residents frequently slept on floors if a flood of women and children had arrived at once and if all the bunk beds were full. The British Embassy was like another world. I knew the other two felt the same way, and we trailed disconsolately out and headed off to lunch with Lindy Boggs on Capitol Hill.

I was dismayed to discover that under President Carter's administration wine was no longer served on formal occasions. I thus had to endure the meal totally sober. Usually I could drink enough to take the edge of the nervousness I had felt since childhood when around important people I didn't know well. As a young girl I had little reason to trust the grown-up world. The residual anxiety was a habit I had trouble overcoming even as an adult.

Lindy Boggs had been involved with women's issues for a long time and assumed that we were a like-minded group of separatist feminists. I explained to her that we believed women should have equal opportunities but that, as far as I was concerned, the women's movement was less interested in equality than in promoting an agenda bent on destroying men and the family. I saw the familiar look of disbelief cross her face. She no doubt felt that I had accepted her invitation under false pretences and that when I made my speech she would be seen as a laughing stock. There was nothing I could do about that. I felt I had to try to get the other people at the table to understand my point of view.

My speech was received with polite clapping. Fortunately for me there was no discussion because just then two enterprising young men burst into the room waving their new book in front of the cameras. Instead of demanding that the security guards remove them, the Congresswoman grasped her lifeline to avoid an embarrassing aftermath to my speech. She didn't speak to me again except to shake my hand as I left. As we walked out of the House of Representatives I stood on the step awaiting the car that was to collect us and take us to our next appointment at the Press Club. Just then I remembered the mothers, children and refuge staff who would be standing in front of the High Court in London's Strand demonstrating on my behalf and publicizing the need for refuges for all who needed them. I very much wished we were there with them.

At the Press Club I hoped that we might spot some sympathetic journalists, but it soon became obvious as I described our refuge and our experiences over the years that we had no support for our views. There were no men in attendance. I was used to being interviewed by women journalists at home. Generally back then male journalists did not involve themselves with 'women's issues'. Men had done little to protect themselves from a hardline feminist movement that was trying to boot them out of their family homes and out of their children's lives. The meeting was a farce, and we faced a stony-faced audience of hostile feminists.

Two days later we were booked to speak at Washington's Georgetown University at its Hall of Nations. By this time I was feeling very depressed. Ann Ashby had telephoned to say that we had lost our court case at the High Court. All that remained was for us to appeal in the House of Lords. So now I had the threat of closure or gaol hanging over my head. The four of us were missing our friends in the refuge. It was very hard to feel cheerful after receiving such a cold reception everywhere, and I was aware that I could avoid trouble if I restricted myself to talking purely about women as victims. The audiences on the US tour would react warmly when I discussed giving shelter to children, but as soon as I made it clear that men could be victims of violence I felt an immediate chill, and knew I had lost them.

We missed our daily life in the refuge, and as I watched our film for the umpteenth time at yet another meeting I felt an enormous sense of frustration. Here were graphic images of mothers and children lying in sleeping-bags on our sitting-room floor with their babies snuggled up beside them, and no one seemed horrified. All people wanted to do was to stand up and hold forth about their belief that women and children who came to Chiswick were there because all men were brutes. It didn't matter how many times I told the audiences that a man, Neville Vincent, had given us our building and it was a man, David Astor, who was compiling a list of donors to make sure that the doors stayed open. My audience was blind to reason.

I was looking forward to seeing North Carolina. I had heard much about the place, and I was by then desperate to get away from the cities of New York and Washington. I felt stifled by the atmosphere of hostility and anger that seemed to seep through the steaming vents in the streets. In Washington the neat, cottagey residences in upmarket Georgetown contrasted sharply with the sprawling slums full of unemployed black people. I hoped that we would have time to explore some of North Carolina and try some of its famous food. I wanted to taste southern fried chicken, hush puppies and sweet potato pie.

To our surprise, we found that our hosts there were a very friendly and devout born-again-Christian family. For a moment we looked at one another aghast. I had a sinking feeling that there would be no alcohol in the house. I was proved right. No one smoked, and I realized I would have to tone down my appalling language. The first evening we arrived we spent sitting at a table with the pastor and kindly visitors who brought along potluck food. Instead of the soul food that we had anticipated we were served macaroni cheese, tuna fish drowned in mayonnaise and various strange puddings that we washed down with soft drinks.

I was initially quite happy to be with this company of people, but I was less keen to listen to smug Christian fanatics rejoicing in the fact that they were saved and about to be swept away in the rapture while the rest of us were going straight to hell. I felt duty bound to make it clear that I didn't believe in one exclusive religion – in fact, I didn't believe in any formal religion. This didn't go down particularly well. I lay in bed that night wishing I was back at home with the children and a couple of bottles of good red wine.

The next day we were to lecture at the University of North Carolina at Chapel Hill and show our film once more. I was asked beforehand if we would have time to visit a well-known writer in her comfortable rooms at the Department of Psychiatry. She was a very beautiful woman. She told us about the disadvantages female professors faced in trying to get tenure in their jobs. I knew such discrimination occurred in Britain and said so. In some universities women rarely were offered tenure. However, I told her, I was concerned, too, that female academics were obscuring the complex causes of family violence as they carved out areas of social and historical study for themselves in which they faced no competition, especially on Women's Studies courses, where men's contributions were unwelcome. I said that the idea of women suffering from discrimination in any field was abhorrent, but the remedy was surely not to encourage further discrimination by excluding men.

She didn't disagree and pointed out how difficult it was for heterosexual women in her field with good careers and salaries to find men willing to become their partners because most men felt threatened my their success.

I thought about how hard it had been for me when I became better known than Jack. Women demanded change from men but made little effort to consider whether men would be willing go along with all their demands. The woman in front of me was an example of the dilemma that confronted women who wanted to liberate themselves from the traditional roles carved out for females over millennia. Would it ever be possible to make the biological roles that defined relationships between men and women interchangeable – or was Freud right and biology destiny?

I left North Carolina with an indelible image in my mind of the strikingly beautiful but lonely woman sitting in her room surrounded by her beloved books and knowing that by choosing an academic career she had inadvertently created a situation in which she might never find a partner or have children. Women have biological clocks and men don't. This puts women at a great disadvantage in terms of achieving full equality in employment as well as a fulfilled and happy personal life. It was unfair – but since when was life fair?

We took the train to New York from there and settled back down in Diana's welcoming loft. We had several lectures around New York, and then we were to catch a train to talk and show our film at the University of Rhode Island. There we encountered a hostile group of yelling and abusive feminists. We had two lectures on one day, so we split up and two went off to Vermont in New England while Tina and I took a train to Ann Arbor in Michigan to stay with some professors. The young woman who was waiting for us at the station wore dungarees and a peaked black baseball hat. She led us to her truck. The three of us squashed into her cab, and she drove us to a graceful colonial house in the countryside.

We were greeted by several very friendly women, and the woman with the peaked cap showed us to our bedroom. It was a small room with a large double bed. I had no qualms about sharing a bed with Tina, although I would have preferred my own. Meanwhile I was looking forward to our evening meal.

The food was delicious, and the conversation was general. It was not until after we moved from the table to the living-room that the atmosphere changed. Most of the women settled on floor cushions and passed around joints of grass. I have never been interested in taking drugs apart from alcohol and nicotine, and the only time I seriously tried to smoke weed I ended up with an acute attack of paranoia. I passed on the proffered joints and stuck to wine. In due course one of the women brought out some photograph albums, and I prepared myself for some holiday snaps. The pictures in front of me looked a bit like images of sea anemones.

I passed the album to my friend, and I saw the women on the floor were smirking.

'Cervixes,' said one of them. 'We take pictures of each other's cervix.' I was amazed. One could observe colours from the palest pink to the deepest purple. 'You can see the changes in the colours over our ovulating periods,' the woman explained. I was enchanted. I had never seen a photograph of a cervix before. What did surprise me was that each had the name of the owner and the date that the picture was taken inscribed underneath. At this point my colleague from England got to her feet and muttered something about needing to get to bed. I felt I couldn't join her because I was determined not to let anyone in the room think I was fazed by the pictures.

Instead I carried on chatting and talking about the difficulties of living in a community. Gradually everyone relaxed, and after a couple of hours and many glasses of wine I made my way unsteadily upstairs. The woman with the peaked cap was sitting on a laundry basket outside our bedroom door. She looked distinctly put out. I tried to push the door open but couldn't. I banged on the door and eventually I felt it give a little. I heard my friend drag her suitcase away from the door, and I slipped in.

'I had to throw her out,' she said.

'How very unsisterly of you,' I replied and fell on the bed giggling drunkenly.

27

RHUBARB, RHUBARB, RHUBARB

We were now on the last leg of our US tour, and the next stop was Philadelphia. I was getting fed up with the constant travelling. Because none of us had much money, before we left England we decided to produce a leaflet on Chiswick Women's Aid and sell it for a dollar to interested audience members that came to listen. Our fares had been paid in full, and our accommodation was provided throughout the trip, although often it was student rooms with narrow, hard beds. The cash from the leaflets kept us going from day to day. Besides, we were keen to reach as wide an audience as possible because there were virtually no shelters run along the lines of our refuges on that side of the Atlantic. There were, to be sure, homeless programmes that would take in women on the run from partners, but many of the women put into the accommodation offered were frightened of the other inmates, and it was particularly hard on their children.

Philadelphia proved a very tense experience. We had been asked there by a group called Women Against Abuse who were a small group of dedicated students working downtown. The meeting was held in a big room in one of the black ghettos and the audience consisted mostly of black women. The atmosphere on the streets outside was menacing, and I went into the meeting a little worried about our safety. As I began to speak I could see a lone man pacing up and down at the back of the room. He had his hand in his jacket with a bulge underneath. I wondered if he had a gun. I tried to keep my voice steady as I began to address the assembly about men as victims. As I spoke I could see the man getting visibly more agitated until I decided that it might be better to let him speak rather than work himself up into even more of a state. I pointed at him and asked as gently as I could manage, 'Is there something you would like to say?'

'I'm a rapist,' he said. 'I've been in prison for raping women.' He brought out of his jacket a sheaf of newspaper cuttings. 'No one will listen to me.' He was crying – and I, too, was nearly crying with relief. I felt quite safe now. The tension in the room, however, was palpable. The audience sat in frozen silence.

The man walked towards where I was sitting. 'I need help,' he continued.

I put my hand out to him and said quietly, 'You've come to the right place. I'll help you, and we'll find you a programme where you can get counselling.'

The organizer of the meeting was a very sensible young woman, so I asked her to give him an address so that he could contact her afterwards to arrange a meeting with a counsellor. She complied, and the man left the hall quietly. You could hear a gasp of relief ripple across the room.

After this dramatic episode several women came up later to talk to me and tell of their own horrific experiences. I was always sad that many of them were unable to transcend their violent backgrounds and get on with life, while others were accompanied by their hurt and abused children. They, too, needed somewhere to find comfort and understanding, but I knew it was important to concentrate all my efforts on getting more refuges established. I very much hoped that one day we could extend help and therapy to all those who had been damaged by their familial experiences.

If people sustain horrific car accidents they end up in intensive-care units, but here in the United States I was listening to stories of women who had undergone the equivalent of such traumas behind closed doors. No account was taken of the emotional damage they suffered. Post-traumatic stress disorder was a term that came to be applied to psychological damage sustained in sudden horrific incidents such as car crashes or in the course of warfare, but I believed that the condition explained why so many people I encountered seemed unable to leave their childhood experiences behind.

Post-traumatic stress disorder is well understood by doctors treating soldiers and others returning from armed combat. I have read studies where men have reported finding themselves emotionally thrown back into a particularly violent moment while they were serving in the army. Some, half asleep at home in their beds, had even lashed out and hurt their partners. No one equates the kind of violence experienced in the home with the damage that may occur in armed combat. Trauma inflicted by strangers is deemed as worthy of therapeutic treatment, while private trauma inflicted by partners and relatives is far less often regarded as a matter for professional intervention.

Sexually abused adults often find themselves caught up in situations where they are accused of being paedophiles because they are found guilty of looking at sexually abusive and pornographic representations of children. In most cases they are innocent of the actual abuse of children. Adults who have been abused as children may find themselves compulsively addicted to re-enacting their most traumatic past sexual encounters. Either they choose willing sexual partners or pay others to assault them. Others may use photographic material, including, increasingly these days, online websites. I feel sorry for those who get caught in the full of glare of public hatred when they have assaulted no under-age children but are none the less stuck in their abusive pasts and labelled paedophiles.

After Philadelphia I was to make a speech in Boston. I immediately loved the city, which came as a relief after New York. We were staying in a very smart brownstone in the middle of town. Our host was a young wife with three small children under the age of five. She had decorated her home beautifully, and when we were ushered into the living-room we found her husband relaxing in a large white hammock. He was witty and charming, but I was immediately on my guard. He didn't seem to take any responsibility for the children who were playing on the floor, and when we sat down to dinner his wife did all the work.

After dinner he disappeared, and we helped with the clearing and washing-up, and I held the baby. Soon after the husband came into the kitchen and kissed his wife. 'I'm going out,' he told her and headed out.

I looked at the woman, whose eyes had filled with tears. 'What was that about?' I asked.

'We agreed we would have an open marriage,' she said. 'But how can I have an open marriage with three small children?'

'Do you want one?'

She shook her head. 'At university, where we met, it seemed like a good idea. Everybody was doing it. But since having the children I think it's a crap idea.'

We spent the rest of the evening talking about marriage. I said that it was vital for me to be with someone who would not betray my trust. I explained that I thought there would always be a need for a women's movement because there was a need to find a balance between what men wanted and what women need. Women who want to have children are likely to be vulnerable for many years and perhaps in need of protection, while, I felt, children need both their parents. In the early days of the women's movement most of the women who stood and spoke on platforms were childless, and a great many were unmarried. They advocated a sexual revolution that, to me, seemed to bring in its wake a catastrophic dissolution of society. All the rules that kept men and women aware of their responsibilities towards one another would be swept away.

I could see how the rhetoric of the feminist movement I first heard in the early collectives trickled down to a situation in which the nuclear family was no longer regarded as a desirable unit. A wife and husband were no longer expected to prioritize their children or one another. The sexual revolution seemed to mean that people could put their own selfish physical, sexual and financial needs first. As far as I could see, in this case it was the three small children in the Boston household who were the victims of their parents' poor decision. How was it, I wondered, that a movement that claimed to liberate women ended up liberating men?

I was desperate to get home and hug my own children. I talked to them nightly on the telephone. I knew that Jack was living in the basement of the house, so they were safe and well cared for, but I felt at sea, as though I'd lost my bearings. I had spent too much time in the company of people who questioned my beliefs. I resented the fact that they thought me old-fashioned and out of touch with what was happening in the 'real world'. I tried to argue that not all traditional ways were bad – for instance, it made sense for children to live with their biological parents, but this was now an inflammatory statement. Most of the feminists I encountered did not believe that children needed fathers. They were already living their lives without men.

I have always believed that a successful marriage is probably the happiest and most sustaining relationship humans can achieve. I was well aware that I had failed, and I was envious of my friends who still lived happily together as couples. I didn't accept the research that claimed that children of divorced parents did just as well as children whose parents were married. I had noticed in the refuge that even when a man had been violent towards his partner and her children usually the children expressed love for their absent fathers. They worried about them and were concerned for their well-being. Even though I had to close my men's refuge I found a woman who was willing to open a series of charity shops called Men's Aid, so I could reassure the children that their fathers were not alone and that we were caring for them, too.

Our next invitation was to speak at Denver, Colorado. The event was a two-day conference taking place in a hotel. I stood on the platform and told those assembled how we had developed the small community centre in Belmont Terrace that became our first refuge, but I was aware as I spoke and talked afterwards to journalists that my presence was designed mostly to publicize the existence of another group of women who held views diametrically opposed to my own.

I was driven to a television studio where I was interviewed by two young reporters with glossy hair and perfect white teeth. As I spoke about the terrible experiences of those subjected to family violence I saw their eyes fill with tears, but as soon as I finished they turned their back on me immediately to introduce the next item. In a split second their expression changed dramatically, and as a belly-dancer gyrated in front of me I was expected to transform myself instantaneously into a cheerful and excited fellow viewer. It dawned on me that I really didn't understand North American audiences, because so often my speeches were greeted with a standing ovation, yet my words seemed to have no profound effect. As I gazed at the presenters' vacant faces I realized I could say 'Rhubarb, rhubarb, rhubarb' and few would be any the wiser!

On the last day of the Denver conference a young woman was handed a microphone, and she launched herself into a confident and dramatic account of her partner's brutality. I was bemused. I studied the audience's rapt faces. I wanted to interrupt and point out that a woman who was the victim of a partner's violence was generally ashamed of what had been done to her. The last thing she would wish to do was to stand up in front of a huge audience of strangers and tell her story to the world. It tended to be women who were violent themselves and who had no sense of shame who were willing to seek the limelight.

After the woman had finished her act, I walked over and said quietly to her, 'You should get an Oscar for that performance.'

She laughed and said, 'I gave them what they wanted to hear.'

It was then I realized that Americans expected to be entertained but, in a strange way, were hardened and even numbed by the commercial entertainment on offer. One had to up the stakes to grab their attention. At that stage suffering as entertainment had not yet reached the Britain in terms of true-life films, misery memoirs and so on, but, like everything else we have imported from the United States, it was only a matter of time.

We flew back to London on 4 April, and my children were waiting for me at the airport. Our Staffordshire bull terriers, Sam and Bess, jumped all over me once I arrived back in Goldhawk Road. The two cats, Girl and Boy, rubbed their noses on my face. I flopped down on the mattress in my bedroom, and all the children piled in on top of me.

While I was away they had been busy rehearsing. Mikey's brother Gregory was in a band called Funkapolitan, and they were gigging. Amos and his friend Darren Vaz, another regular in our house, were playing in the local clubs. Mikey was out creating the band that would become Culture Club, but that first night home he and Cleo cooked chicken, rice and peas for dinner. It was good to be home.

28

SUP WITH THE DEVIL WITH A
LONG SPOON

When I got back from the United States David Astor told me that he wanted me to visit Lord Goodman at his flat to discuss the role of the advisory committee. He also wanted me to accompany him to see Anna Freud, daughter of Sigmund. He said that he visited her almost every day and saw Goodman at least three or four times a week. He told me that back in 1938 when he was twenty-six he had been instrumental in getting the Freud family out of Nazi Germany and setting them up in a new home in Hampstead. I was very happy to meet Anna Freud, because I had read her wonderful books about her work with children. I was less than overjoyed to hear that I had been summoned to appear before Goodman in Portland Place.

Before I agreed to let David set up a committee we had a long discussion in one of our morning meetings at the Big House, and it was decided by everyone involved in the refuge that the committee could only advise. There was to be no question of any decisions being made by the committee that would interfere with the running of the refuge by the mothers, nor could there be an attempt to close the front door to newcomers. David attended this meeting, and he readily agreed to the conditions. He was steeped in the traditions of the psychoanalytical movement, and he was already supporting other therapeutic communities across the country. We felt we could trust him, and it was agreed that I should talk to Goodman about our future.

I felt particularly relieved that at last some of the burden of taking care of of the families in the central refuge was going to be lifted from my shoulders. Gradually other refuges were being set up across Britain, but we were still the only one with an open-door policy. From the beginning we had voted that our address should be made public so that any woman trying to escape a bad domestic situation could find us. The other refuges opted to keep their whereabouts secret, so the bulk of the nation's abused women and children still poured through our door. One of the great benefits of the new refuges was that we were able to ask many of them if we could swap mothers and children who did not need our therapeutic care and in return take families they were unable to help.

One major problem we had to deal with was what to do with the boys who arrived with their mothers but who were now sixteen, seventeen or even older. In the beginning, we had no choice but to let them bunk up with their families in the dorms. I had always dreamed of a separate house for the boys that they could call their own. Latterly we had erected two large sheds in the back garden that housed the older boys in bunk beds. They posted a notice on the door that banned all females from entering, and it gave them somewhere to call their own. I was never anxious about the possibility of sexual activity between children. I was more concerned about promiscuous mothers getting involved with the boys. Fortunately there was so little privacy in the house and garden that clandestine relationships had little chance of developing.

David and I were summoned to Goodman's flat at ten o'clock one morning. We were greeted by his kindly German housekeeper. In the hall were a couple of paintings on the wall that took me aback. Until then I had only seen Goodman lying on his back in a hospital bed, and my first impression was of a crude and rather coarse man. He had been very angry at the time, so I thought. As I stood there in his hall I felt that perhaps I had misjudged him. The paintings seemed to depict an Edwardian brothel scene. The men in the pictures were sophisticated bon viveurs, and behind them it appeared that decadent sexual acts were taking place. The paintings seemed an odd choice of art for the man I had met in the London Clinic.

We sat and waited for a while. Eventually Goodman made an entrance. He was in a much better mood this time and made some remarks to David about a discussion he had been having with Harold Wilson, then Prime Minister. His housekeeper came into the room carrying a tray with coffee for us plus chocolate biscuits for Goodman.

David and Goodman talked about mutual friends that could be invited on to the new committee. Goodman made no attempt to speak to me, so I decided to speak to him. I explained to him, as I had to David, that this new committee would have no power except to raise money for the refuge. Goodman had very dark eyes; I was struck by how dead they were. There was no expression as he heard me out. His response was to look at David, who smiled his assent, and Goodman shrugged. I knew then that he would never abide by rules or decisions we made – and I still had a strange chilling sense that he could destroy me.

I was to learn that Goodman's relationship with David was very odd indeed. David, who was just over a year older, having been born in 1912, admired Goodman and considered him an exceptional man. He was very influential politically, and I was to discover that many people believed he was the most powerful man in Britain. David told me that Harold Wilson would never make a decision without consulting Goodman. I suspected that David, too, an unassuming and quiet individual, probably made no decisions without consulting him. I came away from the meeting feeling grateful to David but wishing we did not have to deal with his friend.

That afternoon we had the appointment with Anna Freud. David told me she had asked to see me, and I was nervous. When I was living in Cawsand in Cornwall as a young naval wife Jack had been away on night duty for many days, and I was alone in the house with Cleo, then two years old, and Phoebe her black labrador. What saved me from total isolation was the library bus that came by once every two weeks. They let me take as many books as I liked, and for almost a year I read nothing but Sigmund Freud. The solitude in the damp, dispiriting little cottage gave me the opportunity to spend the evenings in front of a little electric fire reading his books, writing and beginning the long journey of getting to know myself.

I had also read many biographies of the man. I read about his relationship with his daughter Anna, who reputedly never had any personal relationships that could match the intensity of that she had experienced with her father.

I very much wanted to ask her advice about the teenage children living in the refuge. In the early days of the refuge I had massive fights with the education department in Hounslow which sent people round to check that the children were at school.

Attending school was not my first priority for the children. I was more concerned that they be given a chance to settle into the refuge; only when they were ready were they encouraged to go to school. Some had already been excluded from schools back home. They were taken care of by the staff in our playschool. Those who wanted to learn were taught by our staff; those who just wanted to play with the younger children were encouraged in this. The education department in Hounslow was outraged. It wasn't until one of our girls was found standing defensively in the bushes outside Chiswick Comprehensive with a knife that a belligerent little man from the education department agreed I might have a point. I wanted to ask Anna Freud if she felt that I was right in not pushing children into school before they were in the right frame of mind.

I was also curious to see the famous building that David had helped to buy so that Freud could continue his work in London. I was very aware that there was much about his own life that he never really resolved. In particular, I felt he betrayed the young Viennese women who came to tell him of their incestuous relationships with their fathers. At first Freud had recorded their stories, and for many of those women the fact that at last someone was willing to listen to them was a huge step forward. Very soon Freud decided that in giving them an unbiased ear he was threatening his chances of attaining his goal to become the father of 'psycho-analysis', and he turned on the fragile women who depended upon him and diagnosed them as 'hysterics'.

One look at the hand-wringing coterie of acolytes that greeted us in Hampstead made me realize that the institute was now a mausoleum to the great man. Most of the men and women gathered about us wore black and reminded me of a murder of crows. At the top of a long staircase I saw a tiny wizened woman. The crows straightened up and began to whisper among themselves. Anna descended and took David's hands. She was very obviously fond of him, and despite her diminutive stature she gave off a powerful aura. She turned to me, and I was mesmerized by her warm brown eyes.

She led her little troop of courtiers into a long room. There was a large painting of her father on one wall. Underneath was what I assumed was his chair. We stood to attention until she sat down. I reached into my bag for my cigarettes, and a voice thin as rice paper immediately rasped, 'Miss Freud doesn't like anyone to smoke in her presence.' I regretfully put the pack away.

I started off the conversation by telling Anna that I was concerned about my teenagers. I described my battles with Hounslow's education department, and I said I sought reassurance that I was doing the right thing.

Anna leaned back and smiled at me. One of the greatest problems for teenage children, she explained, was that these were the years when a child's inner life was beginning to bloom. Until puberty a child explored the external world of relationships and experiences; then came a time when he or she felt a need to look inwards. Society, she said, complained that children in their teenage years were lazy. Hours of gazing at ceilings and seemingly being unable to stay awake were actually nothing to do with laziness. The sleeping and the daydreaming was a symptom of children's need to explore their internal world, and as far as possible it was imperative that adults leave them alone. The tragedy, she continued, is that it is precisely these years when adults impose their heaviest expectations upon their children.

I felt immeasurably comforted by what she had to say. We then talked about women who returned to previous violent relationships. I expounded my theory that the way the refuge was organized offered an alternative way of interacting with others that could wean a woman off violence just as other therapeutic programmes wean addicts off drugs and alcohol. I talked to her about the intensity of violent relationships and my theory that, when someone had become addicted to the chemicals of fear and flight, if she was exposed to a tranquil environment the drop-off in those chemicals could induce feelings of dread and anxiety. I explained that I had noticed the refuge helped the violence-prone mothers and children most when it was buzzing with activity; it was noticeable that on the rare occasions the refuge was relatively empty some of the remaining mothers couldn't bear the silence and went back to former violent relationships.

Anna became animated and said she understood exactly what I was talking about. She told me that during the Second World War she had been put in charge of the evacuation of thousands of children from London's East End, which sustained the worst of the bombing. Mostly she arranged for them to be rehoused with their mothers, because she was all too aware of the dangers of separating parents from their children. However, she said, once she settled them into safe and secure accommodation she often found that within weeks the mothers had returned to the East End. Many had missed the excitement of the bombing raids and the camaraderie of the underground shelters.

I came away feeling absolutely entranced by her warmth, but I also reflected that on that day I had just met two of the loneliest people I had ever encountered.

I had a vision of Goodman sitting in his opulent flat with his chauffeur-driven car parked outside – all alone except when he was manipulating events to keep him close to the rich and famous. The abiding image I retained of Anna Freud was of her tiny frame sitting in her father's chair under his dominating picture, enslaved by his memory and surrounded by fawning followers. Did any of them truly love and support her? I doubted it. She looked as though her frail body had never been hugged and kissed, but she emanated a great warmth and kindness – in sharp contrast to Goodman, a diabetic who comforted himself with chocolate biscuits.

When I got home that night I embraced my children and felt comforted by their affection. I lay in bed that night and promised myself that whatever happened I would never let events cut me off from the real world and real people. I sensed that David felt cut off from the world I inhabited, and part of the attraction of the refuge was that he could share the warmth of its atmosphere. Often when I looked up in a morning meeting I could see him sitting quietly in a corner. The mothers soon grew used to his presence, and he seemed to me like an emotionally frozen man holding his hands out to the flames of our laughter.

29
MY REFUGE
SUTTON COURTENAY

I was writing articles for *Cosmopolitan* every month. Journalism paid enough to put food on the table and enable me to afford to keep all the extra young people who stayed on and off in our house. Cleo had a heart as big as a cathedral, and if any of her friends was in any kind of trouble she would invite them home. This quite frequently meant that I had irate parents on my doorstep demanding to see their son or daughter. Usually I managed to negotiate a truce between parent and child, but in some cases this proved impossible. I got used to one particularly belligerent father who made it his business to pursue his teenager daughter around west London. He would pass by my house on his nightly prowl and bellow up in the direction of my bedroom, 'Is she there?' – and I would throw open the window and tell him to fuck off.

Like many single parents I found it almost impossible to keep my children in the house after dark. I'd make rules about 'coming home time', but mostly these were ignored. Mikey was out most nights getting his band together and jamming with his new friends George, John and Roy. Amos and Darren carried their DJ equipment from one club to another, but I was never especially worried about their safety because I gave Amos my Harrods Card to flash if they were ever stopped by the police. I knew he was especially likely to be pulled over by the police, not only because he was with a gang of black youths but because he wore long dreadlocks. He found the card invaluable and was often saved from being spread across a car bonnet when he pulled it out of his pocket.

At this time there were fierce battles between the police and the young people in the streets. The notorious 'sus' laws of the time – entitling police officers to stop and search anyone suspected of carrying drugs or weapons and mostly targeted at black youths – meant that young people in the streets could be harassed at any time, and I knew that the black kids in our house were regularly hounded by local police officers.

I was also concerned about the shebeens. These were secret venues for young people to get together at night. The only way you would know if an event was taking place was if you were contacted by the people who were hosting it. The idea was to find somewhere derelict – a squat, for instance – and set up a loud sound system, tell everyone you knew to bring their friends along and to get on with the party before the police arrived to close the place down. The illegality of the event was half the fun, and all the teenagers in my house seemed to melt away late at night. I would sit up in bed into the early hours of the morning counting the heads as they crept back in.

I was very bad at disciplining my children. I had no strategies to make them behave. I was against any form of physical punishment. I remembered all too well my mother's violence towards me and how all she had succeeded in doing was to make me rebel to such an extent that I had made her life a misery. Her heavy hand had contributed to my hatred of her. My only way of dealing with children was to have a few rules that really mattered and make sure we all adhered to them.

Waiting outside the school in Kew for the children at the end of the day, I found myself largely ignored by the rest of the mothers. One day Cleo came back and announced that from now she was going to call me 'Erin'. 'No, you're not,' I told her firmly. 'I'm your mother, and you've only got one of those. You can call me Mum or Mummy and that's that.'

Cleo glared at me. 'All my friends call their parents by their first names,' she huffed.

'I know,' I replied, 'but I'm a parent – not your best friend.' I was aware that almost overnight many parents across the country had seemed to morph back into teenagers. They shared their marijuana joints with their children and joined them at the rock concerts that now took place every summer. I felt as if a generation of parents had decided to abandon their role as adults. The barriers between parents and children came crashing down.

I made it clear to my children that I was not going to tolerate any sort of drug-taking. Some of the boys had girlfriends, but I made it a rule that the girls were not to stay overnight. On the whole I thought that my teenagers were a wonderful group of young people. I learned to tolerate their pushing of boundaries, and I recognized that as long as I was aware that any of them were not yet back home I could take immediate action if any of them failed to arrive back. Amos presented the greatest challenge in this respect. I privately thanked the good Lord for providing me with Trevor and Cass. They kept his exuberant personality in check. 'Don't be disrespectful to your mother!' I often heard one or other of them remonstrating with him.

I knew that as a single mother I was in an isolated position. I had been married for such a long time that I felt rather like Rip Van Winkle. I had woken up in another time and another era. I was completely unsure how to set about finding a social life with people my own age because I'd been immersed in my role as mother since I was twenty-one years old.

I did screw up the courage to invite a man I decided I liked back to dinner one night. He managed valiantly to cope with the crowd of youths at the table, but when they retreated upstairs Amos made it his business to come rushing back into the room while we were having coffee to scream 'Adulterer!' at him. He left very soon after that.

On another occasion I asked an eminent psychiatrist and his wife to come over for dinner, and during the conversation at the table he asked one of the boys staying with us what he did for a living. Kit smiled shyly and said he had just come out of prison. Feeling the need to elaborate, he said he had been convicted of stabbing a boy in a fight. That was a show-stopper in terms of dinner-party small talk. The psychiatrist had dealt with many imprisoned teenagers over the years, but this was no doubt the first time he had sat down for a meal with one. As it happened, I liked Kit and trusted him. He had indeed been gaoled for stabbing a youth in a pub brawl, but I believed him when he said he had actually been innocent of the crime.

I made one more attempt to find myself a social life with people my age, and I accepted a dinner invitation from a couple with children at Unicorn. As soon as Amos saw me leaving the house he stood before the front door with his arms folded. 'What time are you coming home?'

I pushed him away. 'When I feel like it,' I told him. 'I'm your mother, and I decide when and where I go.'

I found myself in an affluent house with the obligatory stripped-pine floors and doors. The hostess was a gibbering wreck who ran in a distracted fashion between the kitchen and the dining-room try-ing to produce a very elaborate meal for eight. I offered to assist and would have been glad of the sanctuary of the kitchen, but she refused to let me help and instead just yelled at her husband as she grew increasingly frazzled. I was sat next to him, and as I was fork-ing out my singed segments of grapefruit from its rind he leaned over and confided, 'I make sure my wife has an orgasm every night.'

'How boring for her,' I heard myself say. He no doubt was think-ing that as a woman on my own I must be gagging for it.

That was the end of conversation with him, so I turned to the man on my left who gave me a blow-by-blow account of sanding his dining-room floor. I wished I had stayed at home with the teenagers.

When it was time to leave, my hostess singled out the man who had been invited to partner me and asked him to take me home in his car. I tried to say this wasn't necessary but got nowhere. He seemed more than happy to oblige. He opened the car door, climbed into the driving seat and lit up a joint. He took a long drag and handed it to me.

Cannabis makes me paranoid and nauseous, so I turned the dope down – much to his surprise. When we reached my house I leaped out of the car and raced to the front door. Behind me I could hear him plaintively calling after me, 'Don't I even get a cup of coffee?' I ran inside slamming the door and decided that this was the last time I was going to try to get myself a social life.

There were, however, more tempting invitations. One day in 1975 David invited me and all the teenagers then living in our home in Goldhawk Road down to Sutton Courtenay Manor House, his country estate in Oxfordshire, for a few days. I immediately fell in love with the beautiful Elizabethan manor. My favourite part of it was the courtyard that led from into the main drawing-room. As one walked across the ancient yellow flagstones the aromatic smell of thyme would waft from beneath one's feet where it grew in the cracks between the paving. The house had endless bedrooms, and we were told that sheep rustlers used to be hanged over a huge oak beam that once supported the roof of a massive hall.

The River Thames ran through the garden. There was a small motor-boat tied up to the bank, and near by was a swimming-pool in the shape of a grand piano. I was given a small corner room with my own bathroom. To have a bathroom to myself was an unimaginable joy. Every time I bent over the washbasin in our one at home other people's hair would float to the surface.

It was good to know the children were safe. The most mischief they could get up to was to roam round the countryside after dark. Several of them, being inner-city kids, had no previous experience of the great outdoors, so it took them a long while to get up the courage even to head out on their own at night. I thus slept soundly.

Mrs Coupland was David's housekeeper, and she ruled her domain. I was trying hard to finish a memoir, *Infernal Child*, about my upbringing, and the snug little library was a perfect place to write. On the mantelpiece was a Victorian china fairing of a woman hitting her husband; it made me laugh. I loved being in the house, and I loved the peace of the river. On one of my first days in Sutton Courtenay I had gone down to the river and seen a large heron take off from the water. I stood transfixed as the bird rose up, flapping his enormous wings and trailing its spindly legs beneath its heavy body.

I took the teenagers down to the manor as often as I could. These would often include Trevor, Ann's son Mark, Darren, Annie and Caron, as well as Cleo, Amos, Mikey and Cass, so there was a sizeable gang of boys and girls.

Many years before, the publisher Victor Gollancz had published George Orwell, who had been a personal friend of David's and who was buried in the churchyard across the road under his real name Eric Blair. David had befriended him, and Orwell had written many columns for the *Observer* while staying at Sutton Courtenay. The image I had of the austere and financially struggling writer and social reformer was somewhat dented by this information. I had sometimes found myself on the receiving end of brickbats from the more ascetic left-wingers who found my somewhat sybaritic lifestyle opposed to their conviction that everyone should live an abstemious existence without rich food, drink or any of life's little luxuries. As far as I was concerned, if the money was available, nothing was too good for the refuge's mothers and children, and despite occasional censure we would open bottles of champagne if we had anything to celebrate.

Before the publication of *Infernal Child* in 1978 I was summoned by Livia Gollancz, the publisher Victor's daughter, to a meeting in central London at the company office. She, like Anna Freud, sat in an imposing room under a portrait of her father. What little conversation there was between the two of us soon ground to a halt, and I got up to leave with an ominous feeling about the book's prospects.

I received a phone call from my editor telling me my book was to have a print run of 3,000 copies. On publication I was duly sent on a book tour to promote it. I spent much time rushing around the Scottish Highlands and elsewhere in Britain giving local radio interviews. I think I was in Ayrshire when a reader phoned in to complain to a radio station that she was unable to track down a copy, as it had sold out. Gollancz duly printed a further 3,000 copies – but its sales staff forgot to tell the bookshops that it was once more available. Instead the books languished in a warehouse. Eventually I bought up all the remaindered copies and distributed them as gifts to visitors to the refuge. This wasn't a bad thing, as it avoided the necessity for me to sit down and explain my motivation for setting up the refuge to journalists and others.

Now that David had marshalled an impressive group of friends to sit on his advisory committee I suggested that we throw a party at his beautiful house in St John's Wood and invite the committee members to meet some of of the residents and staff from the refuge. We would supply the food, and Goodman, David and I would make a speech – and we would not let anyone out of the house until they had made a financial contribution. David was enthusiastic about the idea, and the first party was a great success.

I remembered the diplomatic parties my mother used to give when we lived abroad. They weren't just frothy social occasions; there was always a good reason for them. It was important for my father to maintain relations with fellow diplomats, and sometimes he would want to make an introduction between two people that would bear fruit at a later date. My mother gained a reputation for hosting excellent parties. I used what I recalled of her party-giving skills to give people a good time while wheedling money out of the great and the good.

Goodman had the largest group of friends. They seemed mesmerized by him. He had a very strange charisma. I stood next to him when he made the opening speech at the party, and he seemed visibly to grow in stature in front of my eyes. He was an excellent orator, and he expertly played with his audience, juggling his speech deftly between humour and seriousness.

I had already seen him making a speech when David and I had one of our morning meetings with him in his large flat. I don't know if he thought I'd be impressed by his act. David certainly was. Goodman walked somewhat theatrically over to his living-room window after finishing his coffee and biscuits and started declaiming the speech made by Betsy Trotwood when she first meets David Copperfield. When he had finished I didn't know what to say, so I mumbled a few words and let David congratulate him. I suspected the man was fraudulent through and through, but for the moment there was no doubt he was crucial to the continued existence of the refuge – and he certainly had the power to muzzle Hounslow Council's attack dogs.

A few days after the party I was sitting in the sitting-room of the refuge chatting with a group of mothers when a small hurricane appeared to blow through the front door and enter the room. I recognized two of the women from St John's Wood. One sported a black patch over one eye and carried an elegant black cane. The other I recognized as Sally Ann Howes from the film *Chitty Chitty Bang Bang*. The woman with the patch was Lady Tony Lothian, and she immediately held the floor. She kissed me warmly on the cheek – and told us that she quite often hit her husband. The word quickly went round that a famous actress had turned up, and mothers and children started to filter into the room. Visits like this gave the community a reassuring sense that there were people out there who cared about us. From then on Tony became a personal friend.

Even before David joined us Pete Townshend from the rock group The Who had contacted me and asked if there was any way he could help. Sometimes there was no food in the cupboards at the refuge, and an urgent phone call to Pete would result in a cheque. Roger Daltrey and others from the band would come down from time to time, and I have a particular affection for Roger because he would spend time with the children who crowded around him in the back garden. Any promises he made he always kept, and a number of the boys and girls were given Who T-shirts or LPs signed by the band.

Later, Stewart Copeland from the rock group The Police often came down to a club called the Black Cat in Richmond and would invite mothers there to join him. The mothers were thrilled by this and by the attention they received from those who visited the refuge. When we had a bit of spare cash in the kitty the mothers would generally vote that the new arrivals should get their hair done. Anything we could do to help make those in the house feel good about themselves was important to all of us.

David was thrilled when Goodman offered to find a theatre venue for a benefit concert, and the Advisory Committee got together a selection of acts to raise money for the refuge. Goodman was offered the Adelphi Theatre in the Strand for a concert to be called 'Superstar Sunday'. I was also delighted but less happy when it was made clear that there would be no tickets available for the refuge's mothers. I argued that I could not possibly attend the performance if they were not invited. Goodman sent a message pointing out the mothers would be occupying seats that could bring in revenue. I argued that for all of us it would be a night of rejoicing that we needed to share. In the end I won after threatening not to attend unless front seats were made available to the refuge's mothers. To be honest, I wouldn't have been unhappy to miss the event, as I dislike crowds, but in the event I was there.

On 12 March 1978 I found myself with others in the royal box at the Adelphi, and I was intrigued to discover that there was a tiny lavatory at the back used only by the Queen. I sat on an opulent seat and wondered if she felt as diffident as I when looking down on the sea of faces staring back up at me. They were probably wondering who was up there. I sat embarrassed, hot and sweaty clutching a gin and tonic and wondering how long it would be before I could escape. I could see the mothers in the front row having a great time. Cleo Laine and Johnny Dankworth played jazz. My favourite act was the singer Julie Covington. In the end it was a marvellous and highly successful evening and one I know many of the mothers treasured.

It didn't take long for me to fall out with some of the members of the committee. I was aware that a number of them had no interest in the refuge or the subject of family violence. They were there because of David. A newspaper published a photograph of David, Goodman and me with the caption 'The Three Musketeers'. Goodman was not best pleased, as he liked to keep out of the spotlight.

David meanwhile took me on a tour of his friends. Being dragged around by him made me uncomfortable, and I was unclear as to the value of the exercise. On one occasion he took me to see Roy Jenkins, then a Labour MP in the House of Commons. We climbed some stairs that seemed to go on for ever and ended up in Jenkins's private rooms. He didn't seem particularly pleased to see me, and after handing me a gin and tonic with no ice or lemon ignored me and addressed all his remarks to David. Jenkins reminded me of a puddle of car oil. I thought him a slick, pompous, self-important little man, and I took an instant dislike to him.

On the way out of the House of Commons David showed me a portrait of his mother. He was very proud of her reputation as a good and active MP in her Plymouth constituency. He told me how brave she had been when the bombs were dropping during the war and she had taken shelter in the air-raid dug-outs of Plymouth – and how she could turn cartwheels to entertain people! My favourite story involved the time she insisted on going swimming in the sea in rough weather and David's father Waldorf had tied a rope around her waist and stood on the beach to make sure she didn't drown. David seemed to have a very conflicted relationship with his mother. When she left Waldorf he decided to remain with his father, which meant that David didn't see her for a long time.

On one occasion at Sutton Courtenay he described his ugly divorce from his first wife Melanie Hauser in the early 1950s. He told me of his lengthy efforts to secure custody of their daughter Frances, and when he talked about their epic battles I wondered at the rancour in his voice. This was a David Astor that few people knew, I thought. Most described David as a shy and withdrawn man. I never knew this side of him. There was laughter and a shared sense of fun between us. To hail a taxi when we left Goodman's flat in Portland Place he would put his fingers between his lips and split the air with a piercing whistle. 'Okey-dokey,' he would say as he dropped me off at the refuge after our forays to raise funds. He was proud of his American origins.

His parents were reconciled before his mother's death, and David made sure that she saw none of the photographs of the scandal that took place at Cliveden in Buckinghamshire, his family home, where in the early 1960s the Conservative MP John Profumo embarked on an affair with the call-girl Christine Keeler, a liaison that was to bring down the government. On one occasion, at David's insistence, I met

Profumo. I was sent with a member of David's entourage to a hotel, and we had tea in the lobby. The former MP looked shifty and desperately embarrassed; he twitched nervously the whole time we were there. David loved to champion underdogs – I was another, I thought, as we left the hotel.

Nancy Astor, like my mother, had been a narcissist and exhibitionist. Such people always had to be the centre of attention and basked in the glow of their friends' admiration. Away from adoring crowds, however, they soon reverted to being manipulative bullies. Damaged in early childhood, such individuals retreat into a solipsistic universe, with the rest of the world rotating around their every need and desire.

These dangerous individuals are to be found in senior positions everywhere. Their powerful need for recognition and acclaim drives them, but they often end up on the brink of destruction, because no amount of fame and adulation can assuage the pain of the abuse or rejection they had experienced in early life. The rage they experience is volcanic, and such people usually make bad parents. One of David's relatives told me that he had outraged his mother one day and in retaliation she had a groom take his puppy and shoot it. I was appalled, although I never had a chance to ask David if this was true. It seemed plausible, however.

Because David and I had both suffered from toxic parenting I felt a great bond with him, and when the teenagers and I were at Sutton Courtenay he often came down for the weekend without his wife. He and I would sit convivially in the little library, and I would drink gin and tonics before cooking supper for us all. David was teetotal. I liked seeing him so relaxed, and he genuinely seemed to enjoy being in the house with all the children. Because there were so many bedrooms and so much space I was able to take along many of our Goldhawk Road teenagers at a time. They enjoyed themselves, and it kept them out of harm's way.

I would cook huge meals in the massive kitchen, and in summer we would sit out in the courtyard and use the barbeque. The children were impressed by the history of the house with its antiques and paintings. It was a world away from the mean streets of London. I found it a delight to watch them joyfully leaping in and out of the pool.

I was at Sutton Courtenay for a weekend when I received a

telephone call about a burglary that had been committed near my home. Three young men had been arrested, and one of them, William, was a close friend of the family. I rushed up to London to bail him out. I found a very repentant young man of sixteen waiting for me at Chiswick Police Station. He admitted being involved, and he told me about his eighteen-year-old accomplice, his friend Francis, who had been arrested with him.

When the case came to court I attended to give a character reference on William's behalf and plead for him to be given community work rather than a custodial sentence. This proved successful.

Francis's solicitor meanwhile told me that the youth had no one to speak on his behalf and that since he had been in trouble many times he was likely to go to gaol for a long sentence. My impression was that he didn't deserve this. I offered to speak on his behalf as well, and on seeing the tall young man sitting in a disconsolate heap in the witness box I asked the judge if he would allow me to take him home. I explained that I sometimes took in boys and young men who had been in trouble with the aim of rehabilitating them so that they could become useful members of the community. I described a summer-long project I was setting up for young boys at Sutton Courtenay and the fact that I had appointed a tutor to teach the children in my charge there. I offered to take care of Francis – known as Russ to his friends – for at least two years.

Jack was staying at Sutton Courtenay to spend some time with Cleo and Amos. I didn't tell him about my promise to the judge, but I asked him as a favour to me to attend court at the next hearing to tell the judge that he could confirm that I was willing to take charge of Russ and keep him out of trouble.

Fortunately the judge had heard of me, so he accepted Jack's assurances and allowed Russ to go free. Jack arrived back at Sutton Courtenay Manor looking slightly dazed, while Russ was positively astounded. One moment he was facing years in prison; the next he was walking into a beautiful country house full of teenagers in time for a decent meal.

Russ became a very important part of our lives. He told me how his mother had left him with his Caribbean grandparents and that his grandmother had been a very violent woman. She used to beat him badly and make him kneel on a coconut grater (these were huge affairs with fierce cutting edges) as punishment when she thought he had been bad. She also made him kneel on top of ants' nests. She felt if you 'spare the rod you spoil the child'. Russ was only three years old when he had been left with her, and he didn't join his family in England until he was thirteen. After that he went off the rails.

I had heard similar stories many times before. Some of the young black women in the refuge told of being left by their parents and of being brought to Britain when they were old enough to work and contribute to the family income. Often on arrival they had no further relationship with their parents.

Most Afro-Caribbean couples that left their children behind with relatives worked hard and sent for their children as soon as they could, but in Russ's case coming to Britain had been a disaster. He was really too old by the time he was uprooted to Shepherd's Bush in west London. He had a strong Granadan accent, and he was bullied and beaten up at his London school. One day he was walking down the street when he saw a cardboard box of bananas outside a vegetable shop. Without thinking he helped himself to a few pieces of fruit and carried on down the road. Within minutes he was stopped by a policeman who arrested him for theft. 'I didn't teef,' Russ tried to explain, but of course according to law he had indeed stolen the bananas. He consequently found himself in borstal.

From then on his life had been a nightmare. He couldn't believe his luck when he first met me – and for my part I was glad to have found him. He rapidly became a great role model for Amos. He was the eldest in the family, and before long he and Trevor came to work at the refuge full time. I always felt safe when Russ was around. And all the children looked up to him.

In general I was very lucky that I was surrounded by really dedicated people who came to work at the refuge in Chiswick. Right from the start, males were made welcome to join the staff, often to work with the children; these exceptionally gentle, sensitive men were to make a lasting impression on many of the deeply traumatized mothers and children who passed through the Big House.

I considered David Astor a dear friend and a saviour, but gradually I realized I was merely tolerated by the majority of members of the committee. There were exceptions, of course: Tony Lothian, Sally Ann Howes and Joanna Lumley were there because they genuinely supported the refuge and could appreciate what I was trying to do. Joanna Lumley surprised me, because I was becoming so alienated by the circus around David that initially I couldn't believe that she would be genuinely interested in our work at the refuge, but she proved me wrong. In the years she was on the committee she was very well known and respected as an actress, but none of this ever went to her head, and even though she was incredibly glamorous there was a side of her that I knew was never going to be seduced from her common-sensical attitude towards life. Like me, she was a single-parent mother and had experienced the odd run-in with the press; these factors made me warm to her immediately. I didn't feel she was cocooned by wealth and privilege, and I could always talk to her.

Jim Duffy, the sympathetic councillor from Hounslow Council, Illtyd Harrington, then Labour leader of the Greater London Council, and several others continued to be good friends, but I was unsure how others saw me. As far as I could tell, some of the very affluent committee members were thoroughly alarmed by the mayhem and anarchy in the streets and the palpable wave of hatred towards any-one regarded as middle class. The frantic charitable efforts of some of the people on our committee hid the cynical fact that partying in the guise of charity was regarded as a good thing; moreover, it could all be set against their tax bills.

I got a salutary reminder of how beleaguered the middle classes felt when I arrived at Sutton Courtenay one weekend to find Mrs Coupland with very red eyes and the staff moping about looking very disconcerted. Once we had settled down with a brandy she told me they had been called together to be told that David and family were planning to emigrate to New Zealand. Many of the staff, including Mrs Coupland, lived in tied accommodation with no housing rights. No one had any inkling of what the future would hold.

I was astounded. I jumped into the car and raced back to London. I went straight to David's home and confronted him. He confirmed that he had decided that he, his wife and children should move across the world, and he said sadly, 'I don't think England is the sort of place with any future for my children.'

I left him standing on his doorstep, and as I drove home I felt a sense of dread. If someone as powerful as David felt he was in danger and planned to flee the country, what hope was there for the rest of us?

30
THE BOYS' HOUSE

Once the glittering committee was set up I assumed I could take a
back seat from public life and get on with working in the refuge. I
appointed Ann Ashby to take care of the great and the good while
I concentrated on our problems with Hounslow Council. It had
recently stepped up its harassment of the refuge, and I had received
a warning that it was going to send a posse of staff from its Health
Department one day at the crack of dawn and demand to be let in to
count the mothers and children in their beds.

Fortunately my health officer mole had given me the date they
were coming, so I was there to open the door. They looked rather
startled, indeed alarmed. 'You should be ashamed of yourselves,' I
admonished them. 'Head-counting was the sort of thing the Nazis
did during the war! You'll frighten the children and embarrass their
mothers.' There was a moment's silence, and, shamefaced, they
turned on their heels and went away.

During the 1970s town halls in the larger cities were increasingly
behaving like little Stalinist outposts. Some of those in London had
virtually made a unilateral declaration of independence from their
electors and had taken it upon themselves to persecute anyone who
tried to defy their tyrannical rules. Hounslow, under the fiefdom of
Alderman King, was a classic example. After determining that a
much-loved nursing home for the elderly was to be closed down, he
was incensed that the local people fought back. Their campaign was
well organized and effective, and for a time it looked as though the
home would be saved. In the early hours of the morning, however, a
fleet of taxis and ambulances emptied all the occupants out of the
nursing home before its supporters had time to mount a protest.
The frail elderly people were 'dispersed' all over the borough, while
Alderman King retreated back to his lair to gloat.

The two sheds in the refuge's garden now came under attack

from the health department. I desperately needed proper accommodation where the boys could create a community for themselves. The new refuges for women that were being established refused to admit boys over the age of twelve – some over the age of nine. I tried to reason with the Women's Aid Federation. I got nowhere, because its organizeers insisted that the male children would be as violent as their fathers and abuse the women and girls in the shelters.

I knew from my years of staying at St Mary's during my school holidays that gangs of girls were more likely to represent a problem than boys. To be sure, some of the boys I encountered over the years were violent, as were some of the girls, but physical violence was fairly easily remedied by our highly trained staff who became mentors to the children. We found it was the more manipulative girls who required most of our attention. Time and again when there were stand-offs between the children I reminded them, as I reminded their mothers, that it was not the bomb that caused the explosion that concerned me but the hand that threw it.

Often I would see a boy exploding with rage in the garden and a girl standing on the sidelines looking innocent. When the matter was thrashed out in a community meeting the hand of the girl was exposed. Yes, the boys had to take responsibility for their rage, but it was also necessary for the girls to consider their sometimes provocative and manipulative roles in creating an incident.

I was delighted when Max Rayne, one of Goodman's good friends, offered to pay for a house in the cul-de-sac behind the refuge. Very shortly after acquiring the Boys' House I was able to buy, in addition, a large house that became our school and Playhouse and a smaller coach house next door to the Boys' House. The Coach House became an important part of my dream to create a safe haven for the boys to help them recapture the bests aspects of their childhood. The girls used to go down to the playschool and would join in with caring for the younger children with the staff. Girls could easily show their emotions and be comforted by everyone, while the boys had no such outlet. In the homes they came from they were expected to emulate their violent fathers, be stoical and show no emotion. And some had mothers who, if not physically incestuous, were emotionally smothering.

'He's your son, not your lover,' I would occasionally have cause to say if I saw a mother totally enveloping her son in an armchair in an inappropriate way. Such boys often had a dangerous love–hate relationship with their mothers that could lead to violence towards other women they lived with in later life. In many families where there were no emotional or physical boundaries parents found it easy to find sexual solace and comfort from their children. Freud used to call it the 'mysterious romance of the family'. But there was nothing mysterious or romantic about those relationships. I was outraged that parents would prey on their innocent, vulnerable children and then act shocked when their child became a dangerous or violated teenager.

Joe was a particularly good candidate for the Boys' House. His mother had been promiscuous and given birth to a string of children by various men. He had done his best to act as father to his younger brother and sisters, but at the age of fifteen he struggled to get out of the grip of his mother's incestuous and suffocating affections. One day I was called out to one of the sheds in which he had pinned up a poster on the wall of a naked woman. He had cut out her breasts and vagina, and I could see the pin holes in the poster where he had thrown darts at it. I asked him to take it down and told him that when he had his own room he could put up any posters he liked but that I hoped I could get him some help so that he could come to terms with his violent feelings towards women.

I was further concerned when I discovered that Joe had been volunteering for line-ups at the local police station when rape suspects were participating in identity parades. He seemed to have a fascination with their crimes. Eventually he asked me for help with his conflicted feelings towards the opposite sex, so with his agreement we went to two separate clinics; both regretfully informed us that they could do nothing to help because he had yet to commit a crime. I was appalled. Here was a young man begging for help because he was afraid of what he might do to a woman – and there was none available. His mother eventually moved on after two years, but he returned to ask me if I would let him move into the Boys' House. The other boys were more than willing to take him in. They had known his mother and had witnessed her inappropriate behaviour towards him.

At around this time an agency was established called We The People. It was one of the many groups that came forward to help us in our work. The men involved in the project were unemployed and offered to help renovate our buildings and our squats. I was delighted to receive their support and asked if they would take some of our boys on as apprentices, since they had a variety of skills they could teach them. A number of the women from the refuge also volunteered to work on the project. These men became mentors for my boys' project. From now on there were no welfare payments for the boys; instead they were paid by the hour at the end of each day. It was a great success, and the boys were soon building walls and learning plumbing and painting skills. Tina had the job of doling out the cash. I chose her because she had a gentle, reserved nature. The boys all respected her, and it was a pleasure to see her handling a large truculent teenager who had stayed in bed rather than work and who now faced a day with no pay.

I painted the little flat on top of the Coach House together with the boys. We put a partition across the room; one side was an office and on the other side we created a bedroom and bathroom. We laid down a thick dark shaggy carpet, while a huge mattress covered in a duvet and coloured pillows completed the bedroom. The little flat had a selection of Fisher Price toys including a big wooden fort with soldiers, plus Tonka trucks, puppets and a large selection of soft toys. The boys would lay across the carpet and play with toys they had never had access to in their battle-scarred lives.

During the afternoon I would make appointments to see any of the boys who wanted to talk to me in the privacy of the Coach House. For many of the boys, feeling safe was a completely new experience. I devised the house with the idea that each boy would have his own room. Each had a budget and was allowed to decorate his room as he pleased, in conjunction with his mentor. After we had had our first house meeting there I felt convinced that the project would do much to help the boys look forward to a positive future.

In its early days a tall young man came to see me in the Coach House. He explained that the boys had befriended him and that he very much wanted to become part of our project. He was from a very violent East End family, and he wanted to get away and make something of his life. The boys were keen to have him in the house and immediately voted him in. He took over the cooking, and within a matter of weeks the rest of the boys regarded him as something of a father figure. Now that they had some control over their lives those who needed to were ready to begin to make changes in their relationships with their mothers, fathers and siblings.

By 1978 I was able to purchase another property in the cul-de-sac which became known as the Home for Indefinite Stay. I had always been concerned about some of the women who took refuge with us and were really unable to look after their children by themselves. Many of the mothers were completely institutionalized, having spent all their lives in care. Quite a few were illiterate, and many of them had been not only physically abused by the staff in care homes but also sexually abused. The solution offered by social workers was to take their children into care and leave them to find accommodation on their own. Often such people just faded into the background and became 'skippers', sleeping on the streets. When the weather got cold some of them came into the refuge. The mothers would find room for them on the ground floor. No one was forced to bathe, and we only de-nitted a woman if she requested us to. The mothers would take it in turns to stay up at night to supervise the skippers and make sure they didn't drop lit cigarettes on their mattresses. Most of these women had come from dysfunctional and violent homes. There but for the grace of God . . . , I used to think.

I had become expert at treating bad feet and to some extent diagnosing and treating other minor conditions, since it was always a struggle to find GPs willing take on our transient families. If necessary I would do my best to find a solution for medical problems the women developed. Most of them refused to go near doctors or hospitals.

One of my first clients at the Home for Indefinite Stay arrived escorted by a very caring social worker who told me that she had two parents who were both of 'subnormal intelligence', as they termed it back then. The man was very violent to the mother of his children; she was promiscuous and had made advances to almost every male and female in her block of flats. As a result the family had been shunned by the neighbours, and the children were bullied by others. The social worker said there were six children and if I couldn't take the family in she would have to apply for a care order and take the children away.

I talked things over with the members of the community, and

they agreed to take the family in. Rosie duly arrived with her children, and we settled her into a corner of one of the large dormitories next to a window overlooking the garden. The next morning I came into the sitting-room to find her waiting for me. She came straight up to me and fondled my breasts. I looked down at the tiny plump woman and removed her hands. 'Rosie,' I said 'these are my breasts. They don't belong to you, and I don't give you permission to touch them.'

She giggled.

'Take me upstairs and show me how you have settled in,' I suggested. From the social worker's description of Rosie's abilities I imagined the other mothers would have had to help her unpack. I was therefore surprised to find that her area and bed was the neatest and best-organized area in the room. 'You're not as daft as you make out,' I said and gave her a hug.

She stared at me as if she was making up her mind about something. 'I'm quite clever,' she said.

Rosie had been diagnosed as 'mentally subnormal' by care workers and medical professionals. She didn't read or write, but she could function perfectly well in many other ways, and she could help mother her children. I was, however, concerned about her eldest boy because he was very bright. I could see that he would benefit from a first-class education, and I asked David Astor to help me. He gave me an introduction to a charity that paid boarding-school fees for especially bright children who otherwise could not afford such an education. Within a very short time the boy was ready to go off to school. I didn't regard boarding-school as a long-term solution, but I hoped that some time away from his mother and family would enable him to glimpse a different future. I wanted to give him space to explore his options, and I trusted him to make his own decisions in life.

It was Rosie who made me realize we needed long-stay accommodation. She was my first family in the new facility, and she remained with us for a long time.

I found an excellent couple who were willing to run the project, and they brought with them their two young children. Lillian, aged around forty, was next to join the Home for Indefinite Stay. She also arrived with a very flustered social worker. Lillian had been married, but her husband was in a mental hospital after suffering a nervous breakdown. She had two little boys in tow, and as far as the social worker knew she was illegitimate and had been hidden from the neighbours in her street and hardly ever been allowed out of the family home.

''Ello, fuckface,' Lillian said cheerily when I walked into the sitting-room and found her sitting on a sofa with her two little children playing round her feet.

'I love you too,' I replied, wondering how we were going to get her into a bath. She stank, and her hair was lank and greasy. Her children were thin and unkempt. I called for JoJo who was excellent when it came to hauling filthy mothers into baths. 'One for you, I think,' I muttered and disappeared into the cubby-hole for a coffee and a cigarette.

I was generally impervious to the nits and the scabies that turned up in the refuge. As fast as we cleaned up one section of the community another filthy family would arrive – and we were off again. I used to boast that the nits fell off my scalp drunk on red wine and the scabies were kept at bay by the vast quantities of garlic I consumed. Everyone else scratched and itched.

One night in the mid-1970s Amos came dashing down in a panic. 'My head is itching,' he announced. I checked, and sure enough there were well-fed nits strolling around his scalp. He leaped about dramatically, his long hair whipping round the room. 'Disgusting!' he shrieked.

'Let me see your hands,' I said. He extended them, and I could see red scaly patches between his fingers. Jack also had scabies, and the two of them had to go down to the local fumigating station where they were stripped naked and painted with white liquid by jolly women and then plunged into hot deep baths. There were a number of disadvantages to having a relative running a refuge for homeless people.

Lillian was an intelligent woman who had been stunted by neglect. She soon became a great favourite in the community, and her manners improved. She had a disconcerting habit of letting her menstrual blood leak down her legs and licking it off her fingers. She was a big woman with an explosive temper, so I was asked to deal with this sensitive issue. 'People don't like you doing this,' I said to her shortly after her arrival when she had been persuaded to take a bath. 'It makes us queasy.'

'It tastes nice,' Lillian replied. 'Why the fuck can't I do what I want?'

'Because you fucking well live with other people,' I said. 'I'm going to get JoJo to sort you out with some decent big knickers, and you are going to surprise me by never doing it again! By the way,' I added, 'you smell really nice.' Lillian grinned, and I hugged her.

She had never been mothered. Whatever had happened in that neglected childhood she was always treated as a secret disgrace. Strangely, someone had taught her to type; she had been given copy-typing to do, presumably from a secretarial agency, but she was never given any of the money she earned. The other mothers said that her children ate off the floor and out of rubbish bins if they were not watched. She was incapable of showing any affection to either of them, and once she was settled into the Home for Indefinite Stay I discussed their future with her. Eventually she agreed that they should go back to their father as long as they visited her from time to time. He had recovered from his breakdown and was now in a stable relationship with a loving woman who said she would welcome the boys.

31
GRANDMA

One morning in autumn 1976 Cleo came into my bedroom and said, 'Mum, I think I'm pregnant.'

I was lying on my bed reading, and I froze. I kept my voice as calm as I could as I said, 'Lie down beside me, and I'll feel your tummy.' She lay down, and I put my hand on her completely flat stomach. I felt an almighty kick, and I knew she was right. Not quite fifteen she was pregnant, very pregnant. 'You've got a footballer in there,' I said and smiled at her. 'I'm going to be a grandmother!' I could see the blood pouring back into her white face, and I hugged her. She went off to tell Mikey that her pregnancy was a fact and that I was not angry.

I left it to him to tell his mother that he and Cleo were going to have a baby. Cleo had a very good relationship with his family, and I hoped they would feel as I did that the young people needed all the support they could get. I didn't know Mikey's parents personally, even though his sisters often attended parties in our house, but I knew his mother and father would be as shocked as I. I also felt somewhat guilty about Cleo's condition, because I used to work flat out in the refuge and come home and continue to work on whatever cases were outstanding. Tina and other members of staff sometimes joined me, and we would often work late into the night rewriting legal papers and updating our casebooks. Had I been more available to my daughter she might not have turned to Mikey for love and comfort during her parents' divorce.

When I was pregnant with Cleo I had a flat stomach for the first seven months, so it came as no surprise that Cleo at fourteen weeks didn't look pregnant. I remember thinking that she was sleeping rather a lot, but then teenagers do. I never suspected that she and Mikey were having sex. Maybe that was naïve of me. At Sutton Courtenay I divided the boys and girls into two dormitories at different ends of the house. I put Mikey in a room with Amos a few feet away from my own bedroom.

Cleo was still a child, and she was going to have her own child long before she was emotionally capable of dealing with such a life-changing event. The teenage years of development might be closed off to her, since she was going to have a baby. When I told a few close friends I was amazed that they expected me to be angry with her. How could I be angry? She was pregnant, and the new grandchild was a fact. All I could feel was an immense amount of compassion. I knew the road ahead would be hard and lonely. Her friends would continue to party and experiment with relationships, while she would be living behind a glass wall cut off from normal teenage life.

I was also concerned about the physical and emotional effects of giving birth at such a young age. The pain of childbirth is so extreme that it takes a mature woman to recover without some emotional damage. I was devastated, not only for her and for Mikey, who was trapped in parenthood at the age of sixteen, but also for myself. Only then was I beginning to get a sense of freedom from child-rearing. The children were of an age where I could begin to relax and have some time for myself and my interests. Now I was to be plunged back into looking after a newborn infant. I knew that I would have to bear the brunt of much of the responsibility for this.

Apart from telling Jack, I felt I had to let David know, because I knew if the newspapers got hold of the story it could reflect badly on the refuge. My reputation as a woman fighting for the rights of victims of domestic violence left me vulnerable to attacks from journalists – and I suspected they would have a field day. For once Goodman was helpful. He was Chairman of the Newspaper Publishers Association, and the only paper to print anything was the *Guardian*, and it was just a small paragraph. The rest of the press held off. Nigel Dempster, a well-known gossip columnist, wrote an unpleasant piece in the satirical fortnightly magazine *Private Eye* in which he called my grandchild 'a bastard', but this was to backfire on him, and the journalists on *Private Eye* soon discovered they had very little support for the piece.

I knew Cleo would have to leave Chiswick Comprehensive, but we had Amos's tutor coming in every day, and she was encouraged to work out her own programme of classes. I felt Mikey needed as much support as Cleo did, and he moved in with us full time so that they could support one other and the baby after it was born. My first grandchild was about to arrive, and we had to make the new member of the family welcome.

When the day arrived and Cleo went into labour I watched her leave the house with Mikey and walk down to Queen Charlotte's Hospital down the road. I tried not to cry, but I felt very emotional about her future. I thought it was important that Mikey was with her at the birth and that I should stay out of the way. I sat with the other teenagers waiting for news for what seemed for ever, and hours later Mikey burst through the door shouting, 'It's a boy!' We opened the champagne and celebrated. He said Cleo was exhausted and was sleeping, so I decided to see her the following morning. When everyone had gone to bed I cried myself to sleep. I knew that I had to take the responsibility for the new baby and for Cleo and Mikey because they were both far too young to look after a child.

Before I got out of bed the next day there was a phone call from Cleo to say that she wanted to come home. The other women on the ward were giving her 'funny looks', and her legs hurt from the epidural. She sounded desperate. I leaped into the car with Mikey, and we drove down to the hospital. I parked illegally outside the main entrance, and we raced into the maternity ward. I knew many of the midwives from Queen Charlotte's because many of my pregnant mothers gave birth there, but I also knew how hidebound the nurses on the maternity ward could be. I could also imagine how awkward a fifteen-year-old would feel in a ward full of much older and largely disapproving women.

Once I saw her in her bed I saw that the baby was not with her. I ran to the nursery to find a line of babies crying in their cots. I didn't even need to check the tags to find my grandson. He was wailing loudly, and his tiny fingernails were tearing at his face. He had a thick head of black curly hair, and he looked like his father. I double-checked his tag and found I was right. I picked him up and ran back to the ward where Cleo and Mikey were ready to leave. We tore down the corridor followed by a doctor yelling at us that the baby could die of hypothermia. 'I have central heating,' I shouted back. It was actually a warm spring day, but I wasn't going to argue with the man. I just wanted to get my daughter and her baby home where she could relax and feel safe.

Once tucked up in my old bedroom upstairs Cleo fell asleep straight away, and I carried my grandson downstairs and took a proper look at him. He had enormous brown eyes with huge sweeping eyelashes. He looked immensely fragile. Some babies come into the world solid and grounded. This baby seemed neither of these. He had an otherworldly quality, and I felt fiercely protective towards him. He might not have had the best start in life, but he was surrounded by people who would love and take care of him. I put him gently down beside me on the bed, and he fell asleep.

As I looked down at my grandson that first time I had the most extraordinary moment of thinking that I understood the meaning of immortality. Holding my own children for the first time was miracle enough, but holding my grandchild made me realize that my genes would continue down the line. My lineage stretched from Irish potato farmers from Counties Sligo and Mayo in Ireland, and the Craig family came from Scotland and from Jamaica's Montego Bay. It was an interesting combination.

The next morning there was a loud banging on the door. Everyone was fast asleep. I opened the front door to find a stony-faced woman standing there in hospital uniform. 'I have come to see Cleo Pizzey,' she said curtly, with disapproval in her voice. I was about to tell her to fuck off when she pushed past me and went straight upstairs. I shrugged and went back to bed. The baby was peacefully asleep with Cleo, and there was really nothing the woman could do.

After a while she came downstairs and marched into the sitting-room. She could see the open door leading to my bedroom. She stood in the doorway, her nostrils a-quiver. 'Your grandson', she announced triumphantly, 'has to go back to hospital. He has jaundice.'

'Has it occurred to you that he is mixed race?' I replied. She glared at me, turned on her heel and left slamming the front door. I went up to see Cleo, who was looking greatly recovered. We laughed about the visit, and I went downstairs to make her a cup of tea. The rest of the day was taken up with visitors arriving to see the new baby, and I made tea for everyone and cooked a celebratory dinner for whoever was still there by the evening.

Life became even more pressurized with a baby in the house.

Mikey and Cleo decided to call him Keita. It was an African name and also that of Stevie Wonder's son. I felt as if I was running a marathon with no time to draw breath. I was immensely grateful that Phyllis Pepper, Chiswick's new housemother, came to help me in the house twice a week. I leaned on her for support because she was the only one who knew how tough things were. Most nights I stayed up writing for *Cosmopolitan* or any other magazine or newspaper that might be willing to commission a feature from me. I had a house full of children, and the cost of keeping it running and feeding everyone was enormous.

David told me that he had been warned that a group of people who lived in Chiswick near the refuge were organizing a protest meeting in a local hall. I decided to steer clear. He offered to represent me, and I was very grateful for his support. He reported back afterwards that someone had showed a film of the front of my house and made sneering references about how I forced the neighbours around the refuge to suffer while I lived a privileged life. It was hard not to feel bitter as I sat up late at nights working my way through a pile of bills I couldn't afford to pay. I took no salary from my refuge work because, in spite of the committee and the fund-raising, money there was always relatively tight.

Mikey was still determined to get a band together and managed to get a job in a local music studio. He was out most nights making connections and playing music. Cleo often accompanied him while I took care of Keita. I loved babysitting him. I had a large, comfortable rocking-chair, and we would rock together. He was a very gentle baby with a broad smile, and everyone in our community loved him. Slowly we settled down to live with a new member of the family. Amos found it hardest at first, because he had been the youngest for so long, and now Keita had stolen some of the attention he was used to receiving. But in the end, with just eleven years between them, Keita became Amos's little brother.

Mikey's family wanted Keita to be christened in their local Catholic church, and I was glad of that because I hoped it would bind the two families together. At the christening I looked across at Cleo and Mikey standing next to the font, and I could only pray that they would find the strength to be able to look after their child. They were far luckier than many young parents. They had a big comfortable house to live in, no financial worries, and they were surrounded by a large group of people who were always willing to help out with the baby.

After the christening we went back to the Craigs' house and celebrated the occasion with some of Mrs Craig's famous goat curry. Keita was passed around the family, and after much music and dancing I returned home with some of the children and went straight to bed. There were times in my life when I just had to hand things over to God. I was now living one day at a time, as the demands of the refuge grew larger and more complex. I was juggling David's and Goodman's committee with my battle with Hounslow and the ominously looming court case which could end with me separated from my family and incarcerated in gaol.

32

THE PALM COURT HOTEL

I was at home one evening in 1978 babysitting Keita when there was a knock on the door. Patrick, one of the volunteers from the refuge, stood on the doorstep and said he had a proposition for me. He came in, and we sat down with some wine. He told me he knew of a big hotel in Richmond that had been empty for years. It had forty-five private suites. He and some friends had thought of holding a concert there, but it proved unsuitable. They now had the key, and he was proposing to hand over to me because he knew that we badly needed more space for our very overcrowded refuge. I was intrigued. Richmond was only a short distance from Chiswick, and I had been worrying about where we could squat next.

Patrick was one of an army of people who ran a squatting agency called the Ruff Tuff Cream Puff Agency. The well-known poet and playwright Heathcote Williams had first come up with the idea, and he and his friends also had set up an illegal radio station called Rebel Radio. They were regularly chased across the London rooftops by the police. They went on to squat a number of houses and create the kingdom of Frestonia in and around Freston Road in north-west Notting Hill in 1977. They housed around 120 people and declared themselves independent from the UK. Heathcote was Ambassador to Great Britain while the actor David Rappaport was its Foreign Minister. I was to use many of their tactics when we moved our squatting efforts to a mostly derelict road in Notting Hill Gate. Many Frestonians helped our mothers and children settle down in their new accommodation.

At the refuge we discussed the possibility of squatting the Palm Court Hotel. Everyone agreed it was the right thing to do, and we knew Patrick's associates would help us with the move. I talked to Ann and suggested that she take over the running of the hotel while I would remain in the main refuge in Chiswick. With a community of some seventy-five mothers and children in Richmond I needed someone who would be there full time, and Ann was by far the most experienced of all the staff.

I hired a huge van, and we waited until we knew the caretaker for the Palm Court Hotel was in the local pub. We filled the vehicle with mothers and children with their possessions mostly in black bin bags. Watching them packing up I was struck by how many of the residents had arrived in the refuge with nothing but plastic bags for their worldly goods. Still, leaving their homes with proper luggage would have alerted the neighbours and families that they were departing – and many had walked out on their partners without telling them. To me a black plastic bag had become a symbol of all that these families had lost when they had to run for their lives. Now, however, the families were moving to a beautiful hotel situated on the bank of the Thames with magnificent views over the water. What we might lack in comfort we would make up for in location. I arranged for a reporter and a photographer from the *Observer* to accompany Ann and the families, so that they would have some protection should the caretaker catch them in the act of moving in.

Ann slipped out to a telephone box and told me that everyone was safely ensconced in the hotel – except for the photographer who had been arrested by the police. Those of us who had remained in Chiswick cheered loudly, and as many as possible crammed into my car and we raced over to Richmond. Inside the hotel Ann had got a huge fire going in the massive kitchens. We brought more bedding over with us, and we stayed overnight to protect the mothers and children from possible trouble. Fortunately the caretaker, faced with a phalanx of determined women, did what most men would do on being confronted – he turned tail and was last seen scurrying up the road.

I slept in one of the downstairs rooms with other volunteers and staff. We were woken by the sound of muffled footsteps, and we jumped up to investigate. We stood with thumping hearts waiting for the shuffling footsteps to come closer – and were confronted with a very cross and smelly tramp who was furious that his shelter had been taken over but who soon headed off. We went back to sleep, and by morning we were up making ourselves coffee and tea in one of the kitchens. Our room soon filled up with mothers and children, and we knew before long curious locals and journalists would start to gather outside.

The *Observer* duly printed the story of our takeover, and very soon there was a trickle that soon became a flood of people from Richmond and the surrounding areas who poured into the hotel clutching quantities of food and warm clothing. Cars and vans pulled up constantly disgorging furniture, bedding and blankets. We were deeply moved by the surge of support for the families. For most of the day we rushed round clearing up the derelict hotel as much as we could, while the playstaff came in to keep the children amused.

It was a bitterly cold day a few weeks later when Jill Tweedie from the *Guardian* arrived to interview me at the hotel. It seemed a long time before that she had first introduced me through her press articles to the existence of the newly emerging British women's movement. We sat in a small corner of the foyer of the Palm Court surrounded by people hammering and repairing the building. At first Jill seemed very fierce, but soon her sense of humour asserted itself and we found ourselves discussing all sorts of things quite irrelevant to domestic violence, homelessness and the rights and wrongs of squatting. She, unlike many other women journalists, refrained from attacking me in her writings, and the article she wrote about our takeover of the hotel was actually quite benign.

After this she often entertained me in her huge gloomy flat in Islington and later in the houses she subsequently purchased. She would also invite me to her much-fêted parties. The glitterati of London's intelligentsia would flock to her home, and she had a huge following among the affluent socialists. I was always amused by the diehard radical left who would drop in to gorge themselves on decadent party food and quantities of champagne. Before long she became a very good friend.

Some years after first meeting her, after a bibulous night together, Jill affectionately pulled me towards her and burying her face in my neck muttered, 'I'm sorry about persecuting you. I had to do it, you know.' I knew what she meant. I had been a laughing stock at her parties, and I was aware of that even before I accepted her invitations. I felt like a maiden aunt being wheeled out to amuse the bright young things. In gatherings of her friends I knew that as a group they adhered to a left or far-left vision of Britain's future. I had no political axe to grind, and I refused to share most of their beliefs or views. My philosophy was – and remains – that political ideology would never resolve the ills of the human condition. All of us are personally responsible for one another, regardless of race, creed or colour. Generally when I was attacked by Jill's friends I responded that if they cared to come across to west London and roll up their sleeves, they could help those members of society worse off than them by changing nappies or nailing down floors – instead of engaging in meaningless rhetoric.

Most of the work at the Palm Court was done by We The People, the infinitely valuable band of men, together with some of the mothers and older children. They were soon busy sawing wood, repairing missing floor planks and slapping paint on walls. The electricians among them saw that the electric fittings in the hotel were safe. I banked on public opinion to help keep the lights and gas on; our supporters lobbied the gas and electricity suppliers, and we were able to install gas cookers and replace lightbulbs wherever they were needed. Before long we were able to provide electric fires in the bedrooms so the families were comfortable in the coldest weather.

Everyone was working frantically to improve the accommodation apart from one mother, Sabrina. I found her ensconced in the kitchen with her eyebrow tweezers and a small pot of brown warpaint. 'Bloody hell, Sabrina,' I said, 'don't you think you should be lending a hand?' She gave me a seraphic smile, and I had to laugh.

'I will,' she said, 'when I've done painting on me freckles.' She was a beautiful young woman with four handsome little boys. She had grown up in a violent and sexually abusive household, and, as happens to many from families where sex was regarded as a commodity, she had become a prostitute. She was most unsuccessful at this. She had originally arrived at the refuge with so many police convictions and fines it took ages to negotiate with a probation officer to let her stay rather than slap her back in gaol and her children back into care. Her problem was that she had no sixth sense like her sisters in the oldest profession, and more than once she offered her services to plainclothed policemen. She had a childlike vulnerability about her, and on returning to Chiswick a second time she was pregnant. 'You told me you didn't want any more kids!' I reminded her.

'I know,' she said laughing. 'It was this furniture salesman, Erin – he had such beautiful eyelashes!'

The hotel was full of newspaper reporters and television cameras, and we were happy to talk to anyone who cared to listen about the need for extra refuges across the country to take in any family in trouble. I was aggrieved to note that often when I mentioned the need for men, too, to have refuge in a crisis the press feature or television item would be quietly dropped. It seemed that men were invisible when it came to domestic violence.

At the end of the first day at the hotel I was just about to go when I spotted a large burly man sweeping the floor with a broom. I walked up and asked his name.

'Mike Dunne,' he replied.

'Are you married? Do you have a job?'

He said he had been working for the tax office but had been made redundant. He was married with a place to live.

'Good,' I said. 'You can start work here on Monday.'

Mike became my most trusted member of staff. All the years I worked in the Richmond refuge he was my constant support, and the mothers and children loved him. The permanent team now consisted of Ann Ashby, Michael Dunne, who worked beside me with the women and children, housemother Phyllis Pepper and Tina Wood, who worked on the legal cases. There were so many men and women who engaged in valuable work in the refuge over the years that it is impossible to list every individual, but I am grateful to them all. Trevor and Russ were to become permanent members of staff in due course, and Cleo, Amos, Mikey, Cass, Annie and Ann's son Mark all worked as volunteers at various times.

In the very early days some very gifted people offered to work with the children. Because our situation was so extreme I needed to have staff and volunteers around me who could be flexible. Many of the mothers and children were extremely volatile, and I needed quick-thinking people who could forget their own problems and concentrate on the situation in front of them. Mike Dunne was a great support, and I knew I could rely on him when mothers or children exploded with rage. Normal parents help their toddlers learn restraint when their children are old enough to learn to contain their anger. In our violence-prone families nobody showed any restraint under any circumstances. Any member of a family could lash out and physically damage anyone or anything around them. Once the rage subsided we were left with an emotionally spent individual and usually some physical damage to people or property.

Most institutions and even the more liberal therapeutic communities punish residents if they resort to physical violence. I understood from an early age that children growing up in violent households never have a chance to learn strategies for survival other than using their rage. At my boarding-school most of the fighting and bullying took place in the school grounds so as to avoid punishment by the nuns. At St Mary's, the holiday home, there was little bullying or fighting, largely because Miss Williams had a genius for dealing with the children. If any of us broke the rules or behaved in an antisocial way she created consequences that really inconvenienced us. I never saw her angry. If I broke her rules – as I did when I first came to stay – she merely looked at me sorrowfully over the top of her spectacles and said I could make reparation for my offence by helping the kitchen staff with the cooking for a day. Peeling endless mounds of potatoes soon made me realize that disobeying Miss Williams was not worth while.

I learned to respect her. She taught me to control my behaviour. She was the first adult in my life that I truly wanted to like me. She had driven ambulances during the war, was a Justice of the Peace and a golf champion. She was six foot seven tall and must have weighed around twenty stone. She had a passion for station-wagons that she drove like chariots, and even the naughtiest children behaved themselves when she was around. At school discipline was imposed on us from above. At St Mary's we did what Miss Williams wanted us to do because we loved and admired her. At the end of each day every child had to go to her drawing-room and stand by her chair to say goodnight. 'Goodnight, Erin,' she said as I stood warming myself by the fire in the grate. 'Goodnight, Miss Williams,' I'd reply, and then I could climb the stairs to my dormitory and fall asleep knowing that I was cared for and loved.

In the refuge we talked about how we needed to create a community where we could allow people to learn patterns of new behaviour to replace the old ones. The 'exploders', the women who externalized their anger, had to learn containment, and the 'imploders', those who internalized their rage, had to learn that it was safe to be angry when it was justified. It became apparent that some of the women had to learn verbal means of describing their fear and their anguish. Most violent people find it very difficult to express pain and sorrow. Rage is the default setting; we needed to help each other express the pain without the rage.

Poppy had been found in a carrier bag on a train station and had grown up in care. After arriving at Chiswick she would go out before lunch and get drunk. On one occasion as she entered the main sitting-room in the refuge Mike and I knew she would attack. She came across the floor with her fists swinging – I was to be the first target. It was immediately obvious that she was not attacking us personally; later we realized that she was raging impotently against others including those who had abandoned her in her infancy. I wrapped my arms around her, and she stayed still for a while, then lurched across to Mike. He held on to her while she sobbed and shouted. We had a very large mattress in the room that came in handy because in the end all three of us fell in a heap and she rolled over quietly. We sat on the floor with her while she slept off her drunken rage. In time she learned to talk about her feelings, and gradually the rages subsided and she could talk to us about her bitterness at being abandoned as a baby.

I was aware that although everyone that came into the refuge had experienced violence – and in a few cases emotional rather than physical – the greatest damage was done where children had been subjected to sexual abuse. Freud called incest the 'glue' that held the family together. There was also the sick joke 'Vice is nice, but incest is best – keep it in the family'.

The Fawcett family had come to us on a referral from social services in the south of England. Their social worker sounded desperate when she telephoned the refuge and spoke to the mother on duty. 'No one will have them,' we were told by her. 'The children are teenagers, and one of the boys is very violent.'

'Sounds right up our street,' we agreed, and before long the family arrived tired and dishevelled from their long journey.

The eldest boy, Reg, aged sixteen, was indeed very aggressive, and it became almost immediately evident that the teenage children were used to beating each other up. They treated their mother with scant respect and swore and threatened her with violence. I knew from the social worker's report that everyone in the family had been beaten by the father. He had been gaoled after Reg had told a teacher that their father was sexually abusing his sister. From what I could tell, Megan, the daughter, held a grudge against Reg for airing the family's dirty linen and telling its secret. The father was due to be released, and the social worker was keen to get the family as far away from his home town as possible. I understood her concern, but I wondered how many members of the family were ready to make the break.

I think that a good definition of incest is when the adults in a family put their emotional and sexual needs on to the shoulders of their children. In this case, as in so many cases of family incest, everyone was involved and the whole family shared the secret. There are occasions where one or other parent genuinely doesn't know their partner is molesting the children, but this is rare.

Louise Fawcett had handed Megan over to her father at a very early age. 'Early age' can mean from a few months old when a child is capable of stroking a parent's sexual organs. Megan had grown up in a family where her sexual relationship with her father was never discussed or even acknowledged, and although he beat her like he did the rest of the family he also groomed her with extra attention and frequent gifts. My job was the try to help Louise and her children learn to love and trust one another.

Our first encounter with Reg's violence was when he attacked his sister. His titanic burst of rage left Mike tightly holding on to his legs and me holding his head and shoulders until he finally subsided into my arms. Most people working with violent children are taught to hold the individual from behind, pinning the arms to their side and trapping the child's legs between those of the adults. For a child in a really violent rage being held like this can feel like an assault. Mike and I learned to hold the children close to our faces so that we could talk – even sing if necessary – until the struggling boy or girl recognized that he or she was in safe arms. After several weeks Reg was able to talk about 'the family secret'. He explained that for years he had hated his father for his violence towards the family but also because he was bitterly ashamed of his sister who lorded it over her two brothers as her father's favourite child.

He resented his mother who had made several attempts to leave her husband but always went back dragging Reg and the other children along with her. Reg said he didn't think his mother or sister would ever leave his father for good, but he wanted to make a life of his own and to save his brother. The two boys settled into the community and began to make friends with some of the other older youths. I was interested to see that Megan and her mother kept very much to themselves. Louise was polite and took very good care of her children. It was as if she had mentally distanced herself from her sons and now was concentrating on her daughter. They were like two teenagers giggling and whispering in corners of the room over a boyfriend. But it wasn't a boyfriend; it was Louise's husband and Megan's father. It seemed that in this case the 'glue' would bind them for life.

Around the same time a mother and daughter were brought into the refuge by an army welfare officer. Jean, the mother, had reported her husband, a sergeant-major in his regiment, for sexually assaulting their daughter Dena. The mother seemed very unemotional about the sexual abuse, and the daughter was very angry with her mother. Jean explained that she usually went shopping on a Saturday morning and left her husband with Dena when they would practise karate together. A few days earlier she had left her purse behind and returned to the living-room to collect it when she heard a loud thumping noise coming from Dena's bedroom. She went upstairs to her daughter's room and pushed open the door to find her husband in bed with Dena. There was something about the way she told me the story that made me think she had a hidden agenda. I didn't doubt her, but her telling of it was so controlled that I knew she had some unfinished business.

Dena quickly made friends in Chiswick, and after week or two she came into my cubby-hole to talk. She asked what would happen to her father, and I explained that he was charged with her sexual assault and would be thrown out of the army. She seemed genuinely very upset by this news; she was obviously fond of her father. It took a while for her to admit to me that her father had been having full sexual intercourse with her for several years. She said that her mother had always known about this state of affairs but had preferred to ignore it. A few days later the girl came back to see me and told me that her mother was going to leave her with her grand-parents, because Jean had a lover and planned to make a new life on her own with him,

It transpired that Dena's father had never known his parents. He had been brought up in a succession of care homes, and as soon as he could he joined the army and subsequently made a great success of his career. He was very popular with his company. Jean had told me that at home he was a deeply needy and emotionally immature man. I could see that Dena felt very responsible for her father and for the fact that he was now thrown of the army with nowhere to turn. She said her mother never loved her and that she would far rather live with her father than her grandparents – but, of course, she knew that was no longer possible. She wanted me to promise that she could at least see him. I said I was sure that we could arrange supervised visits after the court case.

The difficulty for Dena and for many other sexually molested children is that everyone around them reacts with horror and disgust as soon as the child approaches an adult for help. I spent a lot of time with her, allowing her to grieve the loss of her father, even though she accepted my reassurances that as the child in the relationship she was blameless. However, it was important that she be allowed to describe her complicated feelings towards her father – including her enjoyment of certain aspects of their erotic relationship. I knew from the years of work I had done with sexually abused children and adults that part of the guilt they carry is that they are not allowed to express their ambivalent feelings. Where children have been raised with an abuser, sexual molestation may become their idea of affection. Before long any loving approach, such as an innocent hug or a touch on the arm, is interpreted as a sexual overture. It can take a lot of work and patience to help children respond to warmth and affection without becoming sexually excited. First and foremost, it is vital that people who work with victims of sexual molestation recognize that not all molesters are regarded by their victims as evil monsters. Indeed the more depraved the molester the more experienced they may be at seducing their victim into an alternative relationship that the victim may find hard to give up.

As soon as Jean realized that I knew of her plans to dump her daughter she contacted the army welfare officer who came and took her away with Dena. He was not interested in the girl's emotional state. A crime had been committed, for sure, and I certainly didn't try to defend the assault against the daughter. I just wanted everyone involved to be clear about the damage that was going to be done to her by the prosecution of her father and her role in giving evidence against him.

In my experience, where there is sexual abuse in the family usually everyone knows. There are exceptions, but even when some members of the family are in denial the other parent is usually an onlooker or else they passively collude. Most of my experience is with women whose children have been sexually abused by their fathers or partners, and the most usual reason is that the mother didn't want to have sex with the man and handed over one or more of their children as a substitute. At present, with our rigid adherence to the letter of the law, children involved in incest are often doubly abused – once by the parent and then by the state.

33
DOING WELL BY DOING GOOD

I quickly found that although the members of the fund-raising committee knew that they had no power to interfere with the daily
running of the refuge I was expected to put in an appearance at
fund-raising meetings and events. Ann was willing to take my place,
but even though I pointed out that she was a far better fund-raiser
the committee members insisted that I attend.

My first fund-raising invitation came from a woman in north
London. Without enthusiasm I removed my usual pinafore, raked
my fingers through my hair, donned a striped poncho and headed
off to see her. I have always had a deficient dress sense. I hated wearing shoes and usually wore knee-length socks and clogs at work.
Most of my clothes had been selected by mothers from the black
bags of donated garments that came through the door.

On one occasion I received a phone call at home. A plummy
woman's voice said, 'I've seen you on the television, and you dress
atrociously! I have decided to send round a few of my clothes. They
will be delivered to your home address shortly.' I was intrigued,
with visions of floaty designer frocks supplementing my meagre
wardrobe.

I wasn't there when a Rolls-Royce pulled up outside my house
and Cleo accepted a big bag of clothes from a grey-suited chauffeur.
That evening we delved into the bag and pulled out a selection of
tailored dresses, most of them seemingly made by the woman's personal dressmaker. My benefactor was evidently bigger than me and
much taller, but there was one top and skirt that was absolutely
exquisite. The labels on the outfit said 'Thea Porter'; the top was
more a work of art than a garment. I was absolutely delighted. I took
the other dresses to the refuge where one of the women was more
than happy to accept them. I have since often wondered how my
benefactor would feel if she knew that her expensive handmade

dresses were helping the mother do business on the forecourts of Charing Cross Station!

The donor called up a few days later, and I thanked her profusely for the Thea Porter outfit. There was a silence down the line; probably some poor maid got the sack. But the woman was right. I rarely looked in a mirror, and I was conscious sometimes as I cleaned my teeth in front of the bathroom mirror that I didn't look at my face at all. A poor body image and a lack of self-confidence may arise from being neglected and rejected, particularly by one's mother. Untouched and unbonded, a child is left in limbo. A baby needs loving validation – preferably from both parents – to develop a sense of self-worth.

I was aware that I should do something about my appearance, but it seemed hopeless, so I raced off to my fund-raising meeting in north London in my poncho. I knew the other women gathering there would be dressed in the latest fashions – and I wasn't wrong. The conversation around the tea table began with the hostess announcing that she was offering the refuge the UK charity première of a major new Hollywood movie. I explained that I couldn't make a decision about the film there and then but that I would take the offer back to the community to canvass the opinion of the mothers. There was an embarrassed silence, and I realized that this was not how donors usually did business. Recipients of their charity would generally show immense gratitude and agree to everything suggested straight away. Several other fund-raising ideas were mentioned. The offer to sponsor a table at the prestigious fund-raising Rose Ball was greeted with applause. I decided that I would give this a miss – even if I was by now the proud owner of a Thea Porter outfit!

After an hour of small talk smoked salmon was served on palebrown bread, accompanied by a very fine white wine. Platters of cakes were scattered around the table, and I drank several glasses of wine to calm my irritation. I felt guilty about feeling so angry. After all, these individuals were gathered together with the intention of helping our refuge. Since David had come into my life I was learning a great deal about how the upper echelons of society operated.

The days when the idle rich would frolic in public without a care in the world were more or less ended. The Depression of the 1930s and the Second World War killed off the assumption that one class could live their idle lives at the expense of the rest. I had shared a flat in London when I was nineteen in 1958. By the end of that year débutantes no longer were being presented to the Queen at Buckingham Palace in order to secure the hand in marriage of rich and, preferably, titled young men. I was eternally grateful that the Royal Family had the sense to withdraw their support from this aristocratic marital cattle market. My mother, however, had been determined that my sister and I should be presented at court, and to that end she carried rolls of tribute silk from her days in Shanghai in readiness to be turned into dresses for this momentous occasion.

I was invited to lavish parties when I first came to London, but very few could ape the grandeur of the pre-war days. The rich were feeling the pinch financially, and it was no longer acceptable to flaunt a life of leisure. The British working class was experiencing a steady loss of jobs, and the closing down of the coal mines in the 1960s and 1970s meant that workers were become restive and more militant. The 1970s was when the class barriers came crashing down, and the ruling classes became aware that they were no longer looked up to or admired. Ever resourceful, they decided not to flaunt their wealth but to reconvene their entertainments under the guise of charity fund-raising. This way they could continue to party and offset the events against tax!

'I would like to suggest', I said nervously, 'that, since this is a meeting to raise funds for Chiswick Women's Aid, could we perhaps save money by having tea and biscuits instead of smoked salmon and white wine?' An embarrassed silence descended on the gathering, and I found myself gazing fixedly at a beautiful Chagall painting on an adjacent wall. I left the house feeling that I had made a fool of myself but rejoicing in the thought that Ann could attend such meetings in future with her liberal charm and her diplomatic ability to keep her mouth shut when appropriate.

I rang the hostess shortly after to express my gratitude for the meeting and tell her the bad news that the mothers had been to the preview of the Hollywood movie and decided to reject the kind offer of a première because they felt the film was too violent. There was a moment's awkward silence, and then she said, 'You cannot be too pure, Erin.' She left me feeling I was an ungrateful bitch.

I was surrounded by children, my dogs, my cat and the love of many of the mothers and children, but I was juggling my responsi-bilities with a weary hand. Money was a constant worry – not just aspects of fund-raising for the refuge but money to live on. I was often so exhausted after a week in the refuge that I spent weekends lying in bed. I seemed to be running faster and faster on a never-stopping treadmill. In addition, I still had the threat of the House of Lords judgement hanging over me. My blood pressure was rocket-ing. I was miserable. Before, my life had been relatively simple. I had my home and my children and the refuge. I navigated between those two worlds quite comfortably, but now I was way out of my comfort zone.

I don't know who gave me a bottle of Southern Comfort one evening, but I drank far too much of the sweet, potent whisky and found myself the next morning in the refuge huddled under a blanket nursing the worst hangover I had ever experienced. A tall, fair-haired man walked into the sitting-room. He came straight across and fell on his knees in front of where I lay in a heap on the mattress.

'I fell in love with you the first moment I saw you,' he told me. Through a thick dark fog I gazed dimly at my clogs parked neatly beside the mattress and forced myself to focus. I recognized him as one of the volunteer carpenters I had met at the Palm Court Hotel. This vision will go away soon, I told myself. But his voice was insis-tent. 'Look at me,' he said firmly but gently.

His name was Charlie, and he was a miracle. He came into my life at a time when it seemed there was nobody there for me. I found myself spending nights crying into my pillow feeling that life was passing me by. Was I always going to be alone and sur-rounded by people who needed me? Here was a gentle giant who was actually interested in my feelings as well as my work. We could leave Chiswick after work and talk and laugh about the events of the day – or any other subject we chose. My children were too young and too involved with their own lives for me to burden them with my financial worries – or the the often fraught circumstances of mothers and children arriving at the Big House. For the first time since I opened the refuge I had a partner who was as involved as I was.

During the day he acted as a volunteer at the Chiswick refuge mending windows, floorboards, broken banisters and holes in the walls. He lived in a squatted mansion in Hampstead, and we would spend several nights a week together.

We settled into a calm, loving relationship. In the middle of the mad circus of my life here was a man who could spend hours discussing the *I Ching* and reading books about Tibetan monks from centuries ago. His gift to me was to give me back my sense of self. Before he came into my life I would occasionally catch a glimpse of myself in a mirror and be horrified to see the unsmiling face before me. I knew that he would be returning to his home in South Africa before long, but for the nine months he was in my life he was a welcome and loving presence. We never really said proper goodbyes to one another. One day I realized he wasn't going to be around any more, and I wished him well.

During our time together if we had time off to ourselves we would drive out of London and have picnics in the countryside. We would sit by a stream watching a bottle of good white wine chilling as it bobbed about in the water, anchored by a stout piece of string. On the bank we would pick at large Cornish crabs dipped in garlicky mayonnaise.

Around then I revived my idea of writing *The Slut's Cook Book*. I knew by this time I was never going to be a Superwoman in the style of Shirley Conran, so I comforted myself by embracing my inner slut. I decided to share my philosophy of life.

In the process of evolving the recipes for the book – simplified dishes from all over the world – Charlie chopped and sliced vegetables by my side. Contentedly we slurped wine and threw garlic and more wine with abandon into our casseroles and stews. When the book was published in 1981 it was a great success, and I realized that out there were thousands of domestic sluts like me.

My children liked him, and so did the dogs and the cat. At last I had a companion. Even if it wasn't going to last it filled a hole in my heart, and I discovered that I could laugh again.

Being happy had an unexpected side-effect. After a few weeks with Charlie in London I drove down to the Bristol house with the children for the weekend. As I walked into the kitchen one of the older boys rushed forward to hug me. 'You're thinner!' he gasped and burst into tears. The rest of the community gathered around the table in the kitchen sat silent. I hadn't even noticed, but now I saw it was true. I was considerably thinner, but I realized almost immediately that it was my bulk that the mothers relied on to cushion them against a hostile world. It didn't take long for me to regain the weight and for my Bristol boy to smile again.

34

THE HOUSE OF LORDS'
DECISION

Charlie brought much love and laughter into my life. I was pleased that the mothers and children liked him. He was welcome in the Bristol house, and he would also accompany me for staff weekends at Sutton Courtenay. This was a very special time for all of us, because most of the staff and volunteers did not have the money to go away on holidays. We had time to ourselves to play, chat and to enjoy a degree of luxury otherwise unknown to us. I was aware that the truly dreadful sights that most of us saw daily could induce a sense of burn-out in our staff. Some evenings in the refuge Mike would hug me hard, and we both tried not to cry as another woman with multicoloured bruises or a baby with a lump on its head where it had been thrown against a wall appeared before us. Sometimes the damage we detected was not even physical; cold, murderous words could turn a woman into a husk of her previous self.

Our time together in the lovely manor house and gardens brought us back to the real world – a place where people did not abuse each other. We spent some of the day discussing families at the refuge, but most of the time we swam in the swimming-pool and partied at night. I even revived the old games I played as a child in the holiday home. Sardines, Rounders and Murder in the Dark became everyone's favourites. We also invented a lethal game called Murder Ball that we played in the large barn at the end of the drive. No holds were barred, and all the aggression from the week was swept away. I returned to London refreshed and ready for whatever was going to happen next.

Our appeal in the House of Lords finally took place in 1977. I remember little about the hearing except that a supportive troupe of mothers arrived late and couldn't get into the chamber, so I sat on my own in my stripy poncho and tried to follow the proceedings. I held my Russian cross tightly and prayed while Lord Hailsham sat on the woolsack and deliberated. He intoned a very long and complicated explanation for why the appeal could not succeed. On my way out I wandered through a long maize of corridors flanked with bookcases and portraits feeling wretched until I rejoined the mothers and staff waiting outside in the car park.

That weekend I was at Sutton Courtenay with David and my children. I got up early to read the Sunday papers that Mrs Coupland laid out on the big kitchen table. She was all smiles because David's application to immigrate to New Zealand had been turned down. I was comforted to read a leading article in the *Sunday Times* in which Lord Hailsham regretted having had to turn down my appeal. Although I knew I had to go back to Acton Magistrates' Court for sentencing I was grateful that he seemed to sympathize with my predicament.

Back in London I was having breakfast with David and Goodman to discuss a meeting that Goodman wanted with Hounslow Council when he brought up the subject of the house next door to the refuge. The building had been a private school. It had been bought by the Labour Party but was never really used. We had often asked the borough if the building could be used as an overflow site for our refuge, but there was never any agreement over this. One week when we were more than unusually full I counted over a hundred mothers and children in our nine rooms. The mothers voted to squat the building to register a protest. Several of the male staff offered to accompany them, and we decided that, in order to ensure that individuals could not be easily be removed by police, people would chain themselves to each other for the duration of the protest.

No sooner had we entered the building and secured heavy chains round the mothers and men than the police arrived to be joined shortly afterwards by more men with huge steel metal-cutters. The shackles were roughly chopped off everyone's legs and arms and they were forcibly ejected.

The next night the mothers crept back out and painted the wall around the property. 'BATTERED WOMEN NEED A REFUGE', their sign said in huge white lettering. I thought it was great, because I hoped that dignitaries on their way to 10 Downing Street from Heathrow Airport would pass by and notice it.

'I want that sign off the wall,' Goodman rumbled angrily.

'I can't get it off,' I told him. 'The mothers won't agree to it.' He glared at me. He hated me arguing with him, but this time I had a plan. 'I need three thousand pounds', I told him, 'for a project involving some of the children at the refuge. I am sure if you can help raise the funds I can persuade the mothers to scrub the writing off the walls.'

Goodman must have been getting considerable grief from Hounslow Council because he chewed his toast for a bit and nodded. I returned to the refuge to plead with the mothers about the slogan, and in the end they agreed to remove it.

In 1978 in Chiswick a small fire in the only single room in the refuge caused fire engines to race to the scene and envelop the whole house in water. There was very little actual fire damage, but the water hosed everywhere made the electric wiring in the house hazardous. Workers at Hounslow Council, no doubt rubbing their hands with glee, announced that mothers and children in the building would have to be dispersed.

When things look hopeless I always pray furiously, and that afternoon I telephoned Save the Children for advice. The charity swung into immediate action, and within a matter of hours the same night portacabins had been set up in the cul-de-sac where we had our playschool and the Home for Indefinite Stay. In a large field behind the Coach House they pitched several enormous tents. The portacabins had toilets and washbasins, and we filled the Playhouse and the Coach House with mothers and the smallest children, while the rest took up residence in the tents.

The next morning Ann and I awaited the arrival of officers from Hounslow Council. We escorted them to the cul-de-sac and the awaiting community, where everyone was settling in. Several of the councillors and officials were obviously pleased that we had found a temporary solution to our crisis, but the grim looks on our detractors' faces made me very happy indeed.

The response from the public was remarkable as soon as word got out. Blankets, sheets, food and money poured in – so much so that we had to hire a large warehouse to store everything. The provisions that arrived took care of all the outstanding needs of the enforced stay in the cul-de-sac and supplied a substantial stock of clothes, bedding and furniture to hand out to mothers when they were ready to move on. The public's generosity also showed Hounslow Council that we were not alone and had national support. What Alderman King never seemed to grasp was that by persecuting us he merely increased this support.

We had to wait for the wiring to dry out before we could move everyone back in. Once the community was re-established in the house I found myself itching to use the camping equipment donated by well-wishers to take the children from the refuge camping for the summer holidays. I have always been a great fan of living as close to nature as possible. Although I had stayed in a caravan I had rarely camped until after my divorce in 1978 when I had taken Cleo, Amos and the other children living in the White House to spend several weeks on the Greek island of Zakinthos.

My one concession to comfort on this trip with the extended family was a personal toilet tent. We set up camp in a large disused potato field. I supervised Russ while he made my loo tent secure. It was a tall and thin with a long zip. Inside I placed a comfortable portable toilet filled with sweet-smelling liquid. The children were strictly forbidden to enter; it was for my use only. The rest of the day we spent in the warm Greek sea, and we sat in a friendly family-run taverna up the hill that night and ate delicious garlicky hummus, salads and grilled lamb and chicken from the barbeque. I looked around the contented faces lit by the table lamps, and I was happy for the first time in a very long while.

After drinking a great deal of Greek red wine I wandered down the hill with the children to go to bed. Before tucking myself into my tent I decided to christen my loo. I sat down and pulled the zip up to my chin. I could see the sea with a big moon painting the beach and the water. I started to laugh and so surprised myself that I rocked and fell backwards. The toilet ended upside down on my chest. It was then I discovered that the children had ignored my command and the loo was full of turds. I was too happy to be cross. I just lay there and laughed helplessly. Trevor, Russ and Amos came running to pull me out off the ground and disentangle me from the guy ropes and toilet. They half carried me down the beach, and we all charged into the sea. The holiday was very therapeutic for me, and I resolved that the refuge's occupants should have the chance to spend some time close to nature away from city life.

Before we left Zakinthos I had discussed my children's project with the Greek family from the taverna who made me a *koumbara*, a sort of honorary godmother to their youngest daughter at her wedding. Mama Gina and I discussed the possibility of bringing some of the children out to the island for a holiday. I explained that her family would need enormous patience with them but reassured them I would bring enough adults along to ensure that the children were well supervised. The Greek family were happy to let me have the potato field once more; I also decided to rent the small cottage at the end of their garden so that I could spend private time with the children if necessary.

Some of the children in the refuge were a source of great concern to us all, and I promised that if I were able to take them away for a month I could guarantee a change in behaviour in most of them once they returned. I was going to introduce them to the very foreign notion of peace and harmony. On the Greek headland there were just a few tiny shops plus acres of scrubland and coastline. There was nothing to steal, and the only company the children could keep was each other and a scattering of old folk living in nearby small cottages. If they wouldn't choose peace I would force it upon them.

35

JENNY JOHNSON MAKES HISTORY

In 1976 the long-awaited Domestic Violence and Matrimonial Proceedings Act had become law. This new legislation gave a power of arrest along with an injunction to keep violent men (only men, not women) away from their victims. I was grateful to the many feminist legal experts who had worked so hard to create the new legislation. Before this change an injunction had no teeth. It meant that women who were cohabiting no longer had to take out criminal proceedings against their violent partner. They now had the same rights as women in married couples to ask for an immediate injunction. Even more importantly, a woman could now apply for an injunction from the court without evidence of divorce or separation proceedings. This was a huge step forward, and while we were grateful for the legislators' hard work we were concerned because they had not allowed men to give evidence about their experience of domestic violence. Social services, the police force and other agencies were undergoing new training, and I was baffled as to how men could be entirely excluded.

The Act did not, however, protect the housing rights of anyone living in a common-law relationship where the violent partner was the sole tenant. I was incensed by the injustice of this. Most of the refuge women were living in common-in-law relationships, and I was particularly upset when a woman called Jennifer Johnson turned up with her beautiful little girl and told us about the dreadful violence she had experienced at the hands of her partner, who was the official tenant of the family home.

Tina took the case to our brilliant solicitor Alured Darlington, and they fought for the right for a child of a relationship to be spared eviction. It was a long, arduous battle. We were asking to overthrow the rights of a man to his castle. This was a right that had been enshrined in law from time immemorial. As the case proceeded from the High Court to the House of Lords we held our breath. At last the decision came down, and the little girl and her mother were safe. The law was changed so that cohabiting couples had the same rights as married couples.

The national press made much of this decision, which was dubbed the 'Mistress Charter'. There was much harrumphing from various male pundits, but we got out bottles of champagne and celebrated. But much as we recognized the value of these changes in the law that now gave very real protection to women and their children, we were aware that in many of the cases we saw the law was useless if one was dealing with someone with a serious personality disorder.

A few months after the change in the law came about I received a telephone call from one of my most gifted family-law solicitors. He was sobbing down the phone because he said he had forgotten my warnings and advised a woman to return to the matrimonial home with the protection of an injunction with a power-of-arrest clause. She had taken his advice, and that night her husband gained entry to the house and stabbed her to death. The law can be implemented only if people are willing to obey it. Otherwise it is useless. Only the very rich have personal bodyguards to keep away dangerous people. Most victims of domestic violence never will have such security. The only solution if anyone gets involved with a dangerous partner is to get away – far away.

I knew after my House of Lords appeal had failed that sooner or later I would be called back to Acton Magistrates' Court for sentencing. The prospect kept me awake at nights and made my blood pressure soar, as I feared being separated from my children. I was not worried for myself otherwise. So many of my mothers had been in gaol I knew I would be among friends. I often accompanied women whose partners were in prisons on visits. One prisoner governor was very annoyed when I suggested that, for a number of his female inmates, prison was as much of a club as the Athenaeum or Boodles. I felt the injustice of constantly being threatened with prison. Over the years I had been forced to break the law on many occasions, because had I not done so to protect the lives of mothers and children I knew I could never forgive myself.

Yet again I was forced into a crisis of conscience when a mother arrived at our door with her five children. Amina was from Morocco and had been married under her local law. She joined her husband in England and had his children. He was constantly unfaithful and beat her regularly, but she was afraid to leave because she had no right to stay. He eventually decided he no longer wanted her or the children because he wished to get married to another woman in Britain. He thus ejected Amina from the matrimonial home. She came to us because she was fighting deportation with her children, all of whom had been born in the United Kingdom. It was her solicitor who recommended she come to us, because all legal remedies had been tried, and the mother with her children was about to be arrested.

Amina and her children were a very welcome addition to the refuge. She was a warm, caring person and wonderful with all the children. She had a large bruise on her face as a result of her attempt at a last plea with her husband. She was terrified of being forced to return to to her country. She had no relatives to turn to, and with five children to feed she feared they would languish and starve in Morocco.

My first idea was to ring the National Council for Civil Liberties and ask the organization to take the case. A chilly voice informed me that they no longer took personal cases; they only made policy. I was left with a dilemma.

The only way I could resolve Amina's problem was to invent a new background for her and for her children. This involved some very creative paperwork. Before long we were able to rehouse the family safely elsewhere in London. I often think about them and hope those children went on to be good and happy citizens of the country in which they were born.

I had come across a case where the NCCL had taken up the cause of a man who had been born illegitimate and was raised in a large Victorian mental hospital in north London. Susan appeared in the refuge complaining about her partner Ted. She was an enormous woman who arrived trailing a pack of children behind her. His problem, she explained, was that he was very violent and she was tired of the fighting and the shouting. They met while Ted was still at the the hospital. He had been incarcerated there because his psychiatrist doubted that he would ever be able to forge a normal life in the community. He had a long history of violent behaviour but had been given a responsible job in the hospital which he undertook very successfully. He worked in the kitchens, and he was in charge of costing and ordering all the food. Undeterred by the implications of removing Ted from the one place he could call home, the NCCL decided that his civil rights had been infringed and proceeded to get him released.

While he remained in the hospital Susan was very happy with the arrangements. She worked as a prostitute at one of the major railway stations, but the couple managed to exercise their marital rights to the extent that she now had a large brood of children. After a successful court case resulting in the setting of a very important legal precedent that created considerable press attention Ted was set free. The local housing department, in recognition of the couple's changed situation, offered them a new-build four-bedroomed terraced house in Islington. Susan soon discovered that Ted was frightened and bewildered outside the institution. He had no idea of how to live in close quarters with a wife and children, and he was terrified of leaving the house. He bellowed at people going past the door and hurled abuse at teenagers who played out on the grass in front.

The NCCL had achieved its aim, but apart from helping to rehouse Ted and his family it took no further interest. Paper-shuffling, organizing committees and making policy was the main concern. People tended to be used as political footballs.

Before long Susan had contacted Ted, and he offered to advise us on the grocery shopping for the refuge. 'Ted 'ere,' he would shout down the phone each morning. 'The price of hamburgers 'as gone up four pounds . . .' In the end Susan decided to go back to him, as I knew she would, but a few days after she went home she summoned me for help.

Their house was in the middle of a rather smart terrace. I noticed that there were garages underneath the houses which surprised me. Most people on welfare couldn't possibly afford to buy or run a car. Susan ushered me in, and I saw Ted glowering in a corner with a huge pitchfork in his hand. There was a football-shaped hole in the sitting-room window and glass all over the floor. As I sat down to admire the Laura Ashley wallpaper and the brand-new fixtures and fittings there was a thundering of feet passing by the window and wild teenage laughter. 'The kids torment him,' Susan said. 'That was a football,' she said pointing to the window. At this point Ted launched himself at the window waving his pitchfork.

Islington, like many of the other north London boroughs, was a bastion of the ultra-left, and I had a sneaking suspicion that Ted and Susan may have been rehoused in the terrace so that their titanic fights and his alarming behaviour would result in neighbouring residents asking to be rehoused. The desirable new homes with their designer wallpaper and stylish fittings would thus be made available to the activist cronies of the council's employees. The director of Islington Social Services was not best pleased when I told him of my intention to discuss my suspicions with the local press. However, he bowed to my request for rehousing and counselling for Ted to enable him to learn to live a normal life. Eventually they were provided with more suitable accommodation for their needs.

One of our major commitments at the refuge was to encourage students and social workers on placement to work with us so they could gain experience before taking their degrees. Most of them arrived brainwashed by left-wing tutors. They didn't regard the women in the refuge as individuals with idiosyncratic personalities and foibles; they saw them as the oppressed working class in the process of rising up to take their rightful place shoulder to shoulder with their fellows to fight against the evil of capitalism.

We had people working with us from countries as far away as Korea. Phoey was a slight, athletic young woman who enthusiastically cooked dishes from her Korean mother's cookbook. She was appalled at the amount of time women sat around in the sitting-room throwing cigarettes to and fro and drinking endless cups of tea. She came into the cubby-hole one day to suggest that the mothers should join her in exercise out in the back garden. I was more than happy for her to to try to encourage them in this.

She came into the refuge a few days later clutching a large bag containing Korean flags. During the morning house meeting she explained her programme. She promised the mothers that they would lose weight and feel much better as a result of regular exercise. Everyone – apart from me who has always hated any form of organized exercise – was enthusiastic. The next day Mike and I hid in the cubby-hole until the women were out in the garden, after which we observed the class through the window. It was an impressive sight. Phoey regimented everyone into straight lines, and then they began to wave their flags and bend and stretch. By the next day a few had defected, and the day after that she was down to a handful of women. Several days more passed, and before long she stood on her own doing her exercises and waving her flag.

Another well-meaning trainee social worker had a similar experience. She decided that the mothers should get together to paint the kitchen. The house agreed to buy paint and brushes and collectively expressed approval of the scheme. The next morning began with a gaggle of mothers painting furiously under her supervision. Gradually the women dropped away and sat around on kitchen chairs making encouraging noises to those still working. By the afternoon I returned to find the social worker valiantly painting the walls single-handedly. She burst into tears, and I sympathetically pointed out that part of the problem was that she had made a decision to paint the kitchen and only then roped in the mothers. I had discovered that household decisions were more successful if the mothers decided on a course of action themselves, rather than had it suggested to them. I wasn't worried about the future of our country in the wake of revolution. I could see the revolution's failure writ large on our half-painted kitchen walls.

England in the 1970s was awash with a largely middle-class revolutionary elite made up of the media, Labour Party members, civil servants and the universities who, when faced with the overthrow of capitalism, would find themselves waving banners to encourage the lumpen proletariat. The problem was that the proles, like my mothers, would encourage their new masters to do all the work while they carried on drinking tea and sharing fags.

I have witnessed social and political unrest in countries when the majority of people have little to eat, no state provision of health care and live without hope. I didn't think that situation would arise in Britain as long as we have a welfare state to offer some sort of safety net. A basic guaranteed minimum living standard had created an underclass too opiated to revolt.

36
DANNY FLIES IN

All through the years I ran the refuge my sister Kate – she had changed her name from Rosaleen probably because she got tired of being called 'Rogey' – remained very close to me and my family. But just before I was due to leave for Zakinthos with the staff and the children we heard a rumour that my brother Danny was going to descend on my house with his latest girlfriend. I always had mixed feelings about his fleeting visits. Normally he came flying through my door wearing a safari suit, big combat boots and with a bracelet made of elephant hair around his wrist. It felt like being struck by a tornado.

My mother always claimed that George Bernard Shaw was a relative of ours; indeed she would tell the story of how when she was a student at the University of Toronto he had visited the city to stay with two of her aunts, and this was when she met the great man. At times she would cock her head on one side and gaze at Danny. 'Ah,' she would sigh, 'look at that Shavian head.' She was convinced that he would become a great author, and I kept my own wish to write a secret. Danny's head looked quite unremarkable to me, and by this time we were supposed to be related to so many famous people that I had lost faith in her stories.

After he left school he found it almost impossible to live with my father's second wife in their little house in Purley; besides, Marjorie, childless herself, had no idea how to deal with a delinquent teenager of eighteen who lay in bed and refused to have his socks washed. Danny was utterly miserable. He discussed his situation with me – I was then twenty-four – and we agreed that he would be better off joining the Rhodesian police who were recruiting at the time.

Danny loved his new life in Rhodesia. He wrote long letters describing his life in the police force, and I heaved a sigh of relief. After leaving the force he made a large sum of money selling houses with his partner and then wrote his first book, *Whispering Death*.

He sent me a copy, and I could see that in his first novel he had managed to come to terms with our mother's cancer. The book included much violence but told a page-turning story, and he brought the Africa I knew from my years in there to life. I was thrilled for him.

The book wasn't published outside Africa, but now he had written another novel which was to be turned into the film *The Wild Geese*, and he was in London to visit his new publisher. He was staying at the Dorchester, he informed me. I was very impressed. The children gathered around the dining-table while Kate and I took care of the food.

Danny had a wide circle of friends and admirers in London. He told us stories of lavish meals and bottles of champagne shared with shining luminaries of the publishing world. I always loved his company. He lived on the edge of his own explosive universe, and his enthusiasm for his latest ventures captured his audiences everywhere.

During dinner he regaled the children with stories of his travels across the African savannah with his faithful Askari who slept at the foot of his camp bed, cooked his meals and on several occasions saved his life. He didn't seem to notice a change in the atmosphere, and I could see the boys shifting uncomfortably in their chairs. Danny finished his last story with an invitation for any of the boys to drop by and have dinner with him should they find themselves in Rhodesia. Trevor spoke for all of them when he pointed out to my brother that the only black people that Danny invited to his table were servants to wait upon him.

During his previous visit we had an awkward moment when he explained that he could see very real problems ahead for the white settlers in Rhodesia. I suggested that he bring his family back home to England.

'But, Erin, who will saddle our horses?' he said.

'Someone with blue eyes,' I suggested. There was a great gulf between me and my brother. I grew up in a household where my father regularly screamed 'Boy!' at our African cook in Dakar. My mother treated the women who worked for us abroad as mindless robots. I was aware that my parents' behaviour to their staff was wrong, and I tried to reason with them. I do believe Danny genuinely cared about the people who looked after him on his farm in

Rhodesia, but his attitude was benevolent and patronizing, and it made me uncomfortable. But we were so far apart in our beliefs that it was impossible even to discuss the subject.

He spent his first leave from the Rhodesian police sleeping on my sofa in our tiny little sitting-room in Buckingham Gate. I was delighted to see him and pleased and relieved that he seemed to have made a successful career for himself. When he left I was so excited about his African adventures that I wrote down my impressions of his new life. *Punch* magazine offered to publish the article, and I was paid fifteen guineas for my first published piece of writing. Danny was not at all pleased when a copy of the magazine turned up in his mess in Rhodesia.

He was even less pleased when I sent him a copy of my childhood memoir *Infernal Child*. I didn't know that Danny had reinvented himself as a scion of a famous family. He was mortified to have his friends discover that his father was born into a violent, alcoholic family and that his mother was dysfunctional and cold. Kate and I had no such problem. We were always very aware of the realities of our lives. Kate was far more bonded and forgiving of our mother than I was, but there was no friction in our memories. Danny was fourteen when our mother died, and like many men he preferred to keep his mother on a pedestal. In my experience very few men are able to be realistic about their mother's violent tendencies or propensity to sexual abuse. Men can sometimes admit in private that their partners are violent and dangerous – but not their mothers.

In Danny's case my mother had not been physically violent towards him. She always wanted a boy, but when he changed from being her 'little prince' and became a normal grubby seven-year-old she dumped him in preparatory school. There he was tormented by the other boys because he had turned up after being incarcerated under house arrest in China and was 'different'. He was badly bullied and had his head flushed down the lavatory on a number of occasions. He was a fearful child, and after being beaten up a few times he developed a stutter. In spite of my mother's prophecies Danny failed to become a genius at school, and he suffered from her neglect and my father's jealous bullying.

The shadow that lay between us began with *Infernal Child*, but he was generally unhappy about my turning my hand to writing. As much as I tried to convince him that we would never attract the same readership for our books I know he bitterly resented what he saw as an encroachment on his territory. In this he was supported by his editors, and before he died tragically young he confessed that a promise had been made to him that he would never be known in the publishing world as 'Erin Pizzey's little brother'.

Danny was determined to become an internationally famous writer like his great hero Wilbur Smith. My brother was a fantastic storyteller and often held us all spellbound when after a meal and plenty of beer he would lean back in his chair and describe the books he was planning to write. Sometimes I tried to warn him that if he talked out the whole story he might not be able to get it down in print later on, but he didn't listen. I knew that the discipline of sitting down to write for months and sometimes even years was hard for him. I comforted myself with the fact that my next book, *The Slut's Cook Book*, would not cause friction between us.

The visit ended with Danny on yet another hopeless quest to capture the heart of another idealized woman. He was thwarted by her rich middle-class parents who were horrified when Danny pitched up at their Eaton Square townhouse sporting his safari suit and a battered suitcase. 'I love her,' he said fixing me with his periwinkle-blue eyes.

I knew what was coming next. 'I suppose you want to marry her?' Danny was an incurable romantic in the best Irish tradition.

'Of course,' he said. 'Her parents have whisked her off to their villa in Spain, but I have the address and all I need now is an engagement ring.'

Danny knew that everything my mother owned had been taken by my father, and all we had left of her possessions were a few pieces of her much-treasured jewellery. He promised that this time his love was for ever, and he planned to go off to Spain, pitch his tent as close to his beloved he could get and lay siege to her. Alas, he was unsuccessful. He parted with our mother's engagement ring, a beautiful aquamarine set in white gold. His beloved disdained his love but kept the ring.

He went back to Africa after hugging his two sisters and vowing that when he became rich and famous he would take care of us for the rest of his life.

37
BACK TO THE MAGISTRATES' COURT

Cases were now flooding in thick and fast, as word got out that we would fight to the death on behalf of those who asked for our help. None of these people had any money, and by offering support and taking on government agencies, law courts and social services we quickly built up a reputation that caused the courts and most of the establishment to fear and resent us.

One morning in 1977 a young woman called Pauline arrived at the refuge. I found her talking to Mike Dunne, and she told us her story. She was desperate because she had escaped with her two boys from a very violent relationship. She tried to cope on her own as a single mother, but she fell into a deep depression and finally took the boys to her local social services and asked for them to be taken into care. She warned that she was afraid that they might suffer from neglect through her persistent depression.

The children were placed in the care of her partner's step-parents. Pauline tried to warn social services that they were not suitable carers, but she was ignored. Shortly afterwards the boys were spotted in the back garden by neighbours tied to a dog kennel during the day. One of the boys was taken to hospital and died of starvation. Pauline told us that a third inquiry was to take place in the Wirral up north, and she wanted to be able to go up and give evidence because she had been denied access to the surviving child. She hoped that by insisting that she tried to warn social services that the step-grandparents were dangerous she could at last be given visiting rights to her remaining son. I didn't hold out much hope. Social services across the country are their own judge and jury, and they will always fight any suggestion of culpability on their part. But for her sake we had to try.

Pauline showed us a picture of the boy, and a feeling of outrage sent my blood pressure soaring. How could those two little boys be tied to a dog kennel overlooked by neighbours and no one called in social services for weeks?

I had first-hand knowledge of the indifference of neighbours. I was seventeen years old in 1956 when the our neighbours in the town of Axminster knew that my mother was lying dead in our house and that her three children were incarcerated with their terrifying father who refused to release her body for burial.

My sister, my brother and I were locked in Hunthay, our Devonshire house, for six days while my mother decomposed in the dining-room. Miss Williams, who had looked after us in her holiday home for a number of years, could have taken action against my father when she came to pay her last respects to my mother, but she left without saying a word. My mother's doctor came after my mother had been lying there for four days, because my father finally called him to verify she was dead. He left after a few minutes muttering, 'It shouldn't happen to a dog!'

Every evening my father would force the three of us into the dining-room where he lifted the red cloth that covered our mother and made us look at her decomposing body. The smell as the days passed became unbearable. We lay in our beds nightly while my father raged and screamed around the house. Finally the funeral director was called in by my father, and the funeral took place in the church in the middle of Axminster. The local community registered its disapproval of my father by staying away. My father, his three children, his two sisters and a handful of friends stood up to sing 'Jerusalem' before we filed out to bury my mother in the wet Devonshire soil.

It was that first women who came into the refuge, Kathy, who had said, 'No one will help me', who touched my scarred heart and liberated my anger as well as my determination that I would never be one of those indifferent neighbours and turn my back on those in need.

Pauline's children had not only been abused and grossly neglected by their grandparents but also, I believe, by the neighbours with their 'see no evil, hear no evil, speak no evil' policy. We prepared a statement for her, and Mike took her up to the inquiry at Bebington on Merseyside. Throughout the inquiry the social services created a solid wall of denial. Confidential memos had been mislaid, and evidence that should have been given was suppressed. Pauline came back with Mike grateful for our support, but ultimately we felt we had failed her. She did not even get a chance to see if she could get permission to see her child. She remained in contact with us, but I felt that Pauline was now to be added to my list of failures.

Alderman King summoned me to a meeting at the council's offices. This had happened on many occasions, and he expected me to turn up with Ann and several of the mothers. No doubt he was looking forward to bullying us with his account of what would happen once I stood in the dock again at Acton Magistrates' Court. I decided to ask Goodman and David to accompany me to see if Goodman could use his legendary powers of persuasion to encourage Alderman King to back down. It seemed logical that the alderman was in a position to offer a reciprocal arrangement with boroughs across Britain rather than prosecute me for overcrowding. My concern was that he was now so hooked on the publicity he attracted each time he announced another push to close the refuge that he had become a media junkie.

David passed on my request that Lord Goodman attend the meeting, and his huge Bentley duly glided to a stop in front of the refuge. We drove to the massive new building that was now the civic centre in Hounslow. Goodman instructed his chauffeur to ignore the parking signs and to stop within inches of the massive sliding doors leading into the foyer. I watched amused as the horrified flunkeys behind the desk tried to decide whether or not to duck and take cover, but the car stopped just in time, and we alighted. We strode into the hall.

'I'd like you to meet my friends,' I said. 'Alderman King, this is Lord Goodman and David Astor.' For a moment I enjoyed the shock on the councillors' faces.

Jim Duffy was at that meeting, and it was good to see a friendly face. The alderman started waffling. All I had to do, he explained wearily, was to come within the law and I could have anything I liked. Goodman cut him short. A man of King's calibre, he intoned smoothly, should be able to find a resolution to the trifling problem of Chiswick Women's Aid without too much effort. Surely it was just a matter of compromise and diplomacy. Goodman hinted that there might be some political recognition for King if the problem in front of us could somehow be resolved. The alderman duly discovered that he could indeed propose a plan.

I sat and listened to the conversation with disbelief. King promised Goodman he would do everything in his power to see that the refuge was offered sufficient rehousing opportunities for our mothers and children. We could look to his committees to make money available to fill our coffers. With that he stood up to shake Goodman and David by the hand. I followed my committee chairmen with a sinking heart. I had to listen to both of them crowing over their victory. I knew it was rubbish. King wasn't taken in for a minute by Goodman's suggestion of public honours. I imagine he had immense antipathy to both my companions. David would be on his hit list because he was a millionaire and Goodman because he was a millionaire and a 'Labour Party lackey'.

What I didn't tell Goodman or David was that while we were debating the future of the refuge with the council two large caravans were being hauled into the cul-de-sac. Over several years we had travelling families coming into the refuge fleeing violent men. The families found it alien living in a house. Not all of them were used to toilets; we discovered that they were using the sandpit in our garden to relieve themselves. Finally the residents sat down to discuss what we could do to make it possible for the two families to adapt to life within the community. After discussing the matter at length we decided that caravans were our only hope. How I was going to explain this to Goodman I had no idea, but certainly Hounslow Council would take a pretty dim view of the caravans, even if I explained the health hazards of families crapping in the children's sandpit.

The flak didn't immediately come from Hounslow Council but from the belligerent woman who managed the pub on the corner. 'Mrs Pizzey,' she said accosting me in the street, 'I want you to know that you'll never be welcome in my pub!' I was hurt because she had made a good living over the years from the custom of our mothers and staff. I decided that the two families who were to take up residence in the caravans needed chickens to feel at home. I also bought a very large rooster I christened Alderman King. The mothers, children and chickens all settled in happily, and our community congratulated itself on finding a satisfactory solution. Meanwhile I hoped Alderman

King was doing his civic duty and earning his keep by waking the pub landlady each morning at the crack of dawn.

I knew from the research I was doing into violence that there was a very high incidence of it within the travelling communities. Certainly the women who came to stay in our caravans for varying lengths of time recounted horrifying details of physical and sexual violence towards themselves and their children. One of the mothers arrived with over twenty charges of theft, shoplifting and other assorted misdoings hanging over her. The police were still looking for her. After much negotiation and arm-twisting we were able to point out to the police and her probation officer that we had a place for her to stay, she would be supervised and we would work with her. She told me that she had been found at six weeks old hanging in a closet in the family caravan by a neck tie.

One of the other families that settled into our makeshift encampment was Bridget and her seven children. She had never known a life that did not include severe physical and sexual violence. Not all of her sisters and brothers went on to be violent to their partners or their children, but she had chosen a violent lover, and I knew whatever we did or said she would stay with us only for a certain length of time and then she would go back. Gradually she told me details of the abuse she and the children experienced.

Bridget yo-yoed backwards and forwards, but eventually she came in every six months to collect her child benefit, and we welcomed her and her offspring. We were able to ensure that the children were checked over by our doctor and that they went to the dentist. We all worked hard at making secure relationships with the children, and the little cul-de-sac became a second home for the family. Although it concerned us when Bridget went back to her violent partner I had to be realistic. I knew that had I tried to report her partner's violence and sexual abuse she would deny everything and never come to the refuge again.

Our only hope was to influence her as best we could and to offer a vision of a different and better life.

We had more problems when one of our mothers suddenly turned a violent yellow and was diagnosed with hepatitis. She went to the doctor, and the health department swooped down and warned us that she was infectious. Every morning all those in the refuge, including members of staff, had to bring a sample of urine to the housemother to be tested by the health inspector. Within a week or so mothers, staff and children were being hauled off to the local hospital, and a full-scale epidemic was declared.

One morning I came in and to my despair saw a row of ten urine specimens sitting on the desk in the cubby-hole. All the samples were dark yellow. The health inspector collected up a motley assortment of grinning mothers and teenagers, and they were taken off to hospital where the wards were already overflowing with our families. I was increasingly despondent, as I knew that I would be blamed because the spread of hepatitis was caused by overcrowding, and there was no way in the house to isolate anyone.

I was therefore not amused when a few days later all ten of the latest hepatitis 'victims' were delivered back to the refuge in disgrace. They had dipped teabags into their urine hoping to join the fun in hospital with their friends.

One of the long-staying mothers calmed me down by reminding me that I, too, had been guilty of tricking the health department after we had an outbreak of diarrhoea in the house. For days I had struggled with the mothers and the children trying to collect stool samples in time for the health inspectors. Finally we were declared clear of any viruses, but the health inspector insisted that we collect stool specimens for another week. At the time Cleo owned a great dane called Morgan, and I decided to bring in one of his larger offerings and fill the pots with that. My ruse was never discovered, and the health inspector left us alone after that. My friend was right. I regained my sense of humour and welcomed the miscreants back.

No deal was forthcoming from Alderman King after all, and several months after his meeting with Lord Goodman it seemed that he had decided not to keep any of his promises. Thus a date was set for my sentencing.

On 6 October 1977 I put a suitcase in my car and drove to Acton Magistrates' Court. I was horrified to find a gaggle of photographers in front of the court awaiting my arrival. Mothers and children who were former refuge residents had gathered from all over England to be there for the court case, as everyone was concerned that I might be sent to gaol and the Chiswick house would be closed down.

I had prayed frantically most of the night before, and now I was really frightened. All around me was a sea of familiar and much-loved faces. I hated the fact that as frightened as I was it was so much worse for the mothers and children living in the refuge.

The court was packed, but the magistrates did not take long to make their decision.They decided that I should be given a conditional discharge and, provided I turned away mothers and children once we had thirty-six people living in the Chiswick house, I would be safe from the prospect of gaol. To live for so many years with the threat of prison hanging over my head had left me exhausted. All I had wanted was a decision, but it seemed the cat-and-mouse game was not yet over.

I drove back to the refuge with some of the mothers and children. Reporters were outside the house. I walked up the steps to greet a mother and two small children who were standing there waiting for someone to answer the door. 'I have come a long way. Can I come in?' she said. I smiled at her and together we walked inside. I had immediately broken the magistrates' condition.

The journalists asked me what I was going to do now, and all I could say was that there was no way that any one of us would turn a mother and her children in crisis away. I hoped that one day there would be sufficient places in shelters so that this sort of overcrowding would become a thing of the past, but until then we would continue to keep our door open. That night my children were relieved to have me home, and I cried myself to sleep.

'I'm going to write to the Queen,' one of the mothers said.

'There's no point,' I told her. 'The Queen can't interfere in this sort of case.'

I was wrong. A few months later a letter arrived from Buckingham Palace. 'This is not a situation in which Her Majesty the Queen can personally intervene. She has been assured, however, that there is no question of residents . . . being evicted.'

There was a moment's silence when the letter was read out, and we all hugged each other and cheered. Miracles do happen, and as far as I was concerned God answers prayers. I was safe, and now Hounslow would be forced to come up with a sensible and humane solution to the problem of overcrowding in the refuge.

38
AGAINST JUDGE'S ORDERS

I was exhausted after all my fights in court and work at the refuge, and I cheered myself up by daydreaming about the little cottage in Greece and the long holiday to come. But my plans were disrupted when a woman called Glenda arrived at the refuge with her partner and four children. The older children were crying and clinging to her, and her partner John stood silently holding the baby. Glenda explained that she was on the run from a court order to return the eldest three children to her husband, their father. The eldest boy hysterically begged me not to return them to his father. I asked the man to go down to the kitchen with some of the mothers to find the children something to drink and eat.

Britain's family courts have unlimited powers and are virtually self-regulating. During the years I have had dealings with them, although I have encountered the occasional sympathetic and compassionate judge who would put himself out, I have generally found their effect on the lives of parents and children devastating. The judges tend to fail to read the evidence in detail and carelessly rely on that supplied by social services, probation officers and solicitors. I listened to what Glenda had to say and dreaded getting involved.

The story she told was unusual in that, given her husband's background, I found it hard to believe that any judge would consider putting three small children into his care. Glenda's fourth child, the baby, belonged to her new partner John.

Brian, Glenda's husband, had been put into care when he was a child. She told me that his mother was a prostitute who had abandoned him to his father who sodomized him. Eventually he was put into a care home where he killed a boy for refusing his homosexual advances. It was a chilling story. After he strangled the boy with his belt he went into the dining-room and ate a meal. This showed such a disassociated lack of remorse that I could not risk putting him in a position where he might kill again

Brian was put into a remand centre for young boys and later finished his sentence in an adult prison. Here he was mentored and encouraged to finish his studies and came out a plausible and entirely reformed character, or so his probation officer believed.

Brian met Glenda when she was sixteen. She was soon completely dominated and bullied by him. He was violent when he was crossed and beat her, and he was violent towards the children. Glenda went to social services for help, but her husband was adept at manipulating official agencies, and he was very charming and articulate – all things that his wife was not.

After several years on the social services books, with repeated attempts made at rehabilitating the family, Glenda finally made a decision to leave Brian and start a new life with John. Brian called in social services and demanded that he be given custody of the children when Glenda refused to return to him and said she wanted a divorce.

Social services decided to support Brian, even though by then there was a long list of alleged incidents of violence towards Glenda as well as the report of a probation officer who said she witnessed him throwing the eldest boy against a wall in her office. Glenda, John and the children failed to turn up at the court for the custody hearing because Glenda was afraid that the children would be handed over to her husband. Instead they took a train and made their way to the refuge. It turned out that the judge made an order for return and put out a warrant for her arrest. I knew Brian and the police would be scouring the country for her.

I needed to get Glenda to see our solicitor Alured Darlington, and I also needed to be able to hide her where she couldn't be found. Given her story, I could not see the children returned to Brian. I needed time to check out the facts and work out a plan of action. I moved the family into a place of safety and consulted Tina. Glenda's information proved correct, and within a few days there was a knock on the front door early one evening. It was Brian with his solicitor. I told him I had no idea where his wife was, and he went away. I could see why he fooled people. He wore a smart suit, and he seemed a plausible, attractive man.

I discussed the case with Alured and told him that Glenda and her family were now in hiding and that I was demanding a retrial at the High Court in the Strand. Alured appointed a barrister, and they went off to the High Court. I could see that that the family court was in a cleft stick. If they refused a retrial they knew they would have to arrest me for contempt of court. This would attract a huge amount of unwanted publicity. Their only recourse was to agree to a retrial on a point of law, so the request was granted.

Until the court case Glenda, John and the children lived in the Bristol house. There the mothers took them in and made them welcome. They were safe because until a decision was made by the court Brian could not intrude upon the family. Moreover, no one knew where they were until the official solicitor involved in the case was invited to visit the family in Bristol to prepare his report for the court. I was not impressed. He seemed poorly qualified to handle delicate domestic cases, and he soon made it clear that he was unimpressed with my attempts to help the mother thwart the law. I was enraged, as by this time Alured had recorded two hundred counts of violence and abuse committed by Brian. I wondered whether the solicitor had ever bothered to read the file where he would have seen that, quite apart from the domestic violence, Brian very rarely held down a job for any length of time and had a record for petty crime and thieving – unlike Glenda who had no police record at all.

The trial was to last ten days, and Glenda and John came up to London for it while the children stayed in Bristol. The husband was supported by a gaggle of social workers and his probation officer from Leeds. Tina and I sat with Glenda, and we had to endure hostile stares as Brian's supporters scurried in and out of the court to assure the judge that he was indeed a reformed character. Set against Brian's suave, polished performance, Glenda appeared diffident and downtrodden. The night before the judge's decision I was asked by the official solicitor to make sure the children would be in court the next day. I knew then for sure that Glenda would lose her children.

I took John and Glenda back to my home, and we spent several hours hatching a plan. That night her children were brought to my home, and the community was told that the family would be staying the night in the flat at the top of the Playhouse in the cul-de-sac. I decided to create a red herring to placate the judge. As a favour I asked Tina and two other members of staff involved in the case to pool whatever cash we had in our pockets. We handed this over to Glenda; there was just under £100 in total. The couple returned to the Playhouse, and early the following morning one of the mothers collected the family and left with them for Ireland, where in those days there was no extradition arrangement with the United Kingdom. Apart from the £100 for travel expenses, I gave Glenda £1,000 of my own money to start a new life with John and the children there.

After everyone left my house I sat by myself in the sitting-room and cried. I realized I wasn't crying for Glenda and her family – she was safe and surrounded by people who cared about her – I was crying for Brian. Even though I knew he was a danger to his children I knew that as far as he was able he did love them. Thousands of pounds had been spent on incarcerating him in prison, but, like most institutions, they tended to the needs of his body but failed to touch his soul.

Ann and the rest of the staff and mothers had no idea of the whereabouts of Glenda and her family. All they knew was that Tina and the two staff members in on the plan had arrived that morning asking if anyone had seen Glenda, John and the children, who were no longer inside the Playhouse. The four of us went off to the High Court and waited outside while our barrister told the judge that the family had disappeared. After a while I was called into the court. I was handed a Bible, and I knew I was going to commit perjury. The alternative was to have allowed Glenda's children to go back to a man with a track record of violence towards them and a temper that made him dangerous in any stressful situation. There was no way I could be party to handing them over to him and sleep at night.

I took my place on the stand, and the judge smiled benignly down at me. Brian's barrister cross-examined me, and I explained that I had taken Glenda and her new partner John to my house the night before and warned them not to do anything rash. I had asked Tina and the other two members of staff to give some money to the couple so that they could buy a meal, smarten themselves up and prepare themselves for the hearing. The judge asked how much we'd given them, and I said around a hundred pounds. He knew that with that sort of sum Glenda and her family couldn't get very far. I silently prayed as I was examined that my arrangements in Ireland were going smoothly. I had to pretend to be shocked by Glenda's disappearance. My act was so good the judge kindly offered me a chair so that I could sit down and ordered that I should be given a glass of water. As I came off the stand our barrister whispered, 'Excellent performance!' In fact, it was not entirely an act. I had been absolutely terrified of the consequences of my actions.

Tina and the other two members of staff were sworn in, and they duly backed up my account. The judge decided to suspend the hearing until the family could be found, and photographs of Glenda and the children were given to the press. We returned home, and later that night I received an oblique message from the mother who had accompanied the family that they were all safe and she was on her way back. Now it was going to be a game of cat-and-mouse. We hoped Glenda was tucked away somewhere in the Irish countryside beginning her new life with John and the children. Meanwhile the all-powerful family court was left with its case in suspension.

A few weeks later, just as I was getting used to sleeping through the night undisturbed by nightmares of policemen banging on the front door, I got a telephone call from my solicitor John Roberts at Goodman Derrick. Up till this point he had been very patient, even though he had been frankly appalled when I refused to take his advice and return the children to Leeds Social Services. Now he warned me that Brian and his lawyers were going in front of the judge to ask that I and the three refuge staff be hauled into court and questioned once more. I really did not want to lie under oath a second time, so I gathered Tina and the other two members of staff together to discuss the matter in private. Tina decided that a visit to her parents in South Africa was overdue. She booked her ticket within the hour and was gone the next day.

I decided the rest of us should leave the country as well. I knew from my dealings with the family courts that they might put an alert out at the ports and airports, so I raced home, threw camping gear and some clothes into my car, kissed the children goodbye, collected the other two members of staff and made for Portsmouth where we caught the first available ferry to France. I didn't breathe until we were off the boat. The story Ann was to tell the court was that as far as she knew I was heading to Spain to see my new editor about the Spanish publication of *Scream Quietly or the Neighbours Will Hear*.

Joshua and Duane, the two members of staff concerned, were to share the driving on our trip. No one else was to know where we were or where we were actually going.

I knew that the High Court would probably ask Interpol to look out for us, so once we reached France we camped only on unofficial sites. There were no amenities or proper washing facilities, but we felt safe. I hoped that I could keep out of the way until the furore subsided. We took a leisurely drive through the French countryside and cooked meals on the camping gas stove or ate in inexpensive cafés. The cost of the trip came out of my own bank account, because the decision I made to disobey the court was a personal one and had nothing to do with Chiswick Women's Aid. I knew that it was paramount to protect the refuge from the consequences of my actions.

We took our time on the drive and I think all of us felt a great sense of relief now that we were away from England. I was enormously grateful to Joshua and Duane, the two young men who were risking their freedom to defend Glenda's family. Every evening I would telephone Ann from public phones to hear news from the refuge. So far our failure to appear in court had had no obvious repercussion on any of the staff in the refuge. I was afraid that they might be called in and questioned under oath. I also telephoned Cleo to see how she was and get news of the children. During one call she said, 'Guess what, Mum. I'm pregnant!'

I was horrified but asked if she was happy to have another baby. She said she was as surprised as I but didn't want an abortion. She was, however, still only seventeen, and I knew that having another baby so soon would be a strain for her emotionally and physically – as well as being another mouth to feed. I told her I was happy to support her in her decision, and I was genuinely relieved that she had decided to keep the child. At Chartres Cathedral I lit a candle for my grandchild-to-be in front of the Black Madonna.

One night we were staying in a hotel because we were exhausted with the travelling and the camping. We mostly washed in the toilets of petrol stations, but we were all desperate for a hot bath. I phoned Ann and Cleo. Not long after the telephone in my room rang. It was David in a towering rage. This was the first time he had ever raised his voice to me. 'If I'd known', he screamed down the phone, 'how totally irresponsible you are I'd have never taken you on!'

I assumed he was talking about my disappearance, but he wasn't.

Four weeks before we left England I had been asked to a GLC conference to discuss housing issues. I knew Goodman and David were making approaches to the GLC concerning our overcrowding, so as much as I hated conferences I decided to take Mike Dunne with me. We sat through the long, boring discussions and self-congratulatory speeches from other housing agencies and then one of the GLC officials got up to speak.

He said he was going to talk about Paddy O'Connor – my friend who had surreptitiously given us so many GLC houses. I had been very fond of him, although I hadn't seen him for a while. I then discovered that he had died. I also heard that day that he had previously been suspended from his job for supposed 'financial irregularities'. I was devastated by the news.

The official who made the speech about Paddy went on to give a sanctimonious eulogy that would have caused Paddy to puke in his grave. The man he described wasn't the Rabelaisian hard-drinking, foul-mouthed person I had known and loved.

I was so upset that I found myself standing up and telling the assembled company that, for all Paddy's faults, he had not been a thief. I told them that I was outraged that he had been accused of 'financial irregularities' and suspended. I said I suspected that the accusation covered the real reason for throwing him out – that he had overstayed his welcome as the token reformed dosser and that his colleagues were embarrassed by his drinking and wanted him gone. I went on to say that, as far as I was concerned, the GLC had contributed to his death. Well knowing that he was an alcoholic, they had furnished him with a well-stocked bar in his office.

There was a stunned silence and a stuttering, defensive denial from the GLC official.

Mike and I stomped out of the meeting shortly afterwards and went off to a pub to raise a glass to our old friend.

I phoned Paddy's sister shortly before I left the country, and she comforted me by saying, 'Well, at least he died with a drink upright in his hand!'

In my French hotel I was bewildered that David seemed entirely uninterested in what was happening to us in our exile but outraged that I had upset the GLC by my outburst. This was all he wished to talk about. I told him I didn't want to discuss it but that somebody had to defend Paddy – and with that I put down the phone.

We reached Barcelona and made our way to the offices of my Spanish publisher. She greeted us warmly but told us she had received a telephone call that morning to say I was to call Goodman and handed me his phone number. I knew something bad must have happened for Goodman to ask me to phone him, and when I rang him he said that Glenda was back in England, the children were in the care of Leeds City Council, and I should return home. His voice was cold and peremptory. He offered no details, and I didn't ask. I finished my discussion with my editor. She was concerned because members of the Spanish feminist movement were already warning her that they didn't want the book published there, but I was too upset to care. I just needed to get home.

39

CHISWICK CHILDREN GO TO GREECE

Once I was back at home with the children and the animals I felt more secure. Whatever else was going to happen I was comforted to find that Cleo and Mikey had accepted the new pregnancy and were making sensible plans for the baby. It would be a little less than two years since the birth of Keita. The baby was due in January 1979.

I also had to find time in February that year to go to court again with Jack to finalize our divorce. I felt sorry for the judge. He had the most ill-fitting set of false teeth I'd ever seen, and once I began to describe our extraordinary family set-up his dentures nearly fell out altogether. Jack was so nervous I had to hold his hand, which prompted the judge to ask us if we really wanted to split up. I had a bottle of champagne ready on ice to mark the divorce, but neither of us felt like drinking it. There was nothing to celebrate. After seventeen years of marriage, we had failed.

As soon as I could I went down to the refuge to talk to Mike and Ann and find out why Glenda had returned unexpectedly to England. They had been tucked away on a farm, and the children had seemed happy and settled. Mike had been over to see them while I was away and had reported that everything was going well and that she wanted to make a new life for herself and the family in Ireland.

Mike told me that while I was abroad John had come back to England ostensibly to visit his elderly father; in fact, he had approached the *News of the World* tabloid daily to sell his story, and they had duly published it. He returned to Ireland and collected the family and took them to Dublin Women's Aid where he felt they could be protected. Soon Glenda developed jaundice and was taken to hospital. The local social services discussed the possibility of temporary foster-care for her offspring, as its staff intended to respect her wish to keep her family in Ireland.

Her husband Brian meanwhile demanded access to his children, now that he knew their whereabouts, and social services arranged for him to have supervised access. He arrived from Leeds together with a reporter from the *Yorkshire Post*. As the young social worker supervising their reunion was standing on the pavement with the children saying goodbye to their father, Brian suddenly snatched his four-year-old daughter, jumped into the car with the reporter, and the two of them drove off. They crossed the border into Northern Ireland – back to where the the English courts could get to them. Glenda was notified that her daughter had been snatched. She discharged herself from hospital, and a case conference was called. She knew then that she would have to go back to England with the two boys and agreed that they should be returned to Leeds Social Services and put into care.

Tina was still in South Africa. We discussed the latest turn of events. The three of us were potentially vulnerable to the consequences of our testimony at the High Court. We decided that, since it was the summer holidays, the best course of action was that we should take off with the children to Zakinthos as previously planned. For the time being Glenda's children would not be returned to their father, and both parents could see their children in the care home in Leeds – the snatched daughter was now there, too. For the four of us who had been involved in Glenda's disappearance it would be a matter of setting a new date to determine our part in misleading the court.

I flew out to the Greek island a few days before the van was due to arrive with the staff and twelve of the children. It took me almost two full days in the little cottage to stop shaking and crying. I stood at the end of the dusty road that led to the family taverna one evening as the sun was setting. The white van came into view, and I could spot some of the children leaning perilously out of the windows. They jumped out of the vehicle. Amos looked happy and dishevelled, and I gave him a big hug. The Greek family had helped me prepare their old potato field for the tents, and we dug latrines at the back of the site.

The staff were exhausted. Joshua and the others described their hair-raising ferry journey from Dover to Calais. A volatile and difficult boy called Tony had gone out on deck where he had spent most of the crossing hanging over the side of the boat threatening to jump. The other children had enthusiastically encouraged him in this, shouting 'Jump! Jump! Jump!' over and over, while the staff tried to reason with him and haul him back inside. Finally they succeeded. What they all needed now was to finish setting up camp, then come up to the taverna for a relaxing drink and a welcome dinner.

Mama Gina provided an enormous Greek feast. The children tucked into skewers of lamb cooked over charcoal, plates of macaroni cheese, a huge fish lying on a bed of rice and big crisp green salads with shining slabs of white feta cheese. They were too ravenous to be difficult about what they ate, and I sat at one of the tables and heaved a sigh of relief. Until the High Court determined my fate I was safe. The children smiled, excited and content. I looked at their cheerful faces smudged with lamp oil and decided, whatever happened in London, the next few weeks would be happy ones.

I had Trevor and Russ with me, who had the most experience of dealing with children in the refuge. Another volunteer, Steve, was there, too, with his girlfriend. The boys responded particularly well to Russ because they regarded him as 'hard'. He had been in prison and was covered with scars, but they knew that he lived with my family in our home and was a reformed character. Trevor had a brilliantly devious mind, and none of the children could outsmart him. He was also good at making them laugh. His sense of humour came in especially useful during the first few days when the staff had to stand back while the children refused to use the latrines and clean up after themselves.

Trev and Russ knew I was keen that the children learn from their experiences. This principle was a hard one for most of the staff to accept, because the idea that you should leave children to sleep in their stinking tents after they had crapped and peed in them rather than use the latrines was anathema. I felt it was vital that the children learned to cooperate with one another and us over hygiene and similar basic issues. Within a day or two there were large rats running around the tents. Before long the children decided they had enough. They cleaned up themselves and their accommodation and agreed to use the designated latrines.

I was delighted when the boy Tony, within a few days, decided to wait on tables at the taverna. That was the first of my miracles. I never expected much from him. At the refuge he was almost always at the bottom of any trouble, fighting, lying or thieving – and here he was rushing about from table to table putting out bread and cutlery.

Mama Gina took a particular shine to him. She would pat his head, pinch his cheeks and croon over him. 'Good boy!' she said, beaming. 'You, Tony, good boy.' He blossomed.

Liam, another of the more deviant boys, with a history of break-ing into cars, stood in the warm blue Greek sea on the fourth day we were there and screamed at the sky, 'I can't stand the peace!' I was upset for him, but I empathized with his agony and confusion. All the distractions he could create in the middle of a large city like London and among a big crowd of people had evaporated.

For the twelve children there was nothing to distract them and nowhere to hide from themselves. The empty headland stretched for miles. There were a few German tourists camping in the surrounding fields and a few neighbouring cottages – but that was it. Our life centred on the the headland with the beach and the taverna with its peacocks, goats, hens and geese. Most of the day was spent in the sea, lying on the beach and preparing meals and cleaning the camp. On special nights we all ate at the taverna, and gradually during the four weeks we were out there the children calmed down.

The holiday enabled me to really get to know the individual children. Amos was particularly close to Liam, and they would go off off together to fish with members of the Greek family from the taverna. Before long some of the local fishermen with boats encouraged the other children to go fishing, too, and in the evenings we would cook their catches over the camp fire. After lunch I went to the little cottage, and the children knew they were welcome to come and talk to me if they had any concerns. It was there, stretched out on the bed, that Liam confided in me the cause of his regular bouts of constipation.

From time to time his mother had informed me that he needed to go to hospital because of his 'stomach' – it was some mysterious ailment that I never really understood. She assured me it was a long-term condition and that Liam had been treated for it over a number of years. Now in Greece he told me that his mother had, for as long as he could remember, made his two brothers hold him down while she pushed suppositories up his anus. 'It's them that's making me constipated,' he explained. He was, of course, right, and I knew I'd have to tackle his very belligerent mother when I got back. By now I'd had some experience of women who molested their children.

Sometimes their perverse tendencies were disguised as virtuous actions in the care of their children. No one believed that women could be paedophiles. I was aware that they could, but the usual blanket of silence and denial descended if I tried to discuss the subject. In Liam's case something was plainly going on that would need to be dealt with.

Towards the end of the month we decided to have supper and spend the night out in the open on the best beach on the island that was known to us as Horseshoe Bay. We made a huge fire to cook our supper, and while our group sat cross-legged round it with our sausages and baked potatoes we heard voices from the sea. It was a dark night with very few stars, and I saw the children stiffen with anxiety. In their world strangers meant danger. Before long we heard the sound of boats being hauled up on to the beach. We were joined by a large group of Greek fishermen carrying their suppers and skins of wine. They joined us round the fire and began to cook their catch of fish on our embers. They had with them big fat juicy olives and fresh flat loaves, and soon all of us were sharing their meal. After that the men sang far into the night for us before heading off to their beds. Eventually the rest of us fell into a happy sleep on the warm white sand.

In the first two weeks there were times when the children were restless and even explosive in their behaviour. I knew they usually resolved their tensions back home by fighting one another or going off to find something illicit to do. Camp rules forbade fighting. The sanction was to be denied a place at the dinner table in the taverna – and for all the children our taverna nights were a much sought-after treat. If I felt some of them needed a bit of extra excitement and hazard I would create it by telling them to climb on top of the big white van. I would then drive up and down the hills around the camp site. The children clung on like limpets and finally, when we came to a halt, the children jumped down and harmony was restored.

The only major untoward incident occurred one Saturday morning when a street market was taking place near my cottage, and the children went off with their pocket money to buy presents for their families back home. All of a sudden I heard a commotion. I went out to find out what was going on and saw two of the girls, Belinda and Sinead, standing next to a huge and angry-looking stall-holder. A crowd had gathered, and I spotted Mama Gina arguing volubly with the man. Philip, Sinead's brother, was glaring at his sister. Several members of the refuge staff stood around looking bewildered, but I could see that the man was holding several items from his stall, and I knew that Sinead was a persistent shoplifter.

Mama Gina saw me and explained that the girls had stolen the items from the man. He demonstrated how he had turned out their pockets and found them. I stared at the girls. Back in London they normally acted unconcerned when escorted back to the refuge by the police. They could afford to be brazen back home because they knew that since they were under age nothing much would happen – if necessary the shop would write off the stolen goods and collect the insurance.

The crowd was growing more and more vociferous. Mama Gina was in tears of embarrassment. She loved all our children dearly, and now she had been humiliated in front of her friends and neighbours. The girls tried appealing to me with feeble excuses, but I shook my head. 'You stole from the people on this island,' I said.

Back at the camp site the other children made it clear to the culprits that they, too, felt embarrassed. I talked to the girls that evening on their own in the cottage. The three of us didn't go to the taverna that night.

I knew that in many of the violence-prone families shoplifting was the job daughters were groomed to do from a very early age. From babyhood their prams were often stuffed with items stolen from shops. At the refuge I often found girls with stolen goods in their possession. I would take the girls and the items back to the shops concerned and make the children apologize to staff and management. Many of the girls were encouraged by their mothers to steal, so it was not always easy to get them to acknowledge that stealing was a shameful as well as a criminal activity that could get them in trouble.

Once they appreciated the gravity of their offence Belinda and Sinead were contrite that they had upset Mama Gina, as, like all the other children, they appreciated her warmth and concern for them all. They decided to spend the rest of the evening making a card to say 'Sorry' to her. I was glad about this. They understood that what they had done was wrong – and that was a big step in their understanding that this society was very different from the one they had come from.

Many of the boys who arrived at the refuge were involved in criminal activities, too. Bones got his nickname from his skeletal frame. He was tiny for his age, and, chatting to him one day, I asked him what he wanted to do with his life. 'Be a jewel thief like my dad,' he said without hesitation. Bank robbers and jewel thieves were regarded as at the top of the career ladder in Bones's world. He told me that he had been thieving with his father from a very early age. He was small enough to get through tiny windows in the big houses that were his dad's speciality. I hugged him that day and said I hoped he would think about his dad's life in and out of prison and bear in mind how little he had seen of his father as he grew up. Bones was eventually rehoused with his family. Some years later, one dark and gloomy winter's day, I was sitting in the cubby-hole answering desperate letters when I looked up and saw a tall young man in a military uniform in the doorway. Bones had joined the army, and he was on his way to his first posting in Germany.

We only had a few days left on Zakinthos, but that summer the children had come a long way. On the last morning before the camping gear was loaded into the van we had one last swim. I was treading water watching the staff organizing a diving competition off a big rock overhanging the sea. Without being asked, the children formed an orderly queue and waited their turn to jump or dive off the rock. To anyone else watching this would have looked like a normal bunch of kids being supervised by playleaders, but to me it was a miracle. Six weeks earlier the children would have fought and pushed and shoved each other into the sea. That they now waited patiently for their turn and cooperated with one another was an immense step forward. The sight thrilled me.

I kissed Amos goodbye. He chose to drive back with his friends, and I hoped that for all the children the experiences they had had on Zakinthos would stay with them for the rest of their days. Some of them, I knew, would end up in prison or in violent relationships like those of their parents, but I hoped that, whatever happened to them in later life, in their hearts they would always remember the beautiful warm sea, the hot sun, the clear blue skies and the laughter and friendship they found on that Ionian island.

40
CONTEMPT OF COURT

When we got back I was summoned by the Attorney General to the High Court to appear in front of Dame Rose Heilbron who was going to sentence me. I was accused of contempt of court because I had lied under oath – and, of course, I was guilty. At this time I was having difficulty sleeping, and I had frequent nightmares. I knew some of the strain was from the court cases that had hung over my head like dark, threatening clouds for years, but I also had a bizarre impression that my head was full of cotton wool being slowly torn apart. It was a strange sensation and not one that I could put into words. I found myself uttering meaningless sentences. One day I was talking to Tina about things we needed to do, and I heard myself say, 'We must open the garden gate.' I noted the look of surprise on her face, and I gathered my thoughts and corrected myself. 'Sorry, I mean we need to go into the main room and open the post.'

Some of the strain I was under was provoked by the dramatic deterioration in my relationship with David. He called me to his house in St John's Wood a few days after I came back from Greece. Once I was alone in the sitting-room he closed the door, pushed me quite roughly into a chair and said angrily, 'Don't you ever do anything so stupid again! Hiding people against a judge's orders was a crazy thing to do!' His fury and the fact that he pushed me came as such a shock that it took a moment or two to follow what he was saying. He was going on about my 'dark side' and my subconscious and other aspects of my personality I couldn't even follow. He seemed to be suggesting that I was mad and in need of psychoanalysis.

By now I was used to the fact that David expected me to make myself available whenever he wanted to talk to me. On one occasion I was having a picnic with the children on the grass outside the Blue Anchor pub by Hammersmith Bridge. It was late evening, and I saw Tina running across the grass. She was out of breath by the time she

266

reached me. 'David wants to speak to you at once!' she said. Apparently he had tried my house and failed to get hold of me. He phoned everyone who worked for the refuge, and no one knew my whereabouts. He then went down in person to the refuge in Chiswick, but no one recognized him. He wasn't allowed in, and, frustrated beyond belief, he found a telephone box and rang Tina, reversing the charges because he had no money on him. Tina guessed I might be at the pub. To this day I have no idea why he was so anxious to get hold of me. At the time it seemed as though he just wanted me to be at his beck and call.

One of David's favourite places to take me to lunch was the Gay Hussar in Soho, a Hungarian restaurant where its wonderfully eccentric proprietor Victor presided over his guests like a benevolent headmaster. This was where Frank Longford would join us in his attempts to persuade me join his campaign to have Myra Hindley released from prison. She had been incarcerated for life in a secure mental hospital for participating in the horrific killing of several small children. Not only was she party to the terrible events; she had taped the children crying while they were tortured. I was outraged. 'How do you think the children's parents would feel if she were let out?' I once asked.

'They might be a little hysterical,' he said tucking into duck with cherries.

'Hysterical, Frank?' I said. 'If I were them I'd fucking shoot her and then you!'

As a member of the House of Lords Frank could visit any prisoner he liked, and if I were to end up in gaol I could imagine him renewing his efforts on Hindley's behalf while I remained incarcerated in my cell.

One weekend, when I was at Sutton Courtenay with my children, David mentioned that it was his wife's birthday. I was horrified. I bundled him into my car and drove him back to St John's Wood and deposited him on his doorstep. It seemed crazy that he should spend so much time entertaining friends but miss his wife's birthday. I never actually saw her. She was a shadowy figure in his life, as far as I was concerned.

He arranged another big lunch with a very senior member of the police force. The man took great delight in explaining jovially how he instructed his officers to throw marbles under the feet of the police horses restraining demonstrators so that they slipped and fell down. He said this was a good tactic to turn television viewers against the demonstrators.

I decided I had had enough. It was not only the unnecessary lunches but also the fact that I noticed that the hardboiled journalists who dined at the Gay Hussar looked at me with curiosity as though I were David's mistress, and I was not at all comfortable about this. I telephoned David's secretary and told her that in future I would prefer his wife Bridget to be present as well at any public occasion I attended with him. The invitations rapidly dried up.

I was not bothered. My house was full of teenagers, so I didn't want for company at home. Cleo had inherited my mother's talent for throwing parties, and when she lived in the basement with Mikey rock music would pulse through the floorboards drowning out my beloved Mozart quartets. By the end of the decade Amos and Darren would be out every night night lugging their record collections and decks to nightclubs where they played to ecstatic audiences. Meanwhile Mikey was busy putting together the band that would become Culture Club. Sometimes Boy George would drop in to eat with us, while Cass spent most of his waking hours playing bass guitar. All the teenagers were involved in music one way or another. I would come home from the refuge and cook evening meals and we would all sit together round the table and discussed the day's events. Russ and Trevor acted as unofficial house prefects; they saw to it that the house was clean and that the washing-up was done every night. To any visitors that dropped in it looked like a circus, but it was a very comfortable, creative and thriving community of young people.

I found a barrister to represent me for the High Court trial after I was asked by David Jacobs to sit for a second time on his panel for *Any Questions?* This is a well-known BBC radio programme, and I had very much enjoyed responding to the wide range of questions that came from the audience. This time John Mortimer was also on the panel. He was a well-known writer and barrister, famous for winning his cases. After a very boozy dinner that took place before the recording, which he attended with his new and very pretty wife, I got up the courage to ask if he would take me on as his client, and he agreed. I went to bed that night much comforted.

The charming, kindly man whom I had met on this occasion had completely disappeared by the time of my one and only interview with him before the case was to be heard. Mortimer produced a list of demands for me to sign. The first three were trivial, but the final was that I would never again disobey the court. I felt I couldn't sign the document and began to explain why. He immediately lost his temper and started shouting at me. I was astonished, but there was nothing I could do. I knew that where I had a conflict between the wishes of the state or my conscience my conscience would win out. I refused to sign the document, and I faced a furious barrister.

During my time in the refuge I had disobeyed all sorts of court orders, and by now I held the courts in contempt because I fundamentally believed that a court of law was the wrong place to make judgements on the very fragile, delicate and complex matter of human relationships. The law is dispassionate and rational; human relationships are neither. I would continue to follow my conscience, and even John Mortimer's anger would not make me sign a statement that I knew would compromise my beliefs.

One of the documents that Mortimer showed me was a transcript of my evidence given to the official solicitor when he interviewed me about Glenda and the children. I read the first few pages of the transcript and I was puzzled. 'This isn't what I said.' I looked at Mortimer's thunderous face. He brushed this off and continued to bully me to sign his piece of paper. I had always suspected that the family court was incompetent if not corrupt, and before me was the evidence. Many of my words had plainly been altered – there was nothing I could do. I felt as helpless as mothers and fathers must feel when the system closes ranks. The oppressive secrecy of our courts makes it impossible for justice to prevail.

The night before the trial Tina, Joshua and Duane had dinner with me. We joked about the situation, but I had my bag already packed, and I was pretty certain that I was going to gaol. Cleo and Amos were concerned for me, but at least I knew that the older boys would take care of Amos, and, of course, Mikey was there to support Cleo and their children.

Amber, their daughter, had shot into the world in January 1979 after a very short labour. She was a stocky, burly infant with huge black eyes and enormous will. Her brother Keita, not quite two, was not best pleased when she was born, and we had to keep a wary eye on him as he spent a lot of his time stalking her and trying to shoot her with a toy gun. Eventually he got used to having her around, and the siblings became the best of friends.

Keita was a very fragile and emotionally delicate toddler. He loved to draw and paint and had a vivid imagination. I felt very protective towards him because he seemed not firmly anchored to this earth. He was often ill with colds and coughs and a wheezy chest. Amber was totally different physically and emotionally. She was born to command, and if she was crossed she could throw a tantrum that occasionally left her blue in the face and out cold on the floor.

I was deeply upset at the possibility of being separated from my family because I had no idea about the length of the sentence if the Attorney General decided on a custodial sentence.

When I walked into court the morning of 17 June 1979 the press bench was packed with journalists looking remarkably cheerful. I saw the usual two grey-suited women officers from Holloway Prison sitting at the back of the court, and I slid along one of the front benches. We all stood up as Dame Rose Heilbron came into the court and glowered down at me. The first thing she did was to tell the press to leave the court. There was to be no public discussion about the case. I was unhappy about this. My one hope had been that journalists would be able to report the failures of Leeds Social Services and its probation officers, but now the press was effectively muzzled by the draconian rules of the family court. I stood up and declared loudly that if the press was leaving so was I. My barrister galloped after me as I sailed up the aisle towards the door. He grabbed my arm and hissed at me. The judge said something inaudible, and I saw the press returning to their box. I returned to the bench.

The court settled down, and Mortimer rose to his feet. I heard him intone, 'As the prison gates clang behind my client . . .' Suddenly the prospect of incarceration felt very real, and I clutched my cross and mentally said my prayers.

I zoned out of the proceedings around that point until I came round to discover that I was, in fact, not going to go to gaol. Instead I was found guilty and fined £1,000. Only if I were unable to pay was I faced with a nine months' prison sentence.

I left the court deeply relieved but very angry that I should have been found guilty at all. As far as I was concerned, there were extenuating circumstances. Had the judge bothered to read Brian's history I didn't believe he would have considered handing over the children to such a volatile and violent man. The trial Glenda had been granted was a show trial. The judge had no intention of overturning the Leeds judge's order, which is possibly why he appeared to have made no attempt to acquaint himself with the facts of the case.

I was further incensed the day after my own hearing to find that while the judge allowed the press back into the court the gagging order was still in place, so none of the details of the case ever reached the public.

I knew that Glenda was visiting the children in the children's home and so was Brian. I felt devastated that the children were now separated from their mother. I had promised the children they would not go back to their dangerous father, and now my one comfort was that he did not have them in his care.

I was soon due to leave London for a 22-city lecture tour in the United States, but I promised Glenda that I would give her a telephone number through which she could contact me in an emergency.

Physically and mentally I was a wreck. My blood pressure was rocketing, and at times I was finding it difficult to follow what people were saying. I was terribly tired, and my feet felt as though they were shod in iron. I knew I ought not to go on this tour, but I needed the money. I had had a great number of heavy expenses. For one, the barrister's fee for representing me was three thousand guineas.

Jill Tweedie contacted me, and she was rallying all her friends to contribute to my fine and help me pay Mortimer's fee. I was immensely touched.

I hoped that the lecture tour might give me a break. I felt like running away from everything. David was becoming increasingly controlling. Some nights he drove down to my house to push letters through my front door accusing me of ingratitude and bewildering me with references to my inner 'wild child'. I didn't see myself as a wild child, although I did regard my life as out of control. And I couldn't pay my bills. In desperation I spent nights stapling cheques to the constant demands for payment – the cheques would have to be sent back because the staples ruined the machines for cashing the cheques. I would also deliberately put the wrong date or didn't sign the cheques – all in an attempt to buy time.

It seemed the time was approaching when Goodman would achieve what I always felt he had wanted to do. One way or other, he would shift me from my position at the refuge. I felt everything was closing in on me. I had wild dreams and would wake up confused and frightened.

Running away to the United States seemed like a good option just then, and I was glad to get on the plane with a colleague and begin the long journey across North America.

41
RUNNING ROUND THE BEND

Once my feet touched the ground in Chicago the nightmares of the past few months seemed to recede. I was introduced to the officers from the Salvation Army, which had funded the trip, and was delighted to have lunch with them to discuss in detail all the arrangements. Alaska was one of the first places I was heading to, and all I knew about the place was that it was likely to be frozen and icebound. At the other extreme I was to lecture in Jackson, Mississippi, and I knew nothing of that part of the United States, but I was an avid reader of Tennessee Williams, and I was curious to see the Deep South after desegregation.

Flying into Alaska in 1979 I stared out of the plane window at the thousands of miles of bright white tundra that lay below me. There are moments in my life when God's magnificence leaves me breathless. When the plane landed I steeled myself for icy blasts of wind, but as I stepped out on to the tarmac I inhaled deeply and was amazed that the air felt like breathing champagne. The sun was directly hot on my back, and the welcoming committee was composed of a ragbag of individuals dressed as though they had just finished baking, ploughing or working on a farm. This was a welcome change from the hippy-dippy dirndl-skirted sisterhood, the boiler-suited separatist feminists or the grim shoulder-padded executives who usually made up the welcome posse.

We were taken to a huge wooden building where I began my lecture. Before long I was interrupted by a loud thump. I paused for a moment to see a perfectly shod artificial leg lying on the floor. The owner beamed at me. 'Sorry about that,' she said, and her partner scooped up the limb and left to return later with a more reliable appendage. That night we were taken off to the local refuge and met a cross-section of women and their families. The place had a lovely warm, caring atmosphere. The mothers explained that many of

their partners came to Alaska because they had violent and dangerous pasts. Alaska asks no questions. It is a vast state, and most
people eke out a living farming or fishing. Many of these women
had found themselves in violent relationships because they didn't
really know who they were getting involved with. With the men's
history erased so easily, it was also a haven for paedophiles.

That night we stayed in the one big hotel in Anchorage. I was
amused to find the telephone book nailed by a piece of string on to
my side table. To my surprise I found I liked Anchorage and the all
the people I met. It seemed without the 'effluence of affluence' I had
seen elsewhere in the United States. I said my goodbyes with regret,
and we continued on our tour.

I knew as we travelled by bus, train and plane that I was not well.
I struggled to concentrate, and often when I was speaking to an
audience my mind seemed to detach itself from my body. This
disinterested part of me watched my physical self standing on the
stage gesticulating at people in front of me, my mouth forming
words that had no longer any meaning. I was very frightened. There
were, of course, moments of sanity and lucidity, usually when I saw
or experienced something that lifted me out of myself and my preoccupations.

Louisville in Kentucky had a shelter on the top floor of an old
youth hostel. It was run by a mixed group of women supported by
their husbands. They gave us lunch on an old paddle-steamer tethered
to the river bank. The sun shone, and I felt secure and content.

I felt distinctly unsafe when we reached Jacksonville, Mississippi,
however. We came off the plane and were escorted to another large
hall where I stood in front of a sea of white faces. 'Why aren't there
any black women in the audience,' I asked my host. She shifted
about uncomfortably and muttered something about no one having
registered. We were taken to lunch in a local restaurant where
white people sat on one side of the restaurant and blacks on the
other. I gazed across the room and thought that nothing had
changed. The tension was palpable. The whites didn't look at the
blacks or vice versa. Desegregation might have happened in law,
but as far as I could see it had not touched anyone's hearts.

We were to spend the night in the Governor's mansion, a huge
old colonial house rattling with ghosts. The next morning we went

down to breakfast to be served hominy grits, bacon and eggs by a large black servant dressed in a white uniform with white gloves. Nothing had really changed in Jackson, and I was happy to get away from the mossy dampness of the place and to say goodbye to the ghostly trees dripping with vines and distress.

I was glad when the tour ended. I barely made it back to Britain, and within a few days I was on my way to hospital. My doctor decided to take the matter into her own hands and made an appointment for me to see a heart specialist at Charing Cross Hospital. I underwent his tests, and he then sat me down and explained that I was like a fighter pilot who had flown too many times into enemy territory. That made sense. Some nine years of working in the refuge, the squatting, the court cases, David Astor and Lord Goodman, divorce, grandparenthood and, finally, the last lost court case represented far too many forays into unknown or dangerous territory. He was right. I had to bow out for a while, otherwise I risked a fatal heart attack.

Dr Peter Nixon, the heart specialist, had a treatment for me that he termed 'sleep therapy'. I was drugged up to the eyeballs and put to bed only to wake at carefully timed intervals in order to eat and take a bath. I was letting go not just of the recent strains of my life but the more deeply buried wounds that had attached themselves like barnacles to my soul. Drugged, I lay half-conscious, and from somewhere internal I watched events unfold as if on film. Some of them were terrifying, but then the images faded and others took their place. I had no one to interpret my emotions. The psychiatrist that sat by my bed when I was lucid and keen to talk was unable to help. He listened and twitched. He looked more in need of psychiatric help than I.

I did have an angel, though. Often at night, when I struggled out of a sweaty nightmare, I would find a young houseman sitting quietly by my bed. He did his best to listen to my drugged ramblings, but the fact he was there was a comfort in itself.

My sister Kate also came to see me as often as she could, and she brought me fresh green salads to eat. With her I was able to share some of the distressing memories that rose like trout in the River Yarty by our old family house in Devon. Sometimes I woke to find strange faces looming over me. They turned out to be visitors who wished to share their troubles.

On one occasion David came. Everyone was warned that I was heavily drugged and should not be disturbed, but he didn't care about that. As far as he was concerned, he had some argument with me that couldn't wait. I don't remember what this one was about, but fortunately there was another visitor present. I found myself on my knees in bed, with David and I shouting at each other. The visitor hurried off to get help, and as David was ushered out of the room I muzzily wondered what had happened to the quietly spoken man who had championed my cause and who had now become so antagonistic and bitter.

In the middle of my treatment I discharged myself. I was having problems with fellow patients who dropped by to gawp or else sidled in when I was semi-conscious to talk to me. I would awake with a start and with my heart pounding. One male patient tried to climb into my bed in the middle of the night. I managed to fend him off. A few days later I held his hand when his doctor came to tell him that he had terminal cancer of the kidneys. Overall, I felt I'd be better off recuperating at home in the peace of my own bedroom.

Dr Nixon found a wonderful psychologist for me who saw me once a fortnight for nothing. I was back at the refuge and fighting hard to try to maintain the community's autonomy about how the refuge should be run. I was still engaged in trying to hold on to my sanity, but my presence was demanded at committee meetings in David's drawing-room in St John's Wood. I found these a terrible strain. One idea that was mooted was that members of the public should be able to 'adopt' a child, rather like people can adopt children in Africa and contribute to that child's welfare. Everyone thought it was a great suggestion except me.

I knew the refuge mothers would feel that this gesture, however well meaning, smacked of paternalistic and patronizing charity. I tried to argue the case but got nowhere. David felt I was being deliberately destructive, and Saturday-morning meetings at his house were reinstated at which he lectured me on my 'subcon' and my dark side until I sat in a defeated silent heap on one of his chairs and focused on a Picasso drawing on the wall of a strong man in a circus holding up a woman over his head.

I felt caught in a vice. On one hand, I could tell him to fuck off and destroy any chance of the refuge surviving; on the other, I accepted the destructive path we seemed to be taking and risked my health. There seemed no escape. I had been given large doses of valium to take at home, and I was still drinking heavily. The result was that I frequently fell, frightening the children and bruising myself. Russ told me that once when he picked me up after a fall I was mumbling about watching people being tortured on the ship that took us out of Shanghai to be exchanged for Japanese hostages in Lorenço Marques in Mozambique. My mother had told me many years earlier that some of the guards on the ship took my sister and me down to the hold to watch the torture of passengers, I had never wanted to believe her, but I must have repressed those memories for years.

After one particularly volatile altercation at a committee meeting at David's house Tina drove me home in fury after a violent outburst on my part. When she was making a cup of coffee I collapsed on the floor, and she had to get me back to the hospital where she left me safely in bed. The outburst had been triggered by one of the committee members who had plagued me from the moment she was invited to join by David. She was supposed to be a journalist. Her anti-Apartheid husband, Colin Legum, had been rescued from imprisonment or worse in South Africa by David and employed to write about the political situation there for the *Observer*. His wife Margaret maintained that one day she would be the saviour of the black people in her country. My experience of her suggested that the blacks of South Africa were probably better off without her intervention.

Margaret arrived unannounced at the refuge one morning, just after David founded his committee, and said she was taking some of the children back for tea. I tried to explain that I wasn't convinced it was a good idea, but before I could finish Margaret had pulled several of the children clustered around her into her arms and declared, 'I'll take these!' Since Margaret had apparently taken children from the South African slums back home I decided to leave her to it.

I had an anguished telephone call from her later that afternoon. One of the boys, Philip, had slipped into her car in the driveway during tea and, finding the key in place, had reversed the vehicle at speed down the drive until it hit a fence. The children were duly returned to the refuge, and Philip was asked to come into the cubby-hole to explain himself. Margaret, he said, had let him sit in the front seat and change gears on the way over to her house. He had been so excited by this that he had been overcome by temptation. I looked at Margaret, and she just blustered. Later that evening when I was back home she telephoned sounding very angry. She suspected one of the girls, Belinda, of swiping some of her gems while she was showing them the contents of her jewellery case. The girl denied all knowledge of the theft, and no jewellery was discovered at the refuge. I decided that Margaret was a definitely a liability on the committee.

There were, however, some really helpful members of the committee as well, but they generally didn't attend David's meetings with me at his house. I knew that one of the nicest women on the committee was trapped by her husband's violence and his wealth and power. If she did try to leave with her children, she risked losing everything because she had no private money and her husband could afford to employ the best solicitor and Queen's Council that money could buy. Wherever she hid he would track her down. Many years later I wrote a novel about her called *In the Shadow of the Castle* and sent it to her. I watched her two sons destroyed by the violence of their father, and from time to time I still visualize her tired, defeated face. I sometimes think women on the council estates have a better chance of escape from violent men than the woman I knew from David's committee and others from similar backgrounds.

Another affluent woman I met had spent her teenage life on an estate owned by John Paul Getty, one of the richest men in the world. Her mother was known to be one of his twelve mistresses. Claudia had been sent to a well-known public school, but life for her was hard because in those days being the child of Getty's mistress ensured that she was horribly bullied. She came into the refuge with her three-year-old son for a while. She had been very badly bruised by a violent partner and said she needed time to organize her legal situation. We became friends and kept in touch.

One day I had a call from her mother to say that Claudia had been found dead on her kitchen floor with her little son sitting beside her. The death was said to have been an accidental overdose. The newspapers reported the story in lurid detail. I went to see her mother because she wanted to clear her daughter's house. Claudia had told me about her mother's wanton neglect of her, and when I met her I was appalled at her naked hatred of her daughter. The true facts about Claudia's death had been kept from the press. She had ostensibly been on holiday with friends in Afghanistan before she died. She came back carrying a large wooden box hidden in a capacious shawl wrapped around her son. The box contained heroin, and she had secretly stashed the box in her mother's home. It was thought that she had double-crossed the people who were awaiting delivery of the drugs, and it was likely that she had been killed in reprisal.

What bothered me is that her mother showed no grief at her daughter's death. I knew Claudia had suffered from a miserable abused childhood. She had come out as a débutante and tried to make a success of her life, but ultimately she was too damaged by her past with her mother. I wondered as I took some of her belongings to the refuge whether if she had been born in a slum her disturbed behaviour would have been noticed and her family situation investigated. Claudia's mother was able to hide her dysfunction behind the large white porticos of her Holland Park house.

When my children were small I knew a woman who was cruel and neglectful of her children. She had tins and tins of baked beans in her food cupboards. Baked beans on toast was the only thing she fed them. Much of the time they were left in the house while she went out clothes shopping. She never physically assaulted them, but she would scream at them and terrorize them. Her husband worked long hours, and the children were too frightened to speak to him about their plight. Eventually I became so concerned about them that I phoned social services. The person on the end listened, but I heard nothing. Eventually I phoned again to find out whether any action had been taken. 'You didn't tell me her husband was a dentist,' a cross social worker told me. 'Does that make any difference?' I asked naïvely. Of course it did, as I was later to find out. There is one rule for the rich and another for the poor – and the rich can afford lawyers.

When I woke up once more in Charing Cross Hospital I knew I had to stop the downward spiral. If I didn't I was frightened that I could end up in a mental hospital like my paternal grandmother. I was deep asleep one night, and I realized that I was falling feet first down a very precipitous crevasse. I began to panic because there seemed to be no end to this sensation of falling, and then my foot touched solid ground. A voice said, 'There is only one way to go now.' At that moment I knew I had to make a decision. I either fought my way out of the crevasse or I stayed where I was, powerless and out of control. Staying where I was meant that I would be giving up on my sanity, so I struggled my way out of this dark place and back into my hospital bed. The next day I left the hospital for the last time and went home.

42

GOODBYE TO THE REFUGE

In 1981 I received a message from David's secretary to say that Mrs Coupland had complained to his wife Bridget that one of my boys had been sick in bed and hidden the vomit in his sheets. I knew then that we were not welcome at Sutton Courtenay any longer. I was not altogether surprised, because when I had been offered the manor as a refuge for me and my family I had been told by Mrs Coupland that the last incumbent had been a bishop exiled from Namibia and his family had trashed the house. She had recounted the story with a proprietorial gleam in her eye, and I knew it was a warning. I had filled the house with staff from the refuge and my own two children, as well as other young people living in my home. The manor had been a life-saver for some of these children – as well as me. I wondered who had decided I could no longer use the house. It must have been galling for David's wife no longer to have regular use of it – or perhaps Mrs Coupland was genuinely tired of all the extra work. I was always careful to see that we left the house clean and tidy, so apart from changing the sheets there was rarely much to do. I was bereft, because I had come to love the place.

To my great surprise I had a telephone call from David soon after this asking if I would like him to give me Sutton Courtenay as a gift. He knew, he said, that I needed to get out of London because I had to learn to take more care of myself, and he explained that was his way of helping me. I wept tears of exhaustion and gratitude – only to receive a second phone call a few days later to say that he had been advised against proceeding with the gift by his accountants. I could, however, go anywhere I wanted, he said, and choose myself a house. He would pay for it.

Over the three months of my stay in hospital I had time to think about my relationship with him. What I began to understand was that in my family the violence had been overt. My father had bellowed and screamed if he didn't get what he wanted, and my mother did the same. Generally there was no hidden agenda. We three children developed very sensitive antennae, and we were experts in adjusting ourselves to any signal that gave warning of an impending explosion. I had no defence against David's more subtle form of intimidation. I was also blinded to his faults by my gratitude that anyone should take a personal interest in me. My existence had been a matter of indifference to my parents. Most of my life I had felt as if I were an inconsequential shadow in other people's lives. Apart from some lovely months with Charlie – who by this time had faded out of my life – I was very much alone. David had seemed to come into my life as 'a parfait gentle knight'.

He was right about my health. I was indeed thinking seriously of selling my home and moving out of London. I needed to find some space and time for the family and for myself. Ann was well able to take over the day-to-day running of the refuge. Indeed, I had an idea that had always been her plan. I could concentrate on what I do best – working with the mothers and the children.

I was convinced that I should leave London when Cleo telephoned me one evening when I was still at work to say that a small package had arrived without any stamps or a return address. I was alarmed. I immediately told her to contact Hammersmith Police Station and ask them for advice. She telephoned back to say that the bomb squad was on its way. I arrived home a minute before the police and watched officers pile through our front door dressed in black and carrying bomb-disposal gear. After the parcel had arrived Cleo had gingerly placed it at the end of the garden on a ping-pong table. I watched a giant of a man make his way up the garden. He was wearing massive white gloves and a mask over his face. I glanced round and realized I was standing in front of the dining-room windows that overlooked the garden while the policemen were lined up together as far away from the windows as possible. I saw a look of fear on four-year-old Keita's face. He was standing next to Cleo, and she held two-year-old Amber in her arms.

After what seemed for ever the man came back and handed me the opened parcel. It was an oblong block of tofu sent to me by a public relations person who wanted me to write an article about the joys of cooking with it.

I felt really stupid, but the chilling aspect of this incident was that the policeman in charge said that from now, as I was a controversial public figure, all my post and parcels must come to the bomb squad first to be examined. It would then forward letters and packages to me.

I was shaken once more another evening when the house was empty of children and Tina and I were having dinner together. There was a loud knock on the door, and I went to open it. Outside was a very threatening group of young men. They began to shout, 'Erin Pizzey, black, black, black! Out! Out! Out!' I was so shocked I just stood and stared at them. Generally the house was never devoid of teenagers, so the group must have been watching the comings and goings from my home. The chanting went on for some minutes, while I just stood and glared at them. Unnerved, they suddenly turned and ran up the road. Tina wanted to call the police. There was no point, I said, although this was a genuine threat to our household from the racist National Front.

I had never really got used to the picketing and threatening behaviour of the women who used to shout at me when I arrived to speak at public events. I found it very difficult to accept that I was hated by a segment of the British public. I was frightened much of the time, but I knew I couldn't back down from my argument that women who were violent needed help and counselling.

Other refuges refused to deal with women who were alcoholics, drug addicts or who were violent. These women were screened out or if they entered a refuge were soon evicted. To me these were the women who most needed our help. I was outraged that no one would allow women to step off their pedestals and be truly human – least of all other women. Women who failed to become warm, loving mothers were punished and lost their children. The solution to me was blindingly obvious: do what we were doing. Take in problem mothers with their children – and mother them so they can in turn learn to mother their children.

It was unpleasant to know that I attracted so much hostility for my views on domestic violence but worse to know that now I was being targeted at my door by members of the National Front.

In the meantime I scoured the countryside for accommodation with Cleo and other members of the family. All the houses that looked promising were rejected by David for one reason or another – they were deemed to be in poor condition, have dodgy roofs or whatever. It was during one of these excursions that I came across a young woman who listened to my woes and said that she had someone she wanted me to meet. She took me to see a woman who was living in a very big house and running a programme for disadvantaged children. She was another of David's protégés, the young woman explained. All of a sudden what had happened to me started to make sense.

It seemed that David had a habit of picking up women who were in the public eye. He would then find himself in a honeymoon relationship with them. In my case I was particularly vulnerable because I needed him so desperately to help me keep the refuge open. The relationship was bound to turn sour because David, in spite of many years of therapy, had never really come to terms with his damaging relationship with his mother. When we were alone at Sutton Courtenay he often brought out a picture of her in her pearls and talked about the times she spent with him. He spoke of her with such love and longing I was rent with pity – but not for long, because then I would remember his rages and his insistence that I was mad and bad. Now that I had met the woman working with disadvantaged children I knew I could never live in a house owned by David.

In 1981 I was at a fund-raising event for the refuge when I came across a journalist who worked for the *Observer*. She knew of me and talked knowledgeably about the refuge. 'How does one get away from David Astor?' I found myself asking her. I must have sounded insane, but she didn't look surprised. 'You die or you go abroad,' she said.

I was beginning to feel a sense of panic, because now David's telephone calls were becoming more insistent, and then one day I was invited by him to a meeting with a Mr Bunzl, owner of a multi-million-pound business – and another piece of the jigsaw fell into place.

I sat by David's side and listened to Mr Bunzl's financial proposition. He would give our charity £5,000 a year for the next five years, he said. Unlike many of David's associates he was warm and friendly with a lovely twinkle in his eyes.

'You see,' he said to David, 'I, too, have a pet. Ellie. She runs a programme for disturbed young people. I take her here, and I take her there. We visit my friends,' he continued. I didn't look at David. He was shifting uncomfortably in his chair. 'She telephones me in the early hours of the morning. "Darling," she says, "I can't sleep. I owe one hundred and twenty thousand bucks to the bank. What am I to do?"

'I go to Julius – the managing director of a huge steel firm – because we have a business meeting. After the business meeting I squeeze his arm. Julius, I say, give me money for my Ellie and I'll give you whatever you need for your pet. This is how we do business: a little squeeze here and a little squeeze there for our girls.'

David got to his feet and, after shaking Mr Bunzl by the hand and inviting him to our next fund-raising party, we left. I sat in David's car and thought about Mr Bunzl's pet, Ellie. He, like David, was a multimillionaire. Mr Bunzl, according to David's briefing to me before we went to visit him, paid for massive new wings on hospitals. He gave millions to Israel and to many of his other causes. Why did he need to keep his pet in penury? Was it because she was then totally dependent upon his goodwill, as I was with David? Was I a 'pet'?

All this was going through my mind when I got another urgent telephone call at home to say that I was to meet David and Goodman at Goodman's office early the next morning. I was surprised, but I was given no details as to the reason by Goodman's secretary. I hoped for good news. I walked into Goodman's office at Goodman Derrick to be confronted by David, Goodman and Goodman's solicitor. No one was smiling, and Goodman handed me a file with my name on it.

He regarded me steelily. 'You have been accused of stealing a house from your charity.' He sat back in his chair. His huge pendulous cheeks almost obscured the look of triumph in his eyes.

I was shocked, and for a moment I felt a blind sense of panic. I paused, holding my cross. I looked down at the page in the open file. In the memo the address of a property was underlined in red pen. 'Number 9 Coulter Road,' I read out. I looked at the faces before me, bewildered. 'I own that house! My husband Jack and I bought that house to live in long before I started the refuge.' I was startled at what I took to be a fleeting look of disappointment on David's face. 'I have many faults, Lord Goodman, but I am not a thief!' With that I turned and walked out of the room.

What I didn't know then was that Goodman himself was a thief. Years later I discovered that from the 1950s onwards he had been systematically embezzling money from Lord Portman's accounts of which he was the sole trustee – worth around £10 million in today's money – to buy power and influence. Forty per cent of the stolen money went towards bribing senior Labour figures. When he was found out Portman demanded the money back, but Goodman was dying. Portman retrieved about £1 million of the missing money, and a gagging order was issued to last until 2006. I would dearly love to know the names of the people who benefited from the peer's stolen money.

I lost faith in David. His interest in me was, I realized, part of his pathology. His complicated dependence on his mother – long dead – made him destructive to the women in his life, and I was just one in a long line of people who attracted his attention. I could see that David was surrounded by crowds of sycophants who fought for such attention.

He had no concept of money and the cost of living. I saw him send one of his children out because there was no milk in the fridge, and when the child came back with the change David exploded because he was horrified at the cost of a bottle of milk. Meanwhile I had to drive Mrs Coupland to the local cobbler with his much-mended pair of shoes rather than buy new ones. I realized that many rich people brought up by frugal nannies were raised to feel guilty about their inherited wealth. David was so divorced from real life and so spoiled by his claque of admirers and hangers-on that anything he wanted was his to demand – and any time he wanted to contact anyone he was indulged.

The next time I saw Goodman he convened a meeting at the GLC with their top officials. I sat there while he outlined a plan. The GLC, Goodman told me, were offering a quarter of a million pounds to be paid in £60,000 increments to the refuge. He paused for effect. I was to be paid a salary, the sum to be agreed at a later date. I thought that a very smart move: if you are hired you can be fired. There were various structures to be put into place, and, of course, he swore that no woman with her children would ever be turned away. This was a worthless promise, I realized immediately. I got up and said I would have to talk to the community. I told them I could not come to a decision to accept the offer on my own.

The next day at the house meeting we sat down and discussed the deal. The mothers were aware that the house was dangerous and needed rebuilding. After everyone had had their say our final discussion boiled down to the fact that if we refused the money we would lose David and his fund-raising committee. We could lurch on for a while, but eventually we would have to close. If we accepted the money we had to face the fact that the refuge, as we knew it, would change. The huge amount of public money would bring with it scrupulous accounting – and scrupulous accounting brought with it people in suits. Health-and-safety officers would also make their demands, and we would have to accept the changes.

After much tea and many cigarettes the mothers voted to accept the money with the strings attached. I understood their decision. Conditions in the houses were still primitive, and we were all weary of having to make do and mend. I assured them I would stay on to work with them, while Ann would officially take over the running of the refuge with the new title of Director. I, meanwhile, would be designated the Therapeutic Director.

I knew David was waiting for me to object to the GLC's terms. I had always believed that titles created hierarchies and that hierarchies created empires. The problem for charities is that sooner or later they lose touch with the people they originally intended to help. I knew that this was the likely future for the refuge, but I also understood that as an innovator I must be prepared to hand my project over to others and hope that some of my vision would be retained. I agreed with everything Goodman said, because all that really mattered to me was that I could still have time with the mothers and children.

Now that the future of the refuge was secure I no longer needed to jump at David's command. I bought a telephone answering-machine so that I could collect his messages when I was ready. I felt I need not fear his early-morning calls any longer. I did feel guilty when I heard the anger and confusion in his voice when he first had to talk to the machine and not me. Moreover, I myself was upset that our relationship was now so fraught and with bad feeling on both sides that there seemed no way back. I was – and always will be – enormously grateful for his energy and commitment in helping me keep the door open. But in the end appeasing David was too high a price for protecting the future of the refuge.

David and Goodman decided, together with the GLC, to make a public announcement about the new plans for the refuge. For some time I had had a dream that it would be possible to construct a purpose-built refuge in the cul-de-sac. Now I could proceed with my plan. Porter-Wright were appointed architects, and after consultation with the mothers I asked them to create a building representing a woman with her arms folded protectively around a community with an inner courtyard, creating a secluded, secure embrace. The architects produced a brilliant original model of the first-ever purpose-built refuge in the world, and Goodman intended to launch a public preview of the drawings and plans at the GLC. I told David that I wanted to invite Robert Maxwell to the launch. After all, he had offered me money many years back, and now he was fabulously wealthy. He was also publisher of *The Slut's Cook Book* released that year, and I had attended several of his publishing parties at Headington Hill Hall. David, however, was adamant that Maxwell should not be invited.

The GLC event was a glittering affair, and Goodman was standing on a dais with David when I heard a commotion at the back of the audience. Maxwell had arrived at my invitation, and he was pacing up and down behind the audience. He seemed hardly able to contain himself, and when Goodman finished speaking he rushed to the front of the dais and reached out to clasp his hand. I was astonished to see Goodman ignore Maxwell's outstretched hand and turn his back. The snub was hostile and very public. David put an arm around Goodman and ushered him out of the room. Maxwell disappeared, and yet again I wondered about Goodman and his secretive life. I never found out what the great animosity between the two men was about.

Alured Darlington contacted me to say that Glenda's husband Brian had been allowed to take his children home for the weekend. His young daughter Sylvia returned to give the care home staff explicit sexual details of time spent with her father. They were so graphic that the staff realized that she could not have made them up, so the new plan was that the children would eventually live full time with their mother Glenda and her partner John. I was devastated for Sylvia. I had warned everyone that Brian was a danger to his children, and no one had listened. The family court bullied and threatened and found me guilty of contempt rather than listen to the evidence about Brian.

After Margaret Thatcher became Prime Minister in 1979 I had entertained a faint hope that a woman in power might be sympathetic to the idea of changing the law to eliminate some of the shortcomings of the family courts. I had written to her about the issue and got a letter back in reply to say that Margaret Thatcher was 'not interested in women's issues'.

A few months after Ann had been designated Director of the Chiswick refuge in October 1981 she stood on the doorstep as I entered the front gate. 'I've decided that you can no longer come inside the refuge,' she said. 'From now on you can train the staff in the Home for Indefinite Stay.' For a few days while I recovered from the shock I duly met up with some of the staff and volunteers, but I knew that from then I was barred from spending time with the families.

I understood Ann's desire to establish her position as the new Director, but I had not anticipated this move on her part. She never explained why she had decided to ban me from the house altogether and whether she decided on this course of action alone or was acting on David's instructions. I decided not to enquire. My time at the refuge had ended. I decided that the best way to leave was to respect her wishes and not make a fuss. I realized it would be difficult for her to make changes if I was around. Accordingly I spent some time alone with her, and we jointly wrote my resignation letter to the trust.

I cried for some days after I left the refuge. It felt as though a large part of my body had been cut off, and I missed many of the residents and members of staff. But I knew that wherever I went my work would go with me. I didn't need a building or an office to listen and talk to people who needed my help. I had long wanted time to write – in particular I wanted to try my hand at fiction. Now there were no excuses, and if I could make some money through writing I could become independent. Moreover, I could console myself with the fact that there were now refuges all over the world.

At times I had faced personal trauma and pain, but I had tried to turn these experiences into something positive. I used to tell some of the mothers at the refuge that they didn't need university degrees, as they had PhDs in suffering. They learned to put their experiences to use as they took care of each other and offered support. For some people the refuge was merely a place of safety, but for many, including myself, it represented a journey to a new outlook on life. I look back at my years there and my time in hospital receiving therapy, and I am grateful for the insights I gained and the fact that I felt able at last to slough off much of my emotional pain. Those of us who have been rejected by parents may never totally recover from our poor start in life, but in learning to reach out to others we can learn what it is to love and be loved.

Now that there are refuges everywhere I pray that they will be not just places of physical safety but also places where men, women and children can find comfort and be given a chance to transcend their dysfunctional childhoods. I believe that you cannot punish individuals to make them better people, but you can create conditions where those who have been hurt and damaged are given a chance to grow and change.

We need to create a climate in which young people are taught not only about the mechanics of sex but learn more widely about relationships and their responsibilities to one another and to their children. We need to reach out to those already damaged by domestic violence and work with them in our schools and communities so that they can look forward to developing loving, trusting and harmonious relationships with their partners.

Then and only then will we make our homes and communities safe for everyone.

AFTERWORD

By the end of 1981 I was living just a ten-minute drive away from the refuge I had started over a decade earlier. I was still writing for *Cosmopolitan* magazine, but my busy daily life in Chiswick had suddenly come to an end. I missed my contact with the mothers and the children, and I found the sense of rejection I experienced hard to bear.

I knew I had to make a new life for myself and my family. Mikey was increasingly preoccupied with the setting up of Culture Club with Boy George, and I was concerned about Amos who was now fourteen, surrounded by girls and immersed in a music business awash with drugs. I longed for all of us to have some time out. I wanted to take my family away from London and get a complete change of scene for us all.

As long as David led me to believe I could have a house in the country I did think that might be a welcome change, but when that promise evaporated, along with his goodwill towards me, I knew that if I was ever to find peace it would have to be far away in another country. I wanted desperately to get away from him by then – I saw him just a few times after I left the refuge – and from Goodman, whom I never saw after the last GLC meeting I attended. I also wanted to escape the notoriety I had gained from the years I was battling with the far left, the Civil Service and the law courts.

One day I was lying on my bed when I was joined by Amos, and we began to talk about leaving England and moving abroad. I had a big atlas in my bookcase, and we discussed a few options until I remembered that I had once lectured in Santa Fe in New Mexico and been struck by the beauty of the old adobe city with the backdrop of the Sangre de Cristo Mountains and the vast clear-blue skies. 'That's where I want to go,' I told him. I was only too happy to leave a country that for so long had treated me like a criminal for somewhere warm and beautiful. I was exhausted, and my health was shattered.

Cleo asked if she could come with us with her children. Mikey was going join us when he was free, but for the next few years he would be very busy with Culture Club. Cass remained behind. He went on to play with Terence Trent D'Arby on his first album and for many years played bass with Skunk Anansie. Trevor stayed on to work in the refuge and became a social worker. Russ also remained in the refuge for a while but then spent some time abroad with me. Darren Vaz, another of the teenagers from Goldhawk Road, also went on to play music professionally, while Annie Ruddock created the band Amazulu with her friend Sharon.

I knew I would miss all those we left behind, but I was longing to have the time and space to try my hand at fiction. I had wanted to write a novel for years, but to do so seemed like decadence while I was trying to keep the Chiswick refuge and all its offshoots afloat.

I put the house in Goldhawk Road on the market, and it sold straight away. There was no looking back. I did not know it at the time, but I would be away for fifteen years – first in Santa Fe, then down in Cayman Brac, a Caribbean island where I continued to write novels and lived in a fifty-foot-high pyramid on a beach. Finally I ended up in the middle of a forest outside Siena. During that time I not only wrote fiction but continued to be involved in helping victims of domestic violence.

Cleo joined me in the Caymans and finally returned to London to become a social worker, while Amos came back after a year in Santa Fe to develop his own music career. He featured as Captain Crucial on Culture Club's first album, and he continued to write and make records with Boy George. He is now the founder and director of Talenthouse, a website for artists who can upload their work for free and become part of a worldwide creative community.

I meanwhile am back in London living in Twickenham and continuing to work with those who need my help.

INDEX

Please see the Note on the Text on p. 7 regarding names that have been changed. All books mentioned in the index are by Erin Pizzey unless noted.